# THE TV DELUSION

## A PSYCHOLOGY OF BELIEF

# The TV Delusion

## A Psychology of Belief

Simon Day & Joanna van der Leer

**SECOND EDITION**

TruthKey Publishing 2017

*"By doubting, we are led to question: by questioning we arrive at the truth."*

Peter Abelard, French philosopher

Copyright © 2016 - 2017 by Simon Day & Joanna van der Leer

All rights reserved. This book or any portion thereof may not be reproduced or used in any manner whatsoever without the express written permission of the publisher, except for the use of brief quotations in a book review or scholarly journal.

First eBook edition first published in Great Britain in 2016 by TruthKey Publishing.

Second eBook edition published in Great Britain in 2017 by TruthKey Publishing.

Print edition published in Great Britain in 2017 by TruthKey Publishing.

Cover art and illustrations by Joanna van der Leer. Front cover design adapted from an original, "Broken Glass", by Jef Poskanzer under the Creative Commons Attribution 2.0 Generic license. Jef Poskanzer is neither affiliated to nor is an endorser of The TV Delusion.

Print layout by Simon Day.

ISBN : 978-1-545-45413-8

All reasonable efforts have been made to contact the copyright holders but anyone who believes their copyright to be infringed is welcome to contact the authors.

Published by TruthKey Publishing
truthkeypublishing@gmail.com


Printed and distributed by CreateSpace
www.createspace.com

To order your copy, please visit CreateSpace at the above address. Special discounts are available on quantity purchases by corporations, associations, educators, and others. For details, contact the publisher at the above address.

This book is dedicated to Phillip Marshall, Danny Jowenko, Beverly Eckert, Kenneth Johannemann, Christopher Landis, Deborah Palfrey, David Graham, John P. O'Neill, Barry Jennings and all the others who have lost their lives in pursuit of the truth.

# Contents

| | | | |
|---|---|---|---|
| | Preface | ................ | ix |
| | Second Preface | ................ | xiii |
| | Introduction | ................ | 1 |
| 1. | What Is the Truth? | ................ | 9 |
| 2. | A Duel of Truth | ................ | 15 |
| 3. | In Two Minds | ................ | 23 |
| 4. | Beyond the Lemon | ................ | 29 |
| 5. | Black & White | ................ | 35 |
| 6. | What's in a Religion? | ................ | 41 |
| 7. | A Modern Day Religion | ................ | 53 |
| 8. | Good Guys, Bad Guys | ................ | 63 |
| 9. | Canonical Filtering | ................ | 73 |
| 10. | Authority Filtering | ................ | 89 |
| 11. | Religious Labelling | ................ | 97 |
| 12. | Ad Hominem Attack | ................ | 111 |
| 13. | Religious Inferencing | ................ | 117 |
| 14. | Protect the Religion | ................ | 125 |
| 15. | A Madness in Paris | ................ | 139 |
| 16. | Belief | ................ | 155 |
| 17. | Conformity | ................ | 163 |
| 18. | Prison Break | ................ | 177 |
| 19. | An Instrument of Control | ................ | 183 |
| 20. | Brain Waves | ................ | 195 |
| 21. | Hitler: Epitome of Evil? | ................ | 201 |
| 22. | A Health Check | ................ | 219 |

| 23. | Which One Should I Believe? | .................... | 229 |
| 24. | Who Controls the TV? | .................... | 241 |
| 25. | The Canon of the TV | .................... | 253 |
| 26. | Fairy Tales | .................... | 295 |
|     | Conclusion | .................... | 307 |
|     | Glossary | .................... | 325 |
|     | References | .................... | 329 |

# Preface

*"In a time of universal deceit, telling the truth is a revolutionary act."*

George Orwell

---

Back in the 1980s, when I was in my second year of university in England, I met a guy called John. It was the first day of the new academic year, and some friends and I were standing in the entrance hall of the college surveying the new intake of first year students. John wasn't like the other freshmen: he was a head and shoulders taller than most of them, he looked a little older and somehow a lot wiser. The two of us soon got talking and he began to tell me his story.

One year previously, John had started his university education at the same college. He had had to abort his first year's education after just a month and take the rest of the year out. He was starting his course again from the beginning when we met. Being young and not very worldly-wise at the time, I found it hard to envisage an event that would result in such a calamity.

Like many at the time, John's politics were left of centre. Having planned a career in journalism, it was natural that he had become involved with the student union, and all but inevitable that he had landed himself a position as a reporter for the university magazine. At the time, the social phenomenon of religious cults was big news. According to the newspapers and the TV, closed-compound sects of various denominations were springing up everywhere in the UK, the US and around the world. It was therefore not surprising that, for his first assignment with the student rag, he was sent to the local branch of the "Moonies" (or the "Unification Church" to give it its proper name) to conduct interviews and write an article.

When he arrived, John found the resident "Moonies" to be warm and inviting. They suggested that he stay overnight with them in order to fully immerse himself in the cult experience, hoping that, by doing so, he would be able to write a more informed article. As things turned out, one night turned into two, then a week, and, before he knew it, John had become a full-time member of the cult.

At that time, there were several organisations which, at the request of the abductee's family, would turn up at the cult's compound, kidnap the subject and take them to a deprogramming centre to get them "cleaned up". After six months with the cult, John's parents enlisted the help of one of these organisations and had him busted out. After that came a further six months of deprogramming before he was ready to resume his education.

The first question I asked John, probably the first that most would have asked, was why did he not just walk out as soon as he realised he had been lured into the cult? He explained that they had presented him with such a coherent and appealing narrative (the story they told themselves about the world and their place in it) that he felt compelled to stay. After thinking about it for a while, I began to see how these factors might make such a narrative seem both captivating and enduring.

A few years later, I found myself thinking about our conversation and a question sprang to my mind: how would one be able to tell whether or not one was "in a cult"? In my mind's eye I had an image of two people, one "inside" and one "outside", each one pointing at their counterpart and shouting "cult". I was struck by the futility of such a confrontation, and began to ask myself what exactly it was about arguments of this nature that indicated that no progress could ever be possible.

Seeking to answer my own question, my first attempt was this: one is in a cult if one is living in a compound and the narrative one follows is different to that of everyone else. Unfortunately, as soon as this answer came to me, I realised it contained at least one major flaw. If the cult were to increase its size from a handful of members to such a number that it became large enough to fill the town where it was situated, then it would make more sense for the cult members to live on the outside of the compound. The logical place for the remainder of the population would then be the inside. Not only that, but who would we now select to fulfil the role of "everyone else" in order to conduct our comparison of narratives? Would we choose some people from other towns? What if the cult were to grow to encompass those towns too, or even a whole country or continent?

With this chain of thought getting out of hand, I soon realised that my naïve answer was woefully inadequate, so I came up with a new one: one can always tell if one is in a cult if the narrative one follows is false. At this point, two things occurred to me. The first was a question: what do we mean when we say that something is "true"? The second was the realisation that most things are more complicated than they initially appear, but that this complexity is often masked by the presuppositions we make about the world around us.

It was my attempt to unravel these thoughts that led to the writing of this book. I hope you enjoy the ride.

S.D.

# Second Preface

*"History would be something extraordinary, if only it were true."*

Leo Tolstoy

---

It was around the age of twelve that it first occurred to me that something about the world didn't quite add up. At times I struggled at school and, like many, I felt that the subjects we were taught had little relevance to my life. The repetition of seemingly disparate facts gave me little encouragement to study in any great depth. History lessons, the perfect example of this, would often see me leaving the classroom more confused than enlightened. It was like being presented with a jigsaw puzzle with half the pieces missing and without the box.

Science, however, was different. It wasn't just that there was more logic involved, but also that the lessons alluded to underlying processes which were made tangible with real experiments. I had found something that made sense and that I enjoyed. Passing the exams led me on to university and a study of Zoology and Behavioural Psychology. This is where my interest in psychology first began.

Some years later, while working in the medical field, I began to take interest in world events and, more importantly, the way in which these were portrayed in the media. Little by little, I became aware that many of the stories presented on the television, especially those in the news, didn't ring true. The more I subjected these stories to scrutiny, the more the feelings I had experienced in my school history lessons resurfaced.

All this came home to me when, during the financial crisis of 2013, in Nicosia, Cyprus, I was presented with the opportunity to see the mismatch between the media's stories and real events first hand. There, I witnessed a TV camera crew asking local people to form a long line at an ATM so they could be filmed. I had spent a long time walking around the city, and at no other time had I seen any other evidence of long queues, either outside banks or at ATMs, except for the ones on the TV screens. Little did I know it at the time, but this was to be just one of many examples of the divergence between reality and the TV's version of it.

Rather than automatically accepting stories as I had done in the past, I started to question the things I watched and read, and began to do my own investigation. I discovered that there was a huge volume of information at my finger tips that I hadn't even realised existed. It soon became apparent that many of my opinions and attitudes had been formed on the basis of a thin and stilted view of the world. The more I researched, the more I began to develop what I felt was a truer perspective and understanding of the world around me. I had started to take control of the formation of my own opinions. It was at this point that history began to make much more sense to me and, as a result, got a lot more interesting.

One of the most challenging things was learning to process the huge volume of information available, filtering fact from fiction and putting it all together to form the big picture. I learned to appreciate the importance of keeping an open mind in order to reconcile the contradictions which research inevitably brings to light. This was something new to me, having been brought up to accept the homogenous narratives from the television. It dawned on me just how easy it would be to deceive people with half-truths or false information, if these were presented in the right way.

With all this in mind, it struck me how few books existed which dealt with the connection between psychology, deception and the mainstream media. My hope is that you will be encouraged to question and research not only the material covered here but also that which lies beyond the scope of this book. In doing so, I anticipate that you will start to see things rather differently. I hope you enjoy the book and wish you all the best on your journey.

J.V.

# Introduction

*"An error does not become truth by reason of multiplied propagation, nor does truth become error because nobody sees it."*

Mahatma Gandhi

---

We all like to think we know the truth about the world around us, yet pick two random people and a random topic and you are more likely to get disagreement than not. When the chosen topic comes down to a matter of opinion (such as, for example, whether or not the state should stipulate a minimum wage) such disagreement is perhaps inevitable, as it's always possible to see valid points on both sides of the argument. More surprising than this, however, are the cases where we find such discord with topics of a more factual nature, such as, for instance, the laws of physics and their application to the world around us.

An argument between two people is shaped partly by what they understand to be the facts pertaining to the topic at hand. The attitudes of the participants towards those facts and the mental processes that drive the argument, however, play no less a role. It is an attempt at the analysis of these attitudes and processes that is the focus of this book. One thing that makes this challenging is the complex interrelation between these factors.

For instance, consider an example of an attitude such as:

"Nuclear power stations are a bad idea."

a statement such as:

> "There has been a leak of radiation from a power station."

and an opinion that might result from hearing the statement such as:

> "The power station must be decommissioned."

There are at least two approaches we could follow when considering the statement. The first is to accept that the statement is true without question, while the second is to scrutinise the facts behind the alleged radiation leak in order to ascertain whether or not it is true. An individual who holds the attitude above may be more likely to accept the statement as being true without question, and then go on to form the opinion. On the other hand, an individual who does **not** hold the attitude may be more likely to question the statement and, perhaps, arrive at a more balanced opinion.

But there is more to this than meets the eye. Let's suppose for a minute that the leak had been a minor one or even that it had not occurred at all. An individual who first held the attitude above and went on to form the opinion (as a consequence of the misleading statement) would probably find their attitude reinforced as a result of the process. Now, the next time they are presented with a similar statement, they would be more likely to accept it without question, a tendency which, if repeated a number of times, could quite easily lead to the formation of a habit.

This kind of "attitude amplification", to coin a phrase, can lead to the entrenchment of perspective and an unwillingness or inability to see the points of view of others. In extreme circumstances it can even lead to an inability to see the most obvious of facts, even when they are staring us in the face. This realisation is the key to understanding the strong psychological aspect of the way we see and respond to our surroundings.

Many would agree that our experiences play a large part in determining our thoughts and opinions, but few stop to consider the powerful influence of psychology. Even fewer take the extra step to acknowledge that the mind, as it were, has a mind of its own. This may seem like an unusual thing to say, so perhaps the example which follows will make things a little clearer.

We can think of our heart and lungs as machines which operate with one purpose and one purpose alone: to keep us alive. To illustrate this, try a simple experiment: hold your breath for as long as you can. For a while, your lungs "accept" your command and you stop breathing, but, regardless of how hard you try, there will always come a point when your command is overridden. At this point, your lungs step in as if to say: "Hold on a minute, I'm in charge of the breathing around here. If the current course of action continues, the result would be a threat to our existence. I'm going to step in now and take back control in order to remove this threat." The heart goes a step further by refusing to listen to our commands in the first place. It's as if it has already made up its "mind" that there are no circumstances where its pausing, even for a few seconds, would be a good idea.

Of course, this analysis is just a simplified view of what's really going on, but it's sufficient to make the point. When we talk about our lungs "accepting our command" to stop breathing, we know it's not actually the lungs themselves that are doing the "accepting", but just the part of our mind that's responsible for breathing. We could think of it as a dedicated semi-autonomous "mind" that does this on its own, unless we choose to override it. Although its operation can be altered by our conscious mind, the lungs' "mind" has the final say.

Just as easily, we might look at the operation of our legs to reveal more detail about the interplay between mind and sub-mind. The exact nature of the physical activity our legs perform is not only very complex, but also varies quite considerably depending on whether we are, say, walking, running for a bus or jumping over a fence. We are able to choose which one of these activities our legs are to perform and can exercise some basic management of the overall process, such as the direction in which we want to walk, run or jump. The details concerning the placing of each foot and operating all the necessary muscles, however, are delegated to the legs themselves, or, rather, to the dedicated sub-mind that controls them. We might view the choice of activity as being like the selection of a "program" for our legs, a bit like the selection of a CD-ROM to be run on a games console, for example. We choose the CD-ROM we want to use and after that it's the games console that takes over.

So what about the organ we normally think of as our "mind", that is to say our conscious, thinking mind? It too is semi-autonomous, at least in part. Its job is to ensure our continued existence, but, unlike the heart and lungs, which concentrate on short term activity, the mind's job is to focus more on the medium to long term planning. So while, for example, we instinctively withdraw our hand from a hot stove without waiting for our mind to tell us to do so, it's our mind that stops us touching the hot stove again in the future.

The mind has at its disposal a number of different "programs" it can deploy, just as we have seen with the example of the legs. Unlike the legs, however, it is harder for us to verify that this is the case, and there are at least two reasons for this. The first is that it is not possible to directly observe the mind's workings. With the legs, however, this is a simpler matter. We might start, for example, by taking high speed film of them in operation in order to analyse the movement of the muscles. If this did not provide enough detail, we could go a step further and dissect those muscles to analyse their internal structure, as gory a prospect as this might sound. With the mind, we can only observe the behaviour and speech of a subject in order to guess at the mental "programs" operating within.

The second reason for the ambiguity as to the mental "program" is that we rarely tend to exercise any control over which of these is selected by the mind in order to tackle the situations it encounters. Most of the time, the selection is made for us by our unconscious mind.

As an example, consider the instinctive process that's at work while driving a car. Then, by way of contrast, consider the analytical process that presents itself when attempting to solve a problem in mathematics or to find the answer to a clue in a cryptic crossword. At no point do we make a conscious decision to run one "program" or the other, yet clearly **something** has made the choice, as can be seen by the stark difference between the results in each case. Although our mind, in its capacity as a semi-autonomous organ, has chosen the program for us, we do have the **capacity** to make this choice consciously. In practice, however, we very rarely exercise this capacity.

Since the process of "program selection" operates mostly without our oversight, we are normally unaware of the extent of the mental effort we expend during our waking hours. Far from being a defect, this lack of awareness is an inescapable necessity. It has been estimated that our brain performs billions of operations per second, so, if we were ever to be made aware of even a small fraction of these, we would surely be overwhelmed. As a result, our attitude to the question of how our mind works tends to be much the same as our attitude to the operation of our heart and lungs: we don't really care how they work, we are just glad that they do.

In most cases the mind makes the right choice of program to run and, as a result, we are able to act appropriately and get on with our lives. This, however, is not always the case. Going back to the "nuclear power" example, a holder of the initial attitude, the one that is opposed to nuclear power, may unconsciously engage the "blind acceptance" program rather than its "critical thinking" counterpart. If it then transpired that the story of the radiation leak had been false, then the adoption of the opinion might be viewed as unjustified.

This unconscious selection of the "program" may seem like a curious way for the mind to go about its business, but the goal here (from our mind's perspective) is simply to ensure our continued wellbeing. Therefore, if we are to assume that our mind will help us find the truth, we can only rely on this being the case when knowing the truth is concordant with our wellbeing. If ever there were a conflict between the two, we can be sure that the mind would conceal the former in order to enhance the latter.

Needless to say, this is by no means the first book to have been written about psychology, and it probably won't be the last. So what makes this one stand out from the rest? If we were to pick some of the major discoveries of psychology and ask the average person for their views on them, we might expect a dismissive attitude. Many would argue that these theories have little or no relevance to the lives of the average person and so offer little in the way of interest. Most of us seem to assume that we are somehow "immune" to the effects of psychology, and take the view that these processes are things which only ever affect "other people".

Let's take the Milgram experiment[i], probably one of the most widely renowned expositions of practical psychology in history, as an example. Many people are familiar with (or have at least heard of) this piece of research, conducted in 1963 by Stanley Milgram. In this experiment, the subject is asked by a person in authority to administer electric shocks of increasing magnitude to a "victim" (actually an actor), with each increase in shock being accompanied by a more intense scream of pain from the "victim".

For many, the practical applications of this experiment are limited to its ability to "explain" what motivated Nazi soldiers to commit the crimes that were alleged of them. Yet, as we will soon see, the Milgram effect has a profound influence over us all, even though most of us might struggle to see it at first. Throughout the following chapters, our aim is to show how this experiment, and others like it, are relevant to us all today.

Over the course of our journey, we will be looking at both evidence and opinion relating to a wide range of topics from politics to history and to religion. In our quest to illustrate our ideas we will touch on a number of geopolitical events, such as the terrorist attacks of 9/11 and many others. It is not our aim to "prove" or "disprove" any of the narratives we present, but, instead, to use them as a vehicle to explore the mechanisms of thought itself. Where we offer evidence relating to these events, we have made every effort to ensure that we represent the facts in as accurate and unbiased fashion as is possible. But, as will become more apparent over the course of the coming chapters, truth can be a fickle beast and has a tendency to change over time. With this in mind, we strongly recommend that the reader neither believes nor dismisses outright any of the content we explore but, instead, uses it as a catalyst for his or her own unbiased research. Wherever possible, we have provided details of some suitable reference material, but these are suggestions only, and the reader is encouraged to tread their own path.

Whether or not the reader chooses to do this, of course, is entirely up to them, and it is certainly not essential in order to understand the chapters which follow. If there were any prerequisite for the reader at all, then it would be something far simpler: to start their thinking from a point of neutrality when considering new points of view and to resist the temptation to cast judgement based on preconceptions. To illustrate this, we might revisit the example we used at the start of this chapter. Here, we could have quite easily substituted the attitude for its opposite like this:

"Nuclear power stations are a great idea."

In this case it would be the advocates of nuclear power who would be more likely to **reject** the statement without question:

"There has been a leak of radiation from a power station."

and form the opinion:

"The power station must be left alone."

After all, we are not trying to say that opponents of nuclear power somehow have a monopoly on critical thinking.

No matter which way round we word the attitude, statement or opinion, the "programs" of "blind acceptance" (or "blind rejection" in this second case) and "critical thinking" will remain the same. Over the course of the coming chapters, we will be taking a look at these programs and many others like them and see how all this relates to the TV.

# - 1 -
# What Is the Truth?

*"A lie gets half way round the world before the truth has a chance to get its pants on."*

Winston Churchill

---

Sometimes in life, it's the complicated things which receive all the attention, while the simple things are swept under the carpet without a second thought. When two people argue, the crux of the matter often turns out to be a question as to whether a certain fact is "true" or "false". We all suppose we know what is meant when we utter these two little words, but do they really have a strict dictionary definition? What do we mean when we say that an idea is "true" or "false"? When two people each say that something is "true", how do we know that they mean the same thing?

As it turns out, there are many definitions of "truth", and the topic has been a hotbed of debate for philosophers throughout the ages. It's beyond the scope of this book to go into all these definitions, so we'll just focus on the two main ones. For each of these, we'll explore what it means for a proposition ("statement" or "claim") to be classed as "true" or "false".

The first definition we will consider is called *The Correspondence Theory of Truth*. This is the one which most of us would think of if asked for a definition. In this model, a proposition is considered to be true if it corresponds to an actual event or state of the real world, and false otherwise.

As a simple example, consider the following proposition:

"In the northern hemisphere, the stars in the sky appear to rotate counter-clockwise around a point near the North Star."

Under the Correspondence Theory, this proposition would be true if the stars actually **do** rotate in the manner described and false otherwise. In this case, the facts are easy to come by, at least on a clear night, since all we need to do is observe the sky for a long enough period of time. Setting up a camera and taking a shot every ten minutes, then playing the results back as a time-lapse movie would make the rotation easier to observe. This would enable us to conclude whether or not the proposition was true, according to the Correspondence Theory. Incidentally, for those wishing to attempt this experiment in the southern hemisphere, the direction of rotation is clockwise and the central point lies close to the star, Sigma Octantis, which, unfortunately, is too dim to be seen with the naked eye.

In contrast with this, we have our second definition, *The Constructivist Theory of Truth*. Under this model, a proposition is true only if society accepts it as true. In this case, it's a lot harder to pin down exactly where this truth comes from, so we will leave the analysis of its source until chapter 10. To keep things simple for the time being, suffice it to say that we can view this theory as being synonymous with "truth by authority". The nature of this authority can vary significantly depending on the individual we are considering and the society within which they live. Typical examples might include a TV News Anchor, a person in government, a leading scientist (or scientific journal), a religious figure or even one's peer group.

The following is a simple example of a proposition which is true under this model of truth, drawn from popular American culture:

"Bart Simpson is Homer's son."

In this case, we know this is true because Matt Groening, the producer of "The Simpsons", tells us so, and what reason would we have to doubt him? At this point, the reader may argue that the proposition must be false, because Bart Simpson is a fictional character. However, we might also consider this alternative proposition:

"Homer Simpson is Bart's son."

In this case, without doubt, the proposition is false. Once we see this, it's easier to appreciate how the first proposition is, at least in some sense, true.

But enough of the technical definitions: let's look at a practical example and see how our two models compare. Imagine that we are presented with the following proposition, and are set the task of working out whether it is true or false:

"There was a storm last night."

Using the Constructivist Theory, we might decide to turn on the TV to an appropriate channel or look in a newspaper. If the source said that there had been a storm, we would assume that it was true. If, on the other hand, it made no mention of it, we might assume that it was false.

On the other hand, using the Correspondence Theory, we would have to try to ascertain whether or not there actually **was** a storm last night. If it turns out that there **was**, we would say that the proposition was true. If, on the other hand, there was no storm last night, we would conclude that the proposition was false.

So how do we work out whether or not there actually **was** a storm? The simplest way would be to go outside while the storm was in progress and take a look. In practice however, we are usually asking the question after the event, when the lack of the luxury of a time machine makes this impossible. In this case, we would have to try to find some secondary evidence to support the proposition. We could make a good start by going outside (the next morning) to see if the ground was wet and to check whether or not there were leaves or broken tree branches scattered around.

But hold on a minute! What happens if we can't trust the evidence? After all, maybe there was someone outside using a hose pipe the day before, and that's the real reason for the ground's being wet? Maybe there was someone with one of those machines that blows leaves around (we, the authors, have never been able to work out the purpose of those machines) and they had been pointing their machine at the trees' branches?

By entertaining these doubts, we are exercising an important pillar of the Correspondence Theory: the balanced consideration of multiple hypotheses. We will focus more on this idea in due course, but, for now, let's carry on with our thought process.

In order to get a better idea of whether the damp ground was caused by rain or by a person with a hose pipe, we might try and gather some more evidence. If the rain were the cause, it's likely that the damp ground would be quite widespread. Conversely, if it were a person with a hose pipe, we might expect the effect to be limited by the length of the hose. Given this, we can easily construct an experiment whose results would allow us to distinguish between these two hypotheses. We could walk a distance of, say, one kilometre, and examine the ground at every hundred metres along the route. If the ground were found to be damp at most of the points of measurement, this would add weight to the idea that there had been rain. An activity like this encapsulates another important pillar of the Correspondence Theory: the testing of our hypotheses. In walking the kilometre, we have designed an experiment to help us distinguish between our competing hypotheses. We do this by comparing the predictions offered by each hypothesis with the observations from the experiment, an experiment designed specifically to generate a scenario that might correspond to one hypothesis but contradict the other.

We could carry on gathering more and more evidence like this, but eventually we would want to start weighing things up. We might conclude with a statement such as this: "Given the best evidence we have at the present time and the range of hypotheses that have been presented, we can conclude that, in all likelihood, there was a storm last night." Of course, there is always the chance that some more compelling evidence might come along later, or that someone might come up with a new idea; so we must always keep an open mind and be prepared to change it should circumstances dictate.

This leads us to one of the most important differences between our two theories of truth. With the Correspondence Theory, we can never be completely confident that we have reached the right conclusion: we can never be sure that, at some point in the future, further evidence or additional hypotheses might appear. Indeed, in some cases, we might not really be very sure of our conclusion at all. For this reason, it is important that we always express an appropriate degree of doubt along with our conclusion. With the Constructivist Theory, on the other hand, what we think of as the "truth" has reached a terminal state. This is because it always conforms exactly to what's been told to us by the relevant source of authority, and this rarely changes as time goes by. This gives the Constructivist an impression of certainty which can be seen as more comforting than the lack of finality that is always to be felt by an adherent of the Correspondence Theory.

In seeking to deduce which theory of truth has been used to reach a conclusion, we can often get clues by carefully examining the language used by the subject in expressing it. If an absolute certainty is implied, then we might suspect that the Constructivist Theory has been used; while if the speaker has coloured their conclusion with some element of doubt, then we might suspect the use of the Correspondence Theory. Of course, this is just a rule of thumb, but, over the course of the coming chapters, we will identify many more behavioural traits that can give us a more accurate idea as to which mental "program" has been engaged. For each trait, we will first illustrate the concept by means of some simple examples, then go on to formalise it. We have started the ball rolling in this chapter with a light-hearted overview of the Constructivist and Correspondence approaches to the idea of truth. In the next chapter we will offer a more technical approach.

# - 2 -
# A Duel of Truth

*"Dicere enim bene nemo potest, nisi qui prudenter intelligit."*
*(No one can speak well, unless he thoroughly understands his subject.)*

Marcus Tullius Cicero, Roman philosopher

---

In chapter 1 we saw our two theories of truth applied to a simple example, and the reader may be forgiven for thinking that the point was, perhaps, over laboured. The reason why things seemed so clear-cut in that example was that the subject material was not in any way controversial. The outcome of the analysis was of little consequence: with the possible exception of the weatherman, nobody's toes are going to be trodden on if we come out and say that there was or wasn't a storm.

In chapter 15 however, we will tackle a more challenging example where the outcome is of the utmost importance and where the topic is extremely controversial. In these upcoming cases, where there is likely to be an emotional content to our thinking, it is easy to confuse our two theories and so make mistakes. For that reason, it's a good idea to formalise our two approaches before we proceed.

## Correspondence

Starting, then, with the Correspondence Theory shown in Figure 1, and working from top to bottom, we can see the stages which comprise this paradigm. Readers with a

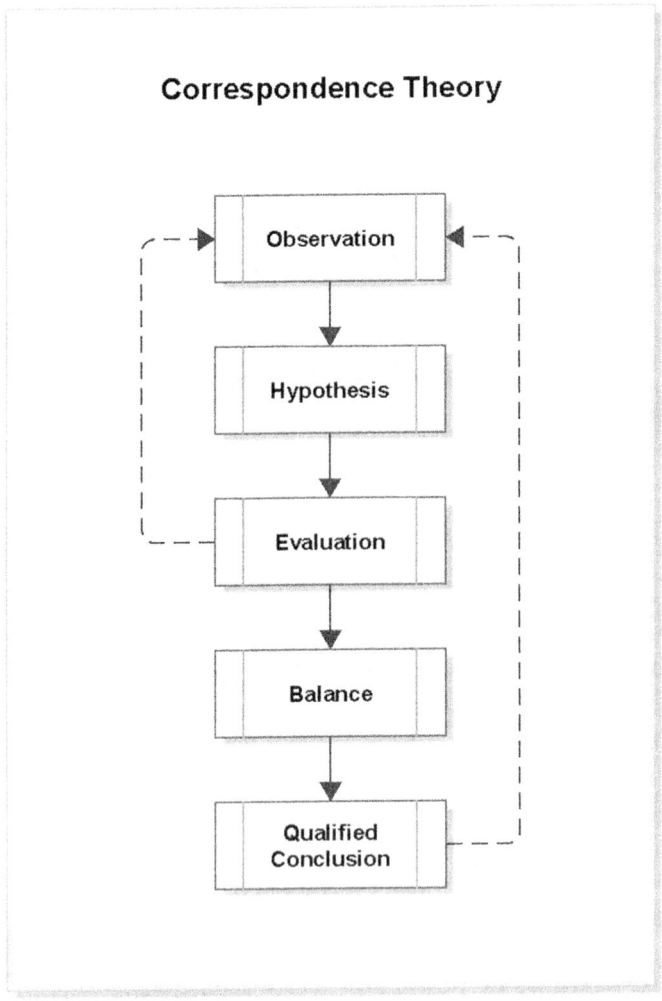

**Figure 1**

background in science or engineering will notice immediately that this is based on The Scientific Method[ii].

The first and most important step is *Observation*. To get this right, we must clear our minds of any theories, explanations or opinions we might have heard from others. In our example from the previous chapter, we started by observing that the ground was wet on the morning after the alleged storm. We must concentrate on making careful observations, without becoming distracted by thinking too much about what we are seeing. But, above all, if we are to truly adhere to the Correspondence Theory, we must take care to record **all** of our observations, no matter how minor they may seem.

Once we have made our initial observations, we can go on to the next step: *Hypothesis*. We should try to come up with as many of these as we can, no matter how unpalatable, since it's important that we do not exclude any possibilities at this stage. Any hypotheses that don't fit the facts will be removed later on, as a natural result of the process we will follow. The more diverse the hypotheses we come up with, the more likely we are to end up with the most accurate answer possible. In the previous chapter we kept the example simple by presenting just two different hypotheses: "storm" and "person with hose pipe and leaf blower".

In the next step, *Evaluation*, we test each hypothesis in turn against each of the observations we made earlier. A hypothesis whose predictions fit well with the observations would score highly, while one which yielded a poor match would be awarded a lower score. During the course of this step, we may find that it is difficult to distinguish between two or more of the hypotheses. In this case we would need to go back and gather some more specific evidence to help us determine which of the hypotheses represented the closest fit for the facts. In our example, we found that we had to gather more evidence to distinguish between the "storm" hypothesis and the "hose pipe with leaf blower" hypothesis. We needed to find out whether the wet ground and the leaf damage were widespread or localised. In Figure 1 we can see this "loop-back step" going from Evaluation to Observation, as shown by the reverse dotted line.

After we have evaluated all the hypotheses, we can proceed to weigh them up in the *Balance* phase. It is important here to take into account **all** the proposed hypotheses, no matter how we might feel about the conclusions they lead to. After all, the ultimate arbiter of the truth is the evidence, not our feelings.

At the end of the Evaluation phase, we arrive at a *Qualified Conclusion*. Continuing with the example from the previous chapter, this time assuming we had decided that the "person with hose pipe and leaf blower" hypothesis represented the better fit, we might say something along these lines: "Given the evidence currently available, it is reasonable to assume that the damp ground and blown leaves were caused by a person with a hose pipe and a leaf blower." The guarded nature of the conclusion is reflected in the use of the word "qualified" in the title of this final phase.

For many, the idea that we might never reach a final conclusion may seem uncomfortable. For a scientist however, this is perfectly normal. There have been many cases throughout history where an established "truth" has been overturned by new evidence, new hypotheses, or even new technology. As an example, Isaac Newton first proposed his theory of gravitation in 1798. It stood as the "truth" for one hundred and seven years until, in 1905, Einstein's theory of Special Relativity explained that Newton's idea was just an approximation. Who knows how we might view Einstein's theory at some point in the future when the next change in "truth" emerges?

## Constructivism

In many ways, the Constructivist Theory can be viewed as the opposite of its counterpart. Whereas we saw that Correspondence had us start with the observations and proceed towards the conclusion, Constructivism starts with the conclusion and works back towards the observations.

Referring to Figure 2 and working once again from top to bottom, we can see that the first step for the Constructivist is to consider a set of *Candidate Conclusions*. To keep things simple, we will assume that each of these is presented by a distinct source of authority. We will have a lot more to say about these sources of authority later in the book, but for now

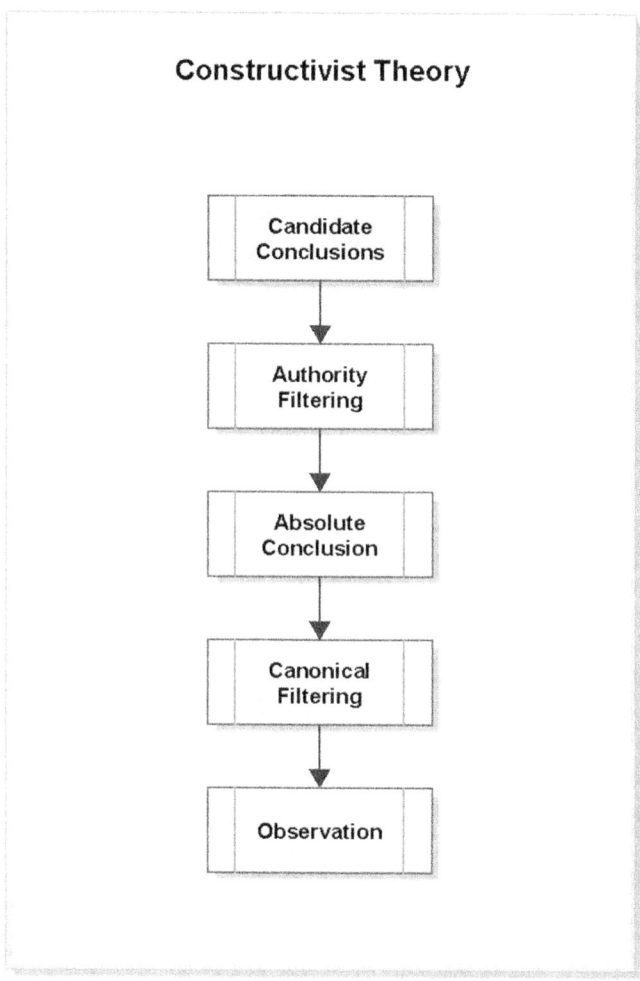

**Figure 2**

we can imagine these to include such people as TV news anchors, members of the government, leading scientists and so on.

The task of the Constructivist is to select one of the conclusions from the available set, but the decision is not made based on the nature of the conclusion but, instead, on the status of the authority figure who presents it. The process of filtering out the unwanted conclusions is termed *Authority Filtering* and can be seen on the diagram as the next step. The details of the selection process are a story in themselves, so we will leave their further discussion until chapter 10.

Once the process of filtering is complete, the Constructivist has arrived at the third step, *Absolute Conclusion*. The adjective "absolute" has been used to qualify this noun because, unlike in the case of the Correspondence Theory, no process of deliberation has been executed, and so there is no need to colour the conclusion with any hint of doubt. We might imagine that the subject either has no interest in weighing things up or that he or she imagines this task to have already been conducted by the source of authority, but such musings would lead us away from our central theme.

At this point it becomes apparent that we face two different possibilities.

The first of these is that the selected conclusion shows broad agreement with the observations. In this case, we might be tempted to say that it makes no difference which theory of truth we use to reach the conclusion, since both routes lead to the same end. Apart from the difference between absolute and qualified conclusions that we have already discussed, there is another, perhaps more important, reason why this is not the case. It turns out that the journey we take to reach a conclusion can often be more important than the destination. This somewhat thorny issue relates to the idea of prejudice and will be the subject of chapter 5.

The second of our two possibilities is that there are one or more significant discrepancies between the selected conclusion and the observations. This eventuality presents the Constructivist with some serious problems, because they are now obliged to somehow reconcile these inconvenient observations with the preselected conclusion. This step, the counterpart of Authority Filtering, is shown on the diagram as *Canonical Filtering*. We will have a lot more to say about this crucial activity in chapter 9, so, for the time being, we'll just say that the unwanted observations are ignored.

The idea of ignoring inconvenient truths in this way may seem a little alien to some, yet this is something we are all used to doing now and again. As an example, it is typical for many of us in the Western world to vote in political elections, with our choice of candidate being based on the promises the candidate makes before the election. However, in the majority of cases, our choice makes little difference since, as soon as our new leaders step into office, they typically break all the promises they made before the election. Deep down, we all know this is going to happen, but it's a truth all too quickly forgotten the next time we step into the polling booth. In our minds, we hold on to the belief that "voting works", and, in order to do so, we must ignore all the past observations that contradict this.

This brings us to an end, as far as the Constructivist Theory is concerned. What should now be apparent, after reviewing this chapter, is that the process of Correspondence and that of Constructivism are very different. Many people take the view that they stand as opposites, since the former starts with an examination of the world and proceeds towards a model that represents it, whereas the latter starts with a model and proceeds towards the world, regardless of whether the world conforms to the model or not. In the next few chapters we will go on to look at how these two theories behave in practice and what kinds of conflict we can expect to see when we put the two of them together.

# - 3 -
# In Two Minds

*"If you would be a real seeker after truth, it is necessary that at least once in your life you doubt, as far as possible, all things."*

Rene Descartes, French philosopher

---

In the last chapter, we introduced a formal definition of our two models of truth. In this chapter, we will build on our definitions by taking a closer look at the practical implications. After all, theories are all well and good, but they are useless until we understand what tangible effects they have on our lives.

When we are faced with the task of what to believe about the world, we are obliged to employ one or other of these two theories of truth. Of course, we all have the potential to choose whichever one we want at any given moment, and, in that sense, we are all equal. In most cases, however, we tend to adopt one or the other by way of habit; a habit that can be hard to break, but which is by no means binding.

When we choose to apply the Correspondence Theory, we tend to seek the truth through careful observation of the world around us and diligent attention to all available detail. This way of thinking tends to lead us to go to any lengths to uncover the truth, no matter how hard a task this turns out to be. The subject matter may vary depending on the individual's taste, but the goal will always be the same: to discover the truth wherever it may be hidden. In some cases, the vista of discovery will be entirely new. It could be a new area of science, philosophy or mathematics, or a new aspect of the world currently unknown to us. In other cases, it could be an already well-known field, but one which, at the time, is largely misunderstood. In these instances, we would probably first have to overthrow the current prevailing "truth" before it can be replaced with our new discovery: a hypothesis that more accurately fits the facts.

Throughout history, the fruits of all the important explorers of science and the physical world have been brought to us by virtue of this way of thinking. The likes of Galileo, Newton, Einstein, Magellan, Curie, Columbus and Cook, to name but a few, could not have achieved what they did without it. Many of them, Galileo for example, had to struggle against the prevailing wrong-thinking of the time. As a consequence, he, and many others like him, experienced persecution in their quest for the truth.

Because of the association with exploration, throughout this book the term *explorers* will be used to describe people when they are thinking in this manner. Wherever the word is used in this way, we will use italics so as to distinguish the psychological type from **actual** explorers such as the ones listed above.

In contrast, when we choose to apply the Constructivist Theory, we do not actively seek the truth at all; at least not the "truth" in the same sense as *explorers* see it. When engaged in this way of thinking, we rely solely on being informed of the "truth" by someone in authority: someone in whom we can place our trust, including, for example, doctors, lawyers, newscasters, plumbers and journalists to name but a few. Of course, this begs the question as to how we go about deciding whom we **should** trust, and this is a topic we will explore in some detail in chapter 10. In this mode, when we are offered new information on a given subject, we are quite happy to accept it when it coincides with the truth as prescribed by our chosen source of authority. Conversely, if the new information conflicts with our pre-existing beliefs, we are likely to reject it.

Whenever we are engaged in Constructivism, our focus shifts away from the facts and observations of the real world and moves towards the word of our chosen authority figures. Accompanying this is a shift in purpose away from the desire to learn about the world around us, and towards the desire of garnering the acceptance of our peers. Because of this tendency to believe what we are told, the term *believers* will be used throughout the book to describe people when they are thinking in this manner. Once again, we will use italics to distinguish the psychological type from **actual** believers (for instance, of some organised religion).

Whenever we use the words *explorer* and *believer*, it is crucial to remember that we are referring to two different mind-sets, parts of the mind which are shared by all human beings throughout the world, the authors included. Indeed, life would be nearly impossible for someone who lacked either one. On the occasions when we apply the terms to a person, if we describe someone as "an *explorer*", for example, then we are referring to a person who is thinking in an *explorer* manner **at some particular moment in time**, nothing more, nothing less.

Of course, it's not possible to say which one of these two "minds" is the "better": they both have their advantages and disadvantages. The *explorer* mind is arguably the better choice when truth is paramount, but its use can be a laborious undertaking, so is unlikely to be the better option for making quick decisions. Of course, it is perhaps the only option in those rare circumstances in which we find ourselves facing some wholly new challenge.

The *believer* mind, on the other hand, is undeniably the easier and far less time-consuming option, producing results much more rapidly. Indeed, for many everyday situations, such as listening to the local weather forecast or checking the result of our favourite sports team, it is the obvious choice because it can free us from much time wasted in unnecessary deliberation. After all, our modern world dictates that we lead busy lives, so there simply isn't the time to analyse everything in detail, especially if the situation seems to be too trivial to warrant it. If we were to imagine a world where the only way we could function was from within the *explorer* mind, it is clear that we would have little time left after all our contemplation, and this might ultimately compromise our survival.

Ignoring, for the moment, the state of balance between these two "minds" within any given subject, it is fair to say that, when averaged across today's society, be it in Europe, the USA or anywhere else for that matter, it is the *believer* mind that gets more air time, as it were. The obvious reason for this is the presence of time constraints, as we have already mentioned. But there is also a more subtle facet to this.

From the dawn of time, humans have lived in tribal groups in order to enhance their chances of survival. In the modern world, we see a similar tendency, but the tribes of yore have been replaced by extended family groups, groups of friends, local communities and even nations. Within such groups, a common belief set is an important building block for a cohesive society. By reinforcing cohesion in this way, one might imagine that the survivability of the group is enhanced, and, as a consequence, so is that of the individuals who comprise it. Given all of this, it's easy to see how the *believer* mind might have come to assume its position of dominance when we consider the idea at the level of society as a whole.

Whatever the reason, the necessity and inescapability of the *believer* mind does present us all with one major problem. For whenever we are inclined to employ the *believer*, we leave ourselves open to the possibility that we might be exploited by unscrupulous authority figures who wish to lie to us for their own gain or for the gain of those who control them.

If we turn our attention back once again to the individual, it would be nice to think that the mechanism for selecting the *believer* or the *explorer* always functioned with perfect efficiency. If this were the case, then, for each and every set of circumstances that came our way, the appropriate "mind" would be selected. Sadly, for the most part, this doesn't seem to be the case. For most of us, the *believer* seems to be the default option to the near complete exclusion of the *explorer*, even in situations where this is not appropriate. While we might regard this as an oddity at this stage, it will become apparent over the course of the book that one of the main contributory factors for this is our own fear. Given this, it is left to the reader to judge the extent to which the individual can be held responsible for the apparent domination of the *believer* mind.

Still more bizarre, perhaps, is the fact that some of us seem to reserve the *explorer* for use solely within certain spheres of our life, and shy away from it in others. For instance, people who are engaged in employment with a technical focus are often well practiced in employing their *explorer* mind while in the office; yet may readily switch to their *believer* mind when they put on their jacket to go home.

Over the course of this chapter, we have described and compared the *believer* and *explorer* minds. Before we finish off, it's probably best to point out the limitations common to each. To put it bluntly, neither *believer* nor *explorer* can **guarantee** us of "success". Sometimes, truth can be a nebulous thing: on the one hand, it is possible for us to be tricked into misinterpreting the evidence; while on the other, it is conceivable that we can be lied to by our chosen authority figures. There is significant merit to be had in viewing the truth as a mutable phenomenon, rather than something that is set in stone.

# - 4 -
# Beyond the Lemon

*"The old scientific ideal of absolutely certain knowledge has proved to be an idol. The demand for scientific objectivity makes it inevitable that every scientific statement must remain tentative for ever."*

Karl Popper, Austrian philosopher

---

Having looked at the characteristics of the *believer* and *explorer* minds in the previous chapter, we will now take the opportunity to develop the idea further by looking at what happens when two people interact. It goes without saying that there are three possible permutations for this, and it will come as no surprise that the patterns of behaviour we can expect to see vary significantly depending on which of the three we examine. In general, we will find a more harmonious interaction in the permutations where each participant adopts the same "mind". When we mix one *believer* and one *explorer*, on the other hand, we should expect a more discordant outcome.

If both parties choose to use their *believer* minds and both follow the same authority figure, the result is usually a reaffirmation of their mutual beliefs and a reinforcement of the esteem they hold for their chosen authority. Whilst such an interaction is unlikely to result in the communication of any detailed information, the result can be a feeling of reassurance for each participant.

If, on the other hand, the participants choose to employ their *explorer* minds, the result is more likely to be a detailed exchange of ideas and information. This may lead to some positive research, with each able to contribute and learn more as a result of the collaboration. The sense of mutual respect that may follow from this can be just as rewarding as that of the previous example.

It's only when we get a *believer* and an *explorer* together that the fun really starts. It's this combination that we will look at here, before refining it with a more formal analysis in chapter 14. The best way to see how such interactions can play out is by means of a role play. In this example, and in many of those that follow, we will look at the interaction between two characters, Edward and Barry, each of whom portrays their own distinct outlook on the world around them. These characters are entirely fictional, and any resemblance that may be seen between them and any real person is purely coincidental.

Let's suppose that Edward makes the following statement (which he claims is true):

> "In my pocket there is a photograph of some lemons."

Now let's suppose that Barry initially rejects this proposition (claims that it is false) for some reason. We will come back to the reasons that he might have for doing so a little later.

At this point, we should not concern ourselves with the question of whether the proposition is actually true or false. After all, it's not the conclusion itself that we are interested in here, but the process we use to resolve the argument and the behavioural traits exhibited by the two characters along the way.

We must now consider the best way for our two participants to resolve their argument and move forward in a constructive manner. For many, the most obvious answer might be that each of them should just look at the photograph in Edward's pocket, if it exists. It seems so simple, right?

Doing this would be an example of the *explorer* mind at work: it seeks to resolve dispute by performing a detailed analysis of the available evidence. Only once both participants had chosen to do this would a detailed investigation be possible, and this might lead to a sequence of relevant questions such as these:

- Are they actually lemons, or could they just be unripe oranges?
- Assuming they are lemons, are they real, or could they just be plastic fakes?
- Assuming they are real lemons, do they seem to be the central theme of the photo, or are they more of a side motif? If they are merely incidental, can the photo really be said to be "of" the lemons?

All these valid, detailed questions can only be answered when both parties are prepared to examine the evidence. If one or more refuses to do so, then the argument can never progress beyond "Yes it is. No it isn't". For many, this kind of argument will bring back fond memories of the school playground.

Now let's imagine that Barry does refuse to look at the photo, yet remains adamant that the proposition is false. Why might he do this? There are a number of possible reasons but, for the purposes of our narrative, we will consider just the one. The reason for this focus will become apparent over the course of the coming chapters.

Let's imagine that, prior to the conversation, Barry's best friend, Charlie, has told him that the photo is actually of some tomatoes. If we imagine that Barry, for some reason, has a hatred of lemons, it's easy to see how he may **prefer** to believe that the photo shows some tomatoes, regardless of whether or not this might be true. For this reason, he may well elect to believe Charlie without question, and refuse to consider the matter further. In this case, Barry is appointing Charlie to the role of authority figure. In this capacity, Charlie has effectively granted Barry the permission to believe in the tomatoes. Barry is likely to accept this permission as, by so doing, his life is made easier: he is no longer obliged to face the uncomfortable prospect of the lemons.

By choosing Constructivism based on Charlie's authority, Barry has shown a preference for using his *believer* mind. But why would this choice make Barry reluctant to consider the evidence? The obvious answer is that, in avoiding it, Barry is seeking to avoid some potential difficulties. If he were to look at the evidence, there is every chance that this might put him in an uncomfortable position in the event that the evidence contradicted his belief. Under these circumstances, Barry would have to take some additional action to deal with the problem. Later on, in chapter 9, we will look at some of the techniques he might use to do this.

Although this example is a trivial and rather contrived one, it does enable us to see some of the factors that underlie the voluntary acceptance of authority that is typical of the behaviour associated with the *believer* mind. If the authority figure is telling us what we want to hear, or what we think we want to hear, we are more likely to accept the statements he or she makes. At the same time, the *believer* is obliged to ignore any contradictory evidence that presents itself, and to exercise diligence in avoiding any discussion of detail.

This example brings to light one of the key differences between statements that emanate from the *believer* mind when compared with those from the *explorer*. *Believer* statements tend to be generalisations and, as such, bear some similarities to political slogans or propaganda. In general, it is not possible to take a *believer's* statement and "drill down" on it to uncover greater levels of detail.

On the other hand, you can take an *explorer* statement and "drill down" towards greater detail as far as you like. In this example, we could do so by asking some of the following questions:

- What attributes of the photo are indicative of lemons?
- What reasons do we have to suppose the lemons are real?
- What differences could we expect to see between a real photo of some lemons and a fake?

This is a process that, by now, should be familiar. It's a similar process to that which we adopted in chapter 1 to work out whether or not there had really been a storm.

In his book, "The Logic of Scientific Discovery"[iii], the 20th century philosopher, Karl Popper, gave us his idea of Empirical Falsification. Popper states that scientific ideas are never entirely proven, but exist for only as long as it takes for them to be falsified. In addition, the only ideas that have any value (from a scientific point of view) are those which are associated with a mechanism by which they **could** be falsified. This does not mean to say that the only ideas that are valid are those that are false, but that a person who is stating a hypothesis is obliged to proffer a mechanism (e.g. some type of experiment or research) that could be used if one were to **attempt** to prove the idea to be false. Without such a mechanism, the hypothesis should not be taken seriously, at least not from a scientific perspective.

Bringing this back to our lemons, we can see that the questions above are commensurate with the idea Popper was trying to encapsulate. For example, if we are to make the assertion that the lemons are real, we might suggest that we obtain five photos of real lemons and five of fake ones. We could then analyse each set to determine which features were indicative of real lemons and which of fakes. For instance, we may notice that the fake lemons all exhibited a waxy lustre which was not present in the real ones. We could then examine the supposed photo in Edward's pocket to see if we could find any of these differentiating features.

In this chapter, we have taken a look at some of the behavioural traits that emanate from the *believer* and *explorer* minds, and seen how to distinguish each by means of a few simple tests. We have shown how the *explorer* mind tends to produce statements that are Popper-compliant, while the *believer* mind tends to offer us indivisible statements which are reminiscent of propaganda.

# - 5 -
# Black & White

*"I'm for truth, no matter who tells it. I'm for justice, no matter who it's for or against."*

Malcolm X

---

In the previous chapter we saw how Edward and Barry's different approaches could be described in terms of the *believer* and *explorer* mind. Some people, however, have less savoury words for the same thing. Revisiting our two friends will help us to understand this.

Imagine this time that Barry is an employer in a large supermarket chain. Let's say that he has a vacancy for a new store manager and that two appropriately qualified people apply for it, one black and one white. We would expect Barry to read both CVs (résumés) then interview the two applicants before offering the position to the better of the two.

However, let's suppose that, at some point in the past, Barry's friend Charlie has told him that all black people are lazy. Perhaps Barry harbours racist beliefs and, as such, finds it convenient to believe what Charlie said. Based on this, he decides to interview only the white applicant and goes on to offer them the position.

At this point, pretty much everyone (quite rightly) would say that Barry's course of action is wrong, and that his unquestioning belief in Charlie's "advice" is just a cover for his own prejudice. In this case, Barry's *believer* mind stepped to the fore, causing him to act in a way that most people would find unacceptable.

Of course, we know that **some** people are lazy, while others are not. We also know that some people are black, while others are not. Furthermore, we know that these two variables are not in any way causally linked. In mathematical terms, we might word this by saying that the two variables are "orthogonal". But, just to add a twist, let's suppose that, in this **particular** case, the black person in question **was**, in fact, lazy.

Now ask yourself this: does this fact make Barry's actions any more acceptable? We can assume that most people would agree that it does not. What is important is the **process** Barry uses to reach his decision, not so much the outcome. In order for Barry to make a fair decision, he would need to use his *explorer* mind, and must also be seen to do so.

We saw the same thing in chapter 1 with our analysis of the storm. Even though we went to great lengths to gather evidence to distinguish the hose pipe hypothesis from the storm one, there is always the possibility that we may have been tricked into thinking there had been a storm by a person with an exceedingly long hose pipe. In this case, we might say that we have arrived at the wrong conclusion, despite the fact that we have followed the appropriate procedure. It is also possible that, while we were being fooled by the long hose pipe, the TV weather channel may have correctly reported the weather with no mention of a storm. In this anomalous situation, we have still "done the right thing" by following the *explorer* process, since doing this gives us the opportunity to question our results and change our conclusion in the event that some new evidence comes to light.

So now we have another clear difference between the two minds. Using the *explorer* mind gives us a greater opportunity to be fair and balanced, while using the *believer* mind may lead us to prejudice and bigotry.

Up to this point, it might be difficult to see how one would **ever** do anything other than simply look at the evidence. After all, it's easy to look at a photograph of some lemons, and it's clear to see that one should conduct interviews before selecting a candidate for a job. But let's see what happens when we consider a different example. Suppose that, this time, Edward makes the following proposition (which he claims is true):

> "There is a three word search term which, when typed into Google, will provide any person of average intelligence with sufficient evidence to prove that the London tube (US: subway) bombings of July 7$^{th}$ 2005 were an inside job."

Once again, we should not concern ourselves with whether this proposition *is* actually true or false. Just as in chapter 4, it's not the conclusion itself that we're interested in here, but the process we use to reach it. If the reader is not familiar with the incident in question, we are referring to the terrorist incident that occurred in London, England, often described as the UK's 9/11.

Whereas before, we saw that the average person would probably want to go ahead and consider the evidence, now, the controversial nature of this new proposition is likely to make those same people reject the idea without any consideration. Or, to put it more simply, most people would probably conclude that Edwards's proposition was false, without any further deliberation or reference to evidence.

But hang on a minute. Before we go any further, what was *your* reaction when reading the proposition? Be as honest as you can. If your reaction was something along the lines of "What are the three words?"[iv], then it was your *explorer* mind that was engaged. If, conversely, your automatic response was one of disbelief and rejection of the notion, then it was your *believer* mind which intercepted the idea before your *explorer* mind could get a look-in. If you experienced the latter reaction then you are in the majority. The most surprising thing about the evidence we refer to here is not that anybody can go and examine it for themselves, but that (nearly) nobody does.

So why do we see this switch from *explorer* to *believer*? Clearly, the answer must have something to do with the nature of the proposition itself, since this is the only thing that has changed. In the second case, when we consider the proposition, it's as if we get a message from our *believer* mind that says:

> "Hang on a minute. We have invested a large portion of our lives in believing we are the good guys and we are fighting the bad guys who are out to get us. If this turned out **not** to be the case, we would have to jettison a good part of our world-view. This is too high a price to pay just for the luxury of viewing a little bit of evidence. Because of this threat, I'm going to step in and take the helm. As far as I'm concerned, there can be no such evidence."

Of course, the idea of having to give up a large part of our world-view is a frightening prospect for many of us, and it is perhaps this fear that is the key to understanding the difference in response between the two scenarios.

The Fear Paralysis Reflex (FPR) is thought to be one of the earliest reflexes to emerge in humans, appearing whilst still in the womb. The reaction is usually characterised by a withdrawal from any sudden, unexpected or threatening stimulus, and is often accompanied by a temporary "freeze". During the withdrawal, the foetus shuts itself off from its environment by producing stress proteins and so becomes literally paralyzed with fear. It is thought that this reflex integrates before birth into the Moro reflex and then, before the age of one year, into the more mature "startle" or Strauss reflex that remains with us into adulthood. This adult reflex is more advanced in that it allows us to consider the stimulus before making a decision as to whether to react to it or ignore it. It is thought that, if the FPR is not fully integrated at birth, this can result in a number of lifelong challenges related to fear. In addition, it has been suggested that even if it **has** been integrated, the reflex may become reactivated later under certain circumstances such as exposure to trauma, injury, toxins or stress.

If this theory is correct, it is reasonable to suppose that the interjection of the *believer* mind may be linked to the manifestation of the fear reflex in its primitive form, and so may be largely involuntary. Putting it another way, we might say that when a possibility is too frightening to consider, the *believer* steps in and offers us an easy way out. We tell ourselves that we don't need to be concerned with the new stimulus and thus award ourselves the opportunity to stay within our comfort zone.

Of course, this leads us on to question the nature of our comfort zone: the world-view that we are trying to maintain. When we look a little deeper, we find that this consists of a belief system that's built around the two simple statements: "We are the good guys. They are the bad guys."

As we will see in chapter 7, this belief system closely resembles a form of fundamentalist religion, albeit a modern-day one. At this point, the reader will be forgiven for thinking that this is a somewhat bold statement to make. After all, an attempt to jump from an unwillingness to consider evidence to the existence of a new religion is probably a leap too far for most. So, before we carry on with this line of thought, we must pause a while to ask ourselves what a religion really is. In the next two chapters, we'll try and answer this question, then pick up this thread again in chapter 8.

# - 6 -
# What's in a Religion?

*"Di immortales virtutem approbare, non adhibere debent."*
(We may expect the gods to approve virtue, but not to endow us with it.)

Anonymous

---

No matter what part of the world you live in, turn on the TV news and it won't be long before you are confronted with an act of supposed terrorism and a narrative to accompany it. More often than not, the story presented will focus on a group of Muslim fundamentalists or extremists. Some accept without question that these stories are genuine, while others reject them with equal vigour. The majority of us, however, will probably take a stance somewhere between these two extremes. But, wherever you stand on this scale, it cannot be denied that a stereotype of religious fundamentalism has been created within the collective mind of our society. The aim of this chapter is to present a simplified model of this stereotype, no more, no less.

Since we are presenting a stereotype, our story should attract no disapproval from the world's religious population in general, the vast majority of whom are decent, rational and peace-loving human beings. By the same token, no indignation need be taken at our attempts to generalise or to conflate ideas which are normally viewed as being distinct. As an example, we will treat the concepts of religious fundamentalism and religious extremism as if they were two sides of the same coin. Of course, we are aware that this is not really the case, but these are the little luxuries one can afford oneself when one is constructing a stereotype.

With this in mind, the reader is invited to suspend judgement until the explanation is complete. Towards the end of this chapter, and also in the one which follows, we will attempt to analyse the extent, or lack thereof, to which we can find any real examples of our stereotype from today's world or from the world of the past.

Having said this, in order for us to talk about religious fundamentalism, we will first need to look at the broader topic of religion in general, a field of human psychology and behaviour which is often grossly misunderstood. The best place to start a story is at the beginning, so we will start the ball rolling by asking ourselves where organised religion comes from in the first place. As for an answer, there are two possibilities which immediately spring to mind:

- Organised religions are created by a god.
- Organised religions are a construct of man.

To make a convincing case for one or the other of these two answers would probably take longer than a chapter, so we'll try and keep things brief by just looking for some pointers, and seeing where they take us.

If religion were truly a divine creation, we might reasonably expect to find a god or gods at the centre of each of the world's major organised religions. In addition, we might expect each god to be unique, by which we mean to say that the god of each religion would have a separate identity from those of other religions. If this were not the case, then two religions which shared the same god would, by definition, be the same religion, given that we have made the assumption that religion comes from a god. But counterexamples of both of these expectations are easy to come by.

The first obvious one is the fact that three of the world's most popular religions not only share the same god, but also recognise each other's prophets, at least to a certain extent. For Christians (two billion followers, worldwide), the god of the Old Testament is the same as the god of the Jews (thirteen million followers). Indeed, the first five books, the Pentateuch, and the Jewish Torah are one in the same. As for Muslims (one billion followers), the Quran tells us that Allah is the same god as the Jewish Yahweh.

A second counterexample presents itself when we consider Sikhism. The Guru Granth Sahib, the holy book of the Sikhs, tells us that god is not a personified entity at all but, instead, can be thought of as the indescribable oneness that lies at the heart of all the world's religions. In some respects, we might consider this concept as being somewhat similar to the approach of Buddhism, in which we see a focus on spirituality taking the place of the worship of a deity. With a little thinking, the reader will be able to come up with plenty more examples of the problems we find when we assume that religion comes from a god or gods.

For these reasons, we have some strong grounds to suspect that religion might be a construct of man and that the god, rather than playing the starring role in the performance, is just one of the characters in the plot. If we accept this possibility, albeit tentatively at this stage, it begs the question as to what exactly it is that resides at the heart of religion. Over the years, various psychologists have attempted to provide an answer to this conundrum and, by doing so, find out where religion comes from. The most promising idea is that it is a cultural phenomenon which began back in tribal times with the notion of "us and them".

In his ground-breaking work, "What Do You Say After You Say Hello"[v], Eric Berne introduces us to the idea of "The Life Positions" which summarise the attitudes of an individual within his or her society. Using his terminology, we can describe religion as the affirmation of the life position: "we're OK: they're not OK." Encompassed by this principle is the idea of an *in-group* of people and an *out-group*. A subject who holds this position will feel themselves to be associated with the in-group, which they will regard as consisting of the "good guys". As part of this process, the subject will tend to identify all others as being part of an out-group, which they will regard as the "bad guys". Typically, the out-group is viewed as not holding the same beliefs as, not sharing the same values as and not adhering to the same customs as the in-group. The differences which are identified between the two groups and the position of "we're OK: they're not OK" lead the adherent, in some cases, to view the members of the out-group as inferior.

An important part of the process is the assigning of a label (for example, "infidels" or "heathens") to the out-group. In our treatment of the photo of the lemons, back in chapter 4, we saw that the goal of the *believer* mind is to avoid detail and analysis, replacing these with a focus on generalisations that are akin to propaganda. As we will see in more detail in chapter 11, the label acts as an instrument to this effect in that it allows the adherent to think of the out-group in abstract terms, rather than seeing it as a collection of individuals.

Now we have the groundwork out of the way, we can begin to construct our stereotype. The model we propose will focus on what we might call the "chain of cause and effect" that drives the adherents of the fundamentalist-extremist religion. This chain is shown in Figure 3, the numbers in parentheses in the following paragraphs referring to the numbers in the figure, the key elements of the model.

It should come as no surprise that the chain starts with a (1) holy book, such as the Bible or Quran. While some of the followers may consult the book directly, many view this process as being too lengthy or arduous. In these instances, the information these texts contain is mediated by a facilitator such as a (2) priest or imam, and is taken on-board in the form of "teachings". The fact that this practice is normally conducted in a place of worship, such as a (3) church or mosque, leads us to make a number of observations about the process.

The first of these is that the adherent enters into it in a voluntary capacity. Some might say that, in some cases, there may be considerable social pressure for them to do so, but few would doubt that there remains at least some element of choice.

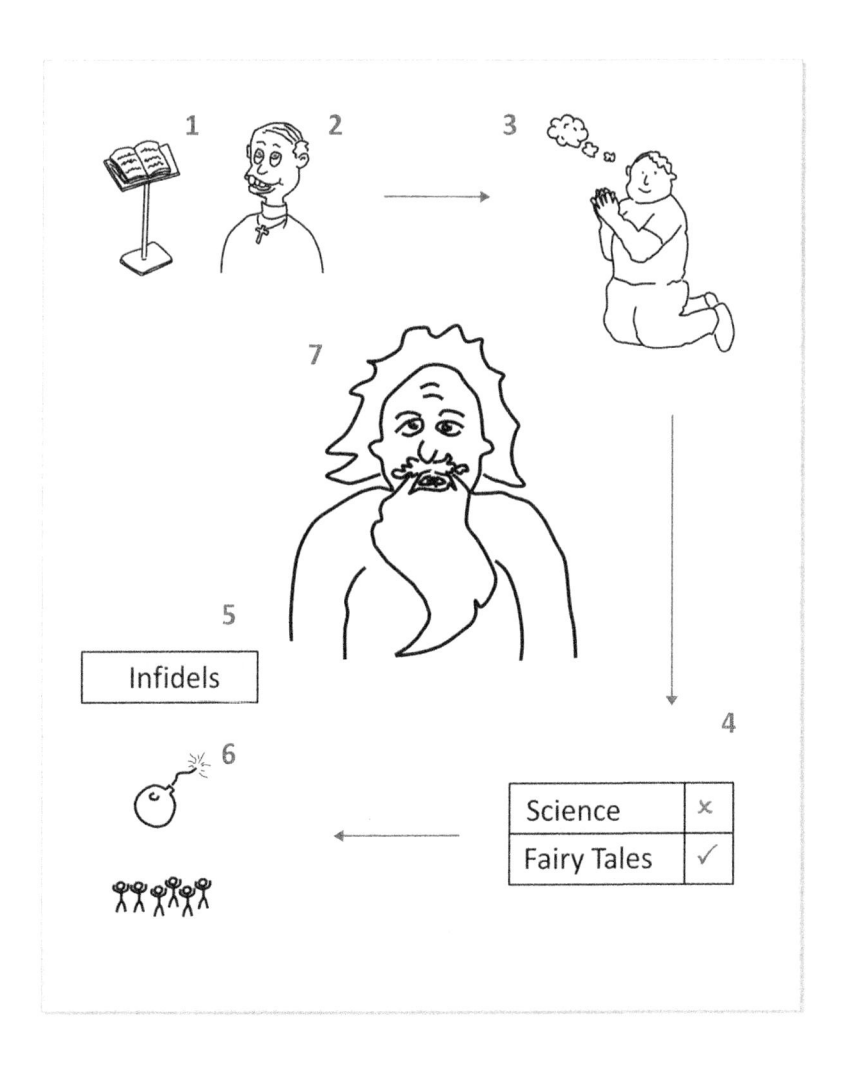

**Figure 3**

The second observation is the fact that, since the adherent has to make a special journey to engage in their indoctrination, a limit is imposed on the efficiency of the process.

In order for the fundamentalist to be welcomed, he or she is required to (4) accept the impossible religious stories that are the canon of the belief system and, at the same time, to deny science, or at least to deny the right of science to interfere with the story. The best way to explore the concept is to select one particular story as an example and analyse it in detail. Here we have selected an example from Christianity, but there is no reason why we couldn't have picked an example from some other religion instead. Our aim, after all, is to illustrate our model, not to criticise any one particular religion.

> "On the third day, at a marriage in Cana, Jesus turned water into wine." (John 11:38-44).

As we have already discussed, one facet of the *believer* mind is the tendency to avoid detailed analysis by focusing just on generalisations. A story such as the one above gives us an opportunity to see this tendency in action. Let's pause to consider the folly that ensues when we attempt to subject it to an analysis such as the following:

> Wine is made from alcohol (13%), water (85%) and other organic material (2%). For Jesus to convert the water into wine he would have to perform an organic synthesis. To do this, he would first have to source the organic material (e.g. methane, ethane or some other material) to be used as the root of the reaction, then conduct a series of organic syntheses to produce the alcohol and the other organic constituents. If the source were to be the water alone, Jesus would have had to first transmute the oxygen atoms into carbon atoms (in some kind of nuclear process) in order to obtain the organic roots for the syntheses.

For a religious story to work, it has to be taken at face value and must not be subjected to this kind of scrutiny, since to do so would be tantamount to saying that it has some scientific basis. Stories like this are non-Popper-compliant, which means to say that they do not offer a mechanism for falsification and so do not qualify as candidates for scientific discussion. This is what we are getting at when we say that the adherent must accept the impossible religious stories and deny science.

When taken as a whole, the collection of stories constitutes the strands that make up the religious narrative which is imparted to the follower. Once again, there are some important observations to be made here. For each individual, the narrative that is absorbed is identical to the one which is imparted to all other followers of the same religion. In addition, the narrative is **different** from that which is received by the followers of other religions. It is this segregation of doctrine, along with the cultural division which results from it, that brings us back to the life position of "we're OK: they're not OK" that Berne described for us so well.

Returning once again to our simplified stereotype, it is easy to imagine how this seemingly deliberate reinforcement of the life position might encourage the (5) labelling of the out-group, perhaps as "infidels", or something similar. The concept of labelling in this specific context, for which we will adopt the term *Religious Labelling*, has such far-reaching implications in terms of both psychology and sociology that a book could be written on this one topic alone. Rather than go off on a tangent at this point, we will leave its further discussion until chapter 11 so we can focus here just on its consequences.

As we have already discussed, the act of labelling encourages the fundamentalist to shift their focus away from seeing the out-group as a collection of individuals and towards a view of them as an abstract concept, and it's easy to see how they might become more inclined to committing (6) acts of violence towards the out-group. For most people, the thought of violence towards an individual precipitates a feeling of revulsion, but the idea of violence against an abstract concept is less likely to provoke this. In some respects, we can view the application of the label as an attempt to dehumanize the members of the out-group, the purpose being to deactivate this reaction.

When considering the supposed acts of violence committed by extremists, some might choose to focus on the culpability of the individual with the bomb. But another way to look at this might be to look upon the extremist as a victim of a wider agenda. When we consider the fact that both the label for the out-group and the life position of "we're OK: they're not OK" are constructed by sources external to the individual, we begin to see how these things might be viewed as instruments of control on the part of the religious leaders. Since this is a theme which we will cover at length in the coming chapters, we will leave it here for now and return, once again, to our stereotype model.

The whole chain we have discussed carries on under (7) the watchful gaze of the invisible being in the sky: the god. Needless to say, we can never be totally sure as to whether or not he (or she, or it?) exists, but we are in a position to make a rational guess. The British philosopher, Bertrand Russell has provided us with some help on this matter with his analogy of the Celestial Teapot[vi]. It's probably best if we allow Russell to explain the concept:

> "If I were to suggest that between the Earth and Mars there is a china teapot revolving about the sun in an elliptical orbit, nobody would be able to disprove my assertion provided I were careful to add that the teapot is ... [too small to see]. But if I were to go on to say that, since my assertion cannot be disproved, it is intolerable presumption on the part of human reason to doubt it, I should rightly be thought to be talking nonsense. If, however, the existence of such a teapot were affirmed in ancient books, taught as the sacred truth every Sunday and instilled into the minds of children at school, hesitation to believe in its existence would ... [attract the attention of the] psychiatrist ... [or the] Inquisitor in an earlier time."

The point Russell was trying to make is that the more outlandish a proposition, the greater the burden of proof that is assumed by its proponents; and it is certainly not the duty of its doubters to "disprove" it.

Earlier in the chapter we suggested that god may not be the central motif in the tapestry of religion, and we have seen how the apparent lack of credibility for his existence would seem to corroborate this idea. What is clear, however, is that he does have an important role to play in the proceedings, so it's only right that we should ask ourselves what that role is. Religion is a subject that can cause much confusion, both for its followers and for those of us who look on from the outside. When we are faced with an idea that doesn't make sense, it can often mean that we are either missing an important part of the puzzle or that one of the parts we do have has been misinterpreted in some way. When the missing piece arrives or the misinterpretation is corrected, it can be a bit of a "eureka" moment.

It is exactly one of these moments that comes to pass when we consider the idea of god in the role of bogeyman. Religious texts tell us that if we live in fear of him, believe the impossible religious stories, deny science and follow the rules we are provided with, then he will grant us eternal life. If, on the other hand, we cross him, it is said that we will be subjected to a life of eternal damnation.

In order for one person or a group of people to exercise control over others, it is necessary for the controller to manipulate one of the emotional drivers of the controlee. In principle, any emotion will suffice, to a certain extent, but by far the most successful one to use is that of fear. A religion's god figure is a construct used by the religious leaders for this purpose. Once the adherent fears the consequences of disobedience, their desire to be their own master dissipates and they tend to relinquish their individual freedom, preferring to become a cog in the machine. Of course, there is also the positive aspect of the coercion, the carrot of eternal life in heaven if we follow the rules, but this is less effective than the stick of fear. When we accept the idea of god's role as mere bogeyman, it frees us to make the mental leap from the view of religion as a spiritual calling to the view that it's just a deliberately constructed power structure. Once we have made this leap, many aspects of religion which previously elicited confusion can be seen in a clearer light.

Now that we have completed the construction of our stereotype, we must ask ourselves the question as to where, if at all, we might find this "chain of cause and effect" playing out in the real world. As we have already pointed out, the narratives supplied to us by our mainstream media all point to the idea that it is very common. Over the course of the coming chapters, we will make the case to suggest that there may be a strong divergence between their messages and the (Correspondence) truth.

Having said this, examples of belief systems which embody such chains are easy to find when we look back in history. To pick just one example from many, we might consider the Albigensian Crusade[vii] which took place from 1209 to 1229 in Languedoc, France. Over the course of twenty years, around a million Cathars, whom the Catholic Church referred to as "Albigensians", were said to have been killed, all thanks to the belief in an unlikely religious story.

Like the Catholics of the time, the Cathars subscribed to a dualistic belief system, which is to say that they held the view that the universe was divided into good and evil. Unlike the Catholics, however, they believed that the Earth was created by the evil guy, the devil, or *Rex Mundi* ("King of the World") to use the name that they knew him by. The idea that the world was purely the creation of the devil was unpalatable to the in-group, the Catholics, who then instigated the crusade against the out-group, the Cathars.

Of course, this is just one example of our chain of cause and effect, but, with a little thought, the reader will, no doubt, be able to come up with many others. What is more, if we choose to see the world through the eyes of the mainstream media, we find the same thing going on today, though, as we have already pointed out, there is good reason to doubt their narrative in most cases.

In this chapter, we have described a stereotype of fundamentalist or extremist religion, taking care to point out the limited scope of its practical realisation. No matter what position the reader takes with respect to this scope, the relevance of the elements of our discussion to the way we think about the world remain unchanged. Thanks to the mainstream media, the stereotype exists in all of our minds, whether we accept it or not.

This brings to a close our examination of mainstream fundamentalist or extremist religion. In the next chapter we will go on to search for some other examples of our stereotype in action, and so discover just how widespread it is.

# - 7 -
# A Modern Day Religion

*"Al-Qaida, literally 'the database', was originally the computer file of the thousands of Mujahideen who were recruited and trained with help from the CIA to defeat the Russians."*

Robin Cook, ex UK Foreign Secretary, The Guardian, July 8th 2005

---

In the previous chapter, we constructed a stereotypical view of a fundamentalist or extremist religion and examined the "chain of cause and effect" which we imagined to be at the heart of it. We pointed out that, although it is easy to find historical examples of the slaughter resulting from this chain, it is likely that such things have all but died out within the confines of mainstream religion as we see it today. The aim of this chapter is to present a modern day belief system that encompasses a model so similar to the one we have described, that we are forced to conclude that we are dealing with an identical phenomenon.

The belief system we will describe is one which is followed by as many as four billion people globally, the vast majority of them unaware of the extent of their devotion. At its heart can be found a chain of cause and effect which is an almost perfect facsimile of our stereotype. It is this striking similarity that gives us good reason to suspect that this belief system represents a virulent form of modern-day fundamentalism. It goes without saying that this assertion will be met with some degree of scepticism from many, but if there is one constant message to be found in the chapters that have led up to this point, it is that scepticism and questioning are behaviours that should be encouraged. Just as in the previous chapter, the reader is invited to suspend judgement until the comparison is complete.

As many will have already guessed, the belief system we are alluding to is the one which emanates from that seemingly innocuous, everyday object, the TV set. To understand how this works, we will start by looking at the corresponding chain of cause and effect, as shown in Figure 4, taking careful note along the way of the similarities between it and the chain described in Figure 3 of the previous chapter.

Since our modern belief system is focused on (1) the TV, it should come as no surprise to see it in place at the start of the chain, assuming the role of the holy book of the last chapter. For the TV, the mediator is not the priest or imam that we saw before, but typically takes the form of (2) the news anchor of the adherent's favourite TV channel.

Whereas in the previous chapter we saw the necessity for the indoctrination to take place in the place of worship, our modern equivalent suffers from no such restriction. In this case, it is typical for the devotee to receive the "knowledge" in (3) the comfort of their own home, in the home of a fellow devotee, in their local pub or bar, or pretty much anywhere else for that matter. Of course, just as before, we must also consider the degree to which the recipient is able to exercise free choice over their indoctrination. Due to the all-pervasive nature of modern TV, it's a lot harder for us to avoid it, and, although very few of us make the choice **not** to own a TV set, even those who make this choice can hardly avoid coming into contact with it at some point during their day. Perhaps it's these factors of locality and omnipresence that mean the TV has around the same number of followers as that of all other religions combined.

In the previous chapter we saw the importance of accepting the impossible religious stories that comprise the canon of the belief system, and the denial of science that this entails. The idea that fictional tales analogous to those of the last chapter are propagated by the TV might seem a pretty bold claim at

A Modern Day Religion 55

**Figure 4**

first, but the following example of such a thing will help to show that this comparison has some merit. The story we will choose goes like this:

> "On September 11th 2001, a handful of men from a group of nineteen, under the command of one with a

beard who lived in a cave, flew two planes into two (from a group of three) buildings in New York. The two planes caused the three buildings to collapse in a manner which directly contradicted both Newton's Third Law of Motion and the laws of conservation of energy, in that all three collapses occurred with acceleration close to that of free fall, without the input of energy that would be required to cause this."

For some people, the contradiction of the laws of physics which is demanded by the story will be self-evident: for others, perhaps less so. In either case, it is outside the scope of this book to explain how this narrative entails the breaking of those laws. For a detailed exposé of this subject, the reader is invited to consult the online article "Evidence for the Explosive Demolition of WTC7 on 9/11"[viii]. Alternatively, any high school physics text book will do the job.

It is worth noting here that the three events we are referring to are the actual "collapses" themselves. In the case of the first two buildings, the duration was around ten seconds. In the case of the third building, the duration was a little less: around seven seconds. We are not talking about the events which led up to this, since these have no bearing on the physics of the collapse.

Just as in the previous chapter, the above story is designed to be taken at face value and does not lend itself to any form of analysis. As with all the narratives which are formulated by, or embraced by the *believer* mind, it is not possible to progress from summary to detail. This can be illustrated by means of the following exercise in folly:

> Newton's laws are fundamental to the way our universe operates, and can be used to predict the motion of all objects, as long as their velocity does not approach the speed of light. The laws of conservation of energy are similarly set in stone. If the necessary energy to cause the collapses was not

present, it means these laws did not apply on September 11th. In this case, we should ask what factors stopped the laws' applying, how the laws should be modified to take into account this hitherto unobserved phenomenon, who orchestrated the deviation from the laws and what mechanism they used to achieve it.

Just as with the story of the previous chapter, this one is non-Popper-compliant, which means to say that it does not offer a mechanism for falsification and so does not qualify as a candidate for scientific discussion. This is clearly evidenced by the above silliness. The fact of the matter is that no man, not even one who has a beard, can ever defy the laws of physics. Just as we saw in the previous chapter, the adherent of the belief system must (4) accept the fairy tales and deny science.

Before we carry on with this thread, it's worth pausing a moment to consider that somewhat emotive phrase: "fairy tales". The reason why this can stir up so much emotion for many is that its meaning is often misunderstood. So often do we see it used as a pejorative term to indicate the speaker's contempt, that sometimes we forget that it can have other, more tightly defined, meanings. It goes without saying that its pejorative sense is very much not the one we wish to imply here. Now, identifying what we **don't** mean is simple enough, but elaborating further on what we do mean will require a chapter all to itself. We will pick this up again in chapter 26.

Central to our modern form of fundamentalism, just as we saw before, is the identification of an in-group and an out-group. In this case, the in-group consists of the Western powers, a group identified as the "good guys" because of their alleged desire to bring "peace and democracy" to the world. The out-group, the "bad guys", comprises the Muslims, who are erroneously blamed for perpetrating the events in the story. They are described as "evil" because they "hate us because of our freedoms". Thanks to the ubiquity of the TV, the dissemination of an identical narrative to a wide audience is ensured. As we saw in the previous chapter, this is a vital step in the formation of the notion of "us and them", and leads to the reinforcement of the life position, "we're OK: they're not OK."

For many people who are sucked in by the belief system, Religious Labelling (see chapter 11) will be the next step. In this case, the out-out group are given the label (5) "terrorists" or "Muslim extremists". Just as before, the fundamentalist's use of the label leads them to take a more abstract view of the, now dehumanized, out-group. The result is that they are now more inclined to tolerate, or even engage in (6) acts of violence towards them, or at the very least to remain silent when such acts are carried out in their name by their governments.

This brings us on to what is probably the biggest difference between our two forms of fundamentalism: the scale of the religious violence. If we take the view that there are Muslim fundamentalists or extremists who conform to our stereotype, we have to accept that, in most cases, these people are armed with guns and with bombs strapped to their bodies. The potential for devastation of these weapons is limited. In the fundamentalism of this chapter, however, the bombs are high-tech devices costing hundreds of thousands of dollars strapped to war planes costing hundreds of millions.

In addition to the monetary cost, we mustn't forget the far greater cost in terms of human life: hundreds of thousands of innocent civilians across Iraq and Afghanistan, all slain because of an impossible lie. If we look at the global "War on Terror" in general, some estimates place a figure as large as four million on the number killed since September 11th 2001. When we compare this figure to the one million killed in the Albigensian Crusade, we begin to get a picture of how far fundamentalism has really progressed in the modern age.

Of course, here we have picked just one example of a modern, fundamentalist fairy tale; and one example alone is not sufficient to build a case to suggest we are looking at a religion. To strengthen our case, we would need to consider some more examples and try to observe a pattern that runs common to all. As it turns out, examples like this are very easy to come by, but, rather than disturb our flow with a long list here, we will leave it until chapter 25 before looking at some of them.

All that remains in our chain now is the (7) central bogeyman, so let's move on and make him the focus of our attention. For more than ten years, this role was played by "Osama Bin Laden", or "Tim Osman", to give him the name he was known by during his time as a CIA asset. So what can we say about his life?

Bin Laden was born on March 10$^{th}$ 1957 in Riyadh, Saudi Arabia, and for much of his later life was quite sick, relying on kidney dialysis to keep him alive. As reported by the New York Times, The Pakistan Observer, Fox News, The Guardian, CNN *et al*, he died, in all probability, on or around December 13$^{th}$ 2001, either directly from this kidney condition, or from a lung complication stemming from it. The various reports show some deviation in the details of the cause and time of death, and the reader is encouraged to perform their own investigation before reaching a conclusion. The example shown in Figure 5 is just one of many.

As was widely reported, he died a second time on May 2$^{nd}$ 2011, following a raid on "his" Pakistan home by US forces. Nobody, we hope, would try to claim that Bin Laden was equivalent to a god, but what is clear is that he does share at least some characteristics with the divine. Jesus Christ, so we are told, also died twice, and we see the same motif repeated in many other mainstream religions.

Laying aside the frivolity, the central point to all this is that, in our modern-day version of fundamentalism, to which we will tentatively assign the name *TVism*, the character of bogeyman is played either by Osama Bin Laden or whoever is conjured up to take his place. Just as we saw in the previous chapter, in order for the leaders of the fundamentalist religion to be able to exercise control over their followers, they must manipulate the fear centres of their subjects. Our governments' creation of the Osama Bin Laden bogeyman, and his successors, is the perfect instrument for the realisation of this strategy. Our fear of them is what coerces us to give up our freedom, and enables us to justify and finance the genocide of millions, often without a second thought.

## Report: Bin Laden Already Dead

Published December 26, 2001 · FoxNews.com

Usama bin Laden has died a peaceful death due to an untreated lung complication, the *Pakistan Observer* reported, citing a Taliban leader who allegedly attended the funeral of the Al Qaeda leader.

Bin Laden, according to the source, was suffering from a serious lung complication and succumbed to the disease in mid-December, in the vicinity of the Tora Bora mountains. The source claimed that bin Laden was laid to rest honorably in his last abode and his grave was made as per his Wahabi belief.

**Figure 5**

So what can we say for sure about Tim Osman (Osama Bin Laden)? It is easy to find evidence of his early life up until his first death, including the time he spent working with the CIA helping them to organise the Mujahideen to fight the Russians. For this reason, it is reasonable to assume that he existed (or "was alive", if you prefer to word it that way) during this period. Between his first death and his second, evidence is much thinner on the ground, and it gets even thinner when we look at the period after his second death. The following three questions are left for deliberation on the part of the reader:
- Was Bin Laden alive between his first and second deaths?
- Was Bin Laden alive after his second death?

- How might your answers to these two questions change if and when a third death is announced?

Over the course of this chapter and the previous one, we have formulated a model for a stereotypical view of fundamentalism. We have shown that, although this model may have little relevance in today's mainstream religions, it is, nevertheless, alive and kicking elsewhere in modern society. Because of the striking similarities we have found between our model and its modern realisation, we have good reason to suspect that we are faced with a new form of fundamentalist religion in the form of TVism. Over the course of the coming chapters we will have an opportunity to delve into this further and see some of its practical ramifications.

# - 8 -
# Good Guys, Bad Guys

*"The propagandist's purpose is to make one set of people forget that certain other sets of people are human."*

Aldous Huxley

---

In the last two chapters we have analysed the chain of cause and effect that exists within a stereotypical view of fundamentalist religion and shown evidence of a very similar chain which exists within *TVism*, a system of belief which we have suggested might be its modern day counterpart. Armed with this knowledge, we are now in a position to resume the thread we left at the end of chapter 5.

At the heart of *TVism* lies the same message that we find in many other religions: "we're OK: they're not OK." When we are presented with a stimulus that contradicts this idea, the threat to the belief system results in a strong feeling of discomfort, and the *believer* mind is forced to take the helm. At the end of chapter 5, we looked at a specific example of such a stimulus: the idea that there might be evidence that the London tube bombing of July 7th 2005 were an inside job. For most of us, our *believer* mind intercepts propositions such as this without allowing our *explorer* to process them. This dictates our reaction to the existence of such evidence, and may explain why this falls in stark contrast to the reaction we see when we are presented with a non-threatening idea, such as the photo of the lemons from chapter 4. Before we continue, it's worth stressing once again that it is not the veracity of this supposed evidence that is the important thing here, but rather our reluctance to consider the idea that it might exist in the first place.

In the example we considered back in the Introduction, we saw how our instruction to hold our breath was superseded by a command from our "lungs" as soon as it conflicted with our survival. The example we see here is analogous to this, with the *believer* mind taking the place of the lungs and the invitation to consider the evidence of July 7$^{th}$ taking the place of the instruction to hold our breath. It's as if the *believer* mind says: "Now hold on just a second: we have got way too much invested in the notion that **we** are the good guys and **they** are the bad guys for me to just let you go examining evidence and upsetting the applecart." This explains why, in this example, the *believer* mind steps up and intervenes in our thought process before the *explorer* mind can get a look in.

Of course, the bad guys' identity changes in an Orwellian fashion according to who we are told the enemy is at any given point in time. For a long while, it was the Russians. After they decided they were no longer going to play the game, some new replacements for the role had to be provided. For a while, it was the Serbs in Bosnia, then it was Osama Bin Laden and his "Al-Qaeda" followers, then it was the new bogeyman of "ISIS". More recently, things seem to have turned full circle with the Russians taking centre stage again. "Enemies" come and go, but the life position of "we're OK: they're not OK" remains the same.

In "The Selfish Gene"[ix] Richard Dawkins tells us how our inclination for altruistic behaviour towards others depends on the extent to which we imagine that we might share some genes with them. The more closely we suppose we are related, so Dawkins says, the more likely we are to act benevolently towards them. The closest match most of us will encounter is the one that occurs between ourselves and our children where, on average, fifty percent of our genes are shared. The only relationship that exceeds this is that of identical twins (one hundred percent shared), and most of us don't have one of those. This suggests that our most altruistic behaviour would be directed towards our children. After this would follow our immediate family, extended family and, behind them, our tribe, whatever the modern-day equivalent of this might be. Last on the list would be people from a different "tribe" or country.

From this starting point, it is logical to surmise that, simply on a basis of genetics, there is likely to be some degree of racism "pre-programmed" into all of us. Most of us have come to realise that there is no rational merit in racism and are careful to avoid it in our conscious thoughts and behaviour. Our unconscious thoughts however, by definition, cannot be subject to such checks.

In chapter 5, we saw how Barry's racism enabled him to readily accept Charlie's suggestion, and how this went on to dictate his behaviour. The same process can be observed when it comes to the fundamentalist religion of *TVism*. Our belief system tells us that Muslims are responsible for acts of terrorism and, as this idea is propped up by our inherent racism (if we may allow this word to apply to a religion rather than to just a race) we are reticent to question the notion. Each time we see some act of violence and are fed the narrative of "Islamic terror", our feelings of racism are reinforced. This, in turn, makes us ever more willing to accept the narrative that similar acts of "terror" in the future are also the result of "Islamic extremism". The result of all this, irrespective of the veracity of the narrative, is a viscous circle of reinforcement.

Before we leave the example of the *believer's* refusal to examine the evidence of July $7^{th}$ 2005, there is one further point that is worthy of note. The act of refusal suggests that, at least in some way, the *believer* mind has already accepted the idea that genuine evidence may exist. After all, if the *believer* were confident that there was no possibility that genuine evidence existed, there would be no harm in letting his or her *explorer* mind examine it. The very act of evasion is a tell-tale sign that the *believer* mind is aware that it has something to fear.

So what happens if, by chance, our *explorer* mind **does** get to see the evidence, despite the best efforts of the *believer* to keep it away from us? When this happens, it can often lead to a psychological phenomenon known as *Cognitive Dissonance*. The best way to understand this phenomenon is to experience it for oneself by conducting a simple experiment, such as the one which follows. Consider this fact about the events of September 11$^{th}$ 2001:

> It is well known that, in New York, the Twin Towers of the World Trade Center were destroyed. What is not so well known is the fact that a third tower, World Trade Center Seven, was also destroyed. This building was not hit by a plane yet "collapsed" with a downward acceleration approximating that of free fall. The event was captured on film from many different angles and can be found with a very simple search of the internet ("Compiled Footage of Building 7's Collapse").

It's worth taking a few moments to view the above video now, even if you have seen it before.

When we watch the video, unaware of the context, our instinct is likely to be to view the building's collapse as a classic example of controlled demolition (assuming we had previously seen an example of such a thing). This is because our *explorer* mind matches the footage against its previous experience and selects those events from memory which offer the closest fit to the new stimulus. The events that are selected are used as a model to interpret the footage and impart meaning to it.

Conversely, as soon as our *believer* mind becomes aware of the context, it is likely to tell us that the building is collapsing on its own for some unknown reason that is somehow related to Muslims. When two parts of our mind are in conflict like this, the result is the feeling of psychological discomfort, *Cognitive Dissonance*, which we mentioned earlier. In this case, the dissonance is created between our religion (*TVism*) and our senses. The result, more often than not, is an emotional response rather than a rational one. Given that there is a religious element to the situation, this emotional response is perhaps inevitable.

The resulting behaviour we can expect to see in the subject varies immensely between individuals. For the *believer*, in the more benign cases, religion "wins" and the subject will use a process called *Erasure* to simply remove the unwanted sensory input. This will be covered in more detail in chapter 9. If the *believer* is put under pressure to provide a response, they may perceive this as a threat to their belief system, and so a stronger emotional response is likely to ensue, perhaps manifesting itself as anger directed at the person who presents the video. If simple Erasure is not possible, there is a wide range of alternative behaviours to choose from. We will place this all together under the banner of *Protect the Religion* and look at it in greater depth in chapter 14.

*TVism* as a religion represents a conveniently packaged system of beliefs that is both palatable to, and easily absorbed by, the *believer*. It satisfies our need to know (or at least **think** that we know) what's going on in the world by supplying us with a comfortable, complete and simplistic narrative. But perhaps more important than this is the comfort we feel in knowing that the narrative we've been handed is the same as that provided to others. For most, the sharing of a narrative with our peers is more important to us than our desire that the narrative be true. After all, it's this feeling of affinity with our peers that makes us feel that we belong to a society: it stops us from feeling like outsiders.

This affinity, of course, is identical to that which we might expect to experience within a mainstream religion. In this case, the narrative with which we are provided is the "knowledge" of what will "happen" to us "after our death" and a set of teachings stipulating how we should behave if we are to achieve a positive outcome from this. Again, mainstream religion not only provides us with a narrative, but also ensures that it mirrors that of our peers, giving us the same sense of unity and "belonging to a society" which we get from *TVism*.

Both *TVism* and mainstream religion feed us with piecemeal chunks of "information", each agreeing with the sum of those that precede them. This creates the illusion that the resulting body of knowledge has been fostered by "experts" who have carried out the necessary investigation on our behalf. Both are power structures which are designed to prevent us from contemplating matters for ourselves by absolving us from the need for critical thinking.

We like to imagine that we are free to think whatever we like about the world around us. Furthermore, we like to think we have free choice over the emotions that accompany those thoughts. We surmise that these emotions emanate from ourselves and that our experiencing them is an inevitable consequence of our freedom of thought. But the reality is that the majority of our thoughts and emotions are merely constructs which result from our devotion to *TVism*. At first sight, this may seem like a bold statement to make, and many may instinctively reject it; but, hopefully, the idea will seem a little more reasonable after reading some of the examples in the following chapters. Since we have already mentioned the topic of racism a few times, we will start the ball rolling here.

Racism is a subject that attracts strong emotion, both for the majority of us who oppose it, and the small minority who support it. When we look at it in some detail, it becomes apparent that the word encompasses a broad spectrum of behavioural traits, some more toxic than others. Although not exhaustive, the following list is an illustration of how we might categorise these:

1. A behaviour which results in direct physical harm to (or even the death of) a person because they belong to some ethnic group;
2. A behaviour which encourages (or finances) the above;
3. A behaviour which results in the social exclusion of a person for belonging to some ethnic group;
4. The use of racist language.

During the UK of the late 1970s, racism commensurate with behaviours 3 and 4 was commonplace. In fact, taking a stand against it would often result in being the victim of abuse oneself. Behaviour 1 was perhaps less common but, nevertheless, it was still a reality. It may be that behaviour 2 also took place, but, if so, it was not as obvious.

While all this was going on, in South Africa, a strict system of apartheid was in place under the leadership of F. W. de Klerk. Under this regime, black people were forced to live separately from white people and, almost without exception, were subject to poorer living conditions and benefited little from government investment. For the most part, they were resigned to their situation, imagining that black people were treated the same the world over. However, those who refused to accept this reality and chose to protest their situation often found themselves facing a violent response. Little mention was made of the story on UK TV, but, instead, shows with openly racist content (such as "The Black and White Minstrel Show") would provide a staple part of viewers' light "entertainment".

Starting in the early 1980s, *TVism* made a change to its official canon by stipulating that it would no longer accept or support racism in this way. As a centrepiece to this policy shift, the slogan "Free Nelson Mandela" was introduced and its uptake by the population at large was both swift and pervasive.

Without question, we would have to agree that this change was a positive one. But, setting aside for a moment the question of our approval, the point we should focus on is the ability of the TV to modify the emotional response of its audience in this way. The topic of Nelson Mandela's incarceration would precipitate feelings of rage and indignation whenever it was broached, yet this had not been a common reaction prior to the TV's change of canon. In the experience of many, behaviours 1, 3 and 4 (from those we listed earlier) began to diminish throughout the UK.

At this point, one might consider an alternative hypothesis: that the change in attitude had nothing to do with the TV, but would have occurred anyway as a result of the public's increased awareness of the situation. It's hard to prove this definitively one way or the other, but the next example will give us cause to suspect that this theory is an unlikely one.

Moving the clock on to the 2010s, a very similar situation to the one in South Africa exists in Palestine (or Israel if you choose to refer to it by this name). Yet the average person would be forgiven for knowing nothing about it, considering the coverage it gets (or lack of it) on the TV. No matter which side of this conflict (if any) we may support, or what ideas we may have as to what caused it, the existence of apartheid based on an ethnic boundary cannot be denied. This is easily evidenced by the physical wall dividing the Israelis from the Palestinians. Not only that, but, just as in the case of South Africa, we can see obvious differences in the quality of life between those living on each of the two sides. On the one hand we see white people living a life of luxury, financed, at least in part, by US tax dollars; yet, on the other, we see brown people living in poverty, their land decimated by war and gradually stolen from them over the course of the years.

This time, unlike in the previous example, we see no significant evidence of any message of condemnation from the TV. As a consequence, there is no mass outcry about the treatment of the Palestinians, even though it is comparable to that which was experienced by the black South Africans under de Klerk. Some have suggested that the reason for this might be because the wall is seen as a necessary barrier against the threat of Palestinian "terrorism" which, so it is alleged, is directed at the Israelis. Others have suggested that the extent of the "terrorism" has been greatly exaggerated by the Israelis and their subservient media in order to justify the land grab that has resulted from the positioning of the wall. Wherever you stand on this debate, it is probably fair to say that there is at least some degree of truth to the notion of Palestinian aggression towards the Israelis, paltry though the evidence is in comparison to the reverse. But who amongst us could honestly say that we wouldn't attempt to defend our country if it were being stolen from us, piece by piece, by some external aggressor who had no right to the land?

To point out that the TV has ignored this particular instance of apartheid is, perhaps, stating the obvious; but what makes this even more galling is the fact that it has also been largely successful in labelling the oppressors as the "victims" and the true victims as "terrorists". Such is the power of our religion, under the directorship and control of the TV, to turn our minds upside-down.

The weapons of oppression that the Israeli government uses against the Palestinian civilians are paid for, in the most part, by US tax dollars. There is no escaping the fact that this behaviour falls squarely into category 2 from our list of racist behavioural traits shown above. But US citizens are not the only ones complicit in such behaviour. The military might of the UK and many other countries is constantly at work throughout the Middle East (in Iraq, Afghanistan, Yemen, Syria, *et al*), killing people and destroying their land and property all under the *canard* of the "War on Terror", perhaps a more accurate label for which might be the "War of Terror".

In this chapter, we have looked at some of the mechanics of the religion of TVism and had a glimpse of the central role that is played by racism. It is ironic to think that, today, we live in a society where racist behavioural traits 1, 3 and 4 are frowned upon, yet category 2 is allowed to continue at a prolific rate, with little or no meaningful discussion. What is perhaps more disturbing is the fact that the feelings of repulsion and anger we feel towards the idea of racism can be turned on or off at the command of our TV.

At this point, we will take a break from the TV in order to focus on some specific aspects of the behaviour of the *believer*. We will resume our analysis of *TVism* and the belief system associated with it in chapter 16.

# - 9 -
# Canonical Filtering

*"Experience has shown, and a true philosophy will always show, that a vast, perhaps the larger portion of the truth arises from the seemingly irrelevant."*

Edgar Allan Poe, American author

---

For the majority of us, every moment of our waking lives brings a plethora of sensation to which we are inclined to ascribe some meaning. To ease this task, we use a variety of mental strategies which we might look upon as a kind of mental toolkit, the parts of which vary from person to person. Examples from the *explorer* kit, for instance, include observation, analysis, balance and interpretation; perhaps even used in this order. A sequence of tools such as this is well suited to the *explorer* paradigm, which starts with a careful and detailed observation of the world then proceeds towards a model that represents or explains it. These tools would serve no purpose in the corresponding *believer* kit, however, where the direction of thought is almost the reverse of that of the *explorer* mind. There would seem to be little purpose for a tool which is designed to expose detail if one's purpose is to avoid it.

All this leads us to the obvious question: what tools are available to the *believer* mind as a substitute for the ones we have described? In this chapter and the four which follow, we will look at some of these, starting here with *Canonical Filtering*. Of course, this list is not exhaustive, and the reader is encouraged to add further examples to it as and when they come across them.

Starting with their preconceived view of the world, the *believer* is faced with an immediate problem when confronted with evidence that contradicts the model. In order to maintain the belief system, we are obliged to rid ourselves of such evidence. We have used the term *Canonical Filtering* since the process involves the filtering of observations to leave just those which match the official, or canonified, narrative.

The best way to see how this works in practice is to follow a simple thought experiment. Imagine a game in which we start with a number of different cards placed inside a black bag. On each card is written an example of an act of geopolitical aggression taken from the last fifty or sixty years. Each round of the game consists of our drawing a card then determining whether or not it represents a genuine act of unjustified aggression. If it is deemed to be so, the chosen card is stuck on a whiteboard in a section headed by the name of the instigating country. If, on the other hand, it is deemed not to be such an act, then the card is simply discarded.

Before we carry on, take a moment to consider which country you think will accrue the greatest number of cards.

So let's look at our first card. Let's suppose we draw one which depicts the events of August 7$^{th}$ 2008, when Russia invaded Georgia in support of the breakaway republic of South Ossetia. Most of us in the West would probably ignore the events leading up to the invasion and have little hesitation in placing this card on the board under the heading "Russia". Let's leave the card on the board and move on to draw the next one.

This time, suppose we pick a card depicting the invasion of Iraq by the US on March 20$^{th}$ 2003, an invasion predicated on what we now know to be the myth of "weapons of mass destruction". This act of US aggression resulted in the deaths of some 200,000 innocent civilians, not to mention the US and Iraqi service men and women who were also killed.

At this point in our game, a strange thing happens. Because our *believer* mind will probably have a hard time facing up to these facts, it is likely that it will step in to deliver a message along these lines:

> "Hang on: our religion says that **we** are the good guys and **they** are the bad guys. The whole idea that this might be an act of US aggression would contradict this belief, so I'm going to ignore this card."

This interjection means that this card is likely to be discarded, with the *believer* forced to construct some suitable means to justify this.

Now, moving on to the next round, imagine we draw a card that depicts the invasion of Vietnam. This act of aggression was precipitated by the Gulf of Tonkin incident (on August $2^{nd}$ 1964) which was later admitted to have been a hoax orchestrated by the US "against" its own forces. The result was the deaths of around two million innocent civilians and a catalogue of horror which spread across the subcontinent.

Once again, we are presented with a problem stemming from the unpalatability of these facts. In all probability, our *believer* mind will intervene with a similar message to that of the previous example. After all, we have invested too much time and effort in believing that we are the "good guys" for a few little facts to get in the way. Again, this card is likely to be discarded, the *believer* probably "justifying" it by mumbling something about "fighting communism" and avoiding an explanation as to why such a fight was necessary.

For the next round, let's pick the card which represents the "annexation" (in the words of the mainstream media) of Crimea by Russia on the March $18^{th}$ 2014. Although this event did involve a military presence on the part of Russia, no deaths were reported as a result of it and, some weeks later, the population of Crimea voted with a majority of 95.5% to become part of Russia. The dissenting 4.5% were suggested to be ethnic Tatars, who had historical reasons to mistrust the "invader". Although some have suggested that the vote might have been rigged, no evidence has been offered to support this idea.

The inhabitants' decision to change nationality was depicted by the media to be the result of coercion, but a brief look at history provides us with a simpler, more plausible explanation. Between 1783 and 1954, Crimea had been a part of Russia, only becoming a part of Ukraine when gifted as a political sop by Nikita Khrushchev. In fact, over the last five hundred years, Crimea has spent less time as part of Ukraine than it has as part of Russia, so perhaps this is why the residents feel a greater affinity to the latter.

Regardless of all this, driven by the label of "annexation" that has been dangled in front of us, our *believer* mind pops up once again, this time creating the idea of aggression instigated by "them" (the Russians) against "us" (Ukraine and their Western backers), and the card goes on the board again under the heading "Russia".

Since the bias that is developing here is easy to see, and in the interests of brevity, we'll just remind ourselves of the main acts of US aggression over the course of the last fifty or so years, all of which seem to have conveniently disappeared down the "Memory Hole":

Cuba, 1961, CIA-directed Bay of Pigs invasion fails.

Iraq, 1963, CIA-instigated coup brings Saddam Hussein back from exile.

Vietnam, 1964-75, US troops wage war against NVA and Viet Cong, killing 2 million.

Panama, 1964, US troops shoot Panamanians objecting to the US theft of their canal.

Indonesia, 1965, CIA-assisted army coup kills 1 million people.

Dominican Republic, 1965-66, US troops and marines land during election campaign.

Guatemala, 1966-67, US Special Services intervene against "rebels".

Cambodia, 1969-75, US military campaign during Vietnam war.

Laos, 1971-73, US directs South Vietnamese carpet-bombing campaign.

Chile, 1973, CIA-backed coup ousts elected president.

El Salvador, 1981-92, US troops aid war against "rebels".

Nicaragua, 1981-90, CIA funds Contras following sale of cocaine (to Americans) and arms (to Iran).

Lebanon, 1982-84, US marines expel PLO and bomb Muslim positions.

Grenada, 1983-84, US troops invade following revolution.

Iran, 1987-88, US aids Iraq in war against Iran and shoots down a civilian jet.

Philippines, 1989, US jets provide air cover for government against coup.

Panama, 1989, US troops oust nationalist government.

Iraq, 1990-91, US forces invade Kuwait and part of Iraq killing some 200,000 people.

Iraq, 1991-2003, US forces execute bombing runs while enforcing no-fly zone.

Somalia, 1992-94, US occupation during civil war.

Bosnia, 1993, US jets execute bombing runs while enforcing no-fly zone.

Haiti, 1994, US military takes action against military government to restore President Aristide after coup.

Croatia and Bosnia, 1994-95, US bombs Serb positions in Yugoslavian war.

Yugoslavia, 1999, US executes bombing runs and effect occupation after Serbia declines to withdraw from Kosovo.

Afghanistan, 2001-14, US forces invade to overthrow Taliban and install Karzai puppet regime, killing some 150,000 people.

Iraq, 2003-14, US invade and overthrow Saddam Hussein regime killing some 200,000.

Haiti, 2004-05, US troops invade after right-wing rebels oust elected president.

Libya, 2011, US execute bombing raids and missile attacks ousting Qaddafi government.

Pakistan, 2005-14, US execute missile, bomb and drone attacks along with covert CIA operations in raids on alleged "Al Qaeda" and Taliban forces.

Syria, 2014-present day, US executes bombing runs against Assad while claiming to be bombing "ISIS".

By constantly glossing over the facts that disagree with the doctrines of *TVism*, and over-emphasising those which support it, we are able to maintain our religious world-view. It's this pattern of non-thinking which allows us to rant about "Russian aggression" and believe that we are stating the obvious. In reality, although there is some evidence of historical Russian aggression, this pales into insignificance when compared to that of the West, and the divergence becomes more apparent as we consider the events of more recent history.

Before we go on to look at the mechanics of Canonical Filtering, it's worth noting that there is a simple methodology we can use to neutralise its effects and restore a more balanced view: a cognitive trick which we will call "reversal".

For instance, in order to re-evaluate our stance on Crimea, we can envisage a hypothetical situation in which Scotland becomes independent from the rest of the UK and decides to become affiliated with Russia. Now, do you think it would be reasonable for England to use military force to recapture its nuclear naval facility at Faslane (in Scotland, UK) in order to stop its falling into Russian hands?

If you are a US resident, you may find it helpful to substitute "Scotland" with "Florida" and "Faslane" with "Jacksonville". Whichever example you pick, it should now be easier to see that Russia's actions were justified, given that the Crimea contains one of the most important bases of the Russian navy at Sevastopol.

## Erasure

So much for the theory behind Canonical Filtering, but how does it work in practice? Once the *believer* mind has identified a set of observations that are to be the subject of the filter, it needs to find a way to apply it in a socially acceptable way. In the majority of cases, this is achieved by simply ignoring the unsavoury details in a process which we will term "Erasure". If, for instance, you skimmed over the list above and have already forgotten the contents, it's likely that your *believer* stepped in and executed this process just a few moments ago.

Erasure occurs predictably when the subject is confronted with information that does not sit well with their preconceived beliefs. During the course of the proceedings, the subject will often remain silent for a moment while staring ahead into the middle distance. This pause is usually followed with a *non sequitur*: an abrupt change of topic. We can surmise that this pause represents the time it takes for the *believer* mind to eradicate the effects of the stimulus.

## Coincidence or Miracle

If the facts are presented in a more robust manner, simple Erasure may not be sufficient, especially if the subject feels that he or she is under some pressure to make some kind of response. In these cases, the *believer* mind has one or two more tricks up its sleeve.

One additional avenue open to the *believer* is to "explain" away the unwanted observations by using the device of *Coincidence*. By now, the astute reader will realise that our use of italics here is meant to signify a specialised meaning to this word.

In normal parlance, the word "coincidence" is used to denote a possible, yet unlikely event. For example, let's imagine that, while on vacation, we bump into an old friend unexpectedly. Putting a figure on the odds of this happening is quite challenging, but we could make an educated guess at somewhere between 1:1,000 and 1:1,000,000, perhaps.

To this we must compare the kind of situation where the odds of an event's happening by chance are incalculably small. A good way to visualise such a slim chance is by saying that we might reasonably expect the event to happen less than once during the lifetime of the universe. In order to distinguish this use of the word *coincidence* from the more usual one, we will use italics as before.

To see how this works, it's worth looking again at a simple example, such as the destruction of World Trade Center Building 7 on September 11th 2001 that was mentioned in chapter 7. For readers unfamiliar with the topic, their attention is drawn to David Ray Griffin's book, "The Mysterious Collapse of World Trade Center 7"[x]. There is also plenty of footage of the destruction available on the internet ("WTC Building 7 Collapse - 23 angles"), and the reader is encouraged to view this, if they haven't already done so, before continuing with the rest of this section.

As is evident from the footage, the building falls straight down through the path of greatest resistance (perpendicular to the ground) with the entire process taking around seven seconds. The destruction is both uniform and orderly, and the zone of destruction (the part of the building that is being destroyed at any given instant) seems to be fixed, out of sight, somewhere near the base of the building. Without speculating on what might have caused such an event, we should instead consider in detail the physical process that must have taken place during it. If the following physical processes had not occurred, we would not have been able to make the observations that can be seen in the clip.

In order to deduce the sequence of events, we must first start with an analysis of the building's construction. It was built around a core of twenty-four upright columns and fifty-seven smaller peripheral columns. Each floor was attached to all of these, giving a total of eighty-one attachment points per floor. Focusing initially on a single floor, in order for the building to fall perpendicularly to the ground, each of these attachment points would have had to have failed at exactly the same moment in time as did its siblings. To see why this would have been necessary, we should pause to examine some alternative scenarios, and consider how these would have affected the observations.

For example, if more of the attachments on one side of the building had failed before the ones on the other, we would expect to have observed some tipping away from the vertical during the descent. Such tipping, were it to commence, would tend to be amplified as the destruction progressed, in the same way that a broom handle balanced upright on one's finger will exhibit angular acceleration once it tips away slightly from the vertical. In actuality, no such tipping was observed.

Taking another example, we could imagine the attachment points failing in some random sequence spread over some period of time. In this case, there would have been a considerable delay in the destruction of each floor, and so the collapse of the building as a whole would have taken a significantly greater length of time, if it were to have happened at all. Again, no such observation was made. The whole building came down in roughly seven seconds: a time which a simple calculation can show is commensurate with that of free fall.

From this analysis, we can conclude that all the attachment points on each floor must, indeed, have failed at the same point in time (experts say that all eighty-one failures would have had to have occurred within a tenth of a second). Without this stipulation, our observation of the free fall collapse, over the period of the seven seconds, would not have been possible.

When we now consider the timing of the destruction of each floor relative to that of the others, we are able to note a similar finesse of timing. After the destruction of the first floor, not only would the eighty-one attachment points of the floor above have had to have failed simultaneously, but this group of events would have had to have occurred at exactly the right point in time after the destruction of its predecessor. More specifically, each floor would have had to have failed and been destroyed when, during its descent, it passed through the point in space where its predecessor had been just moments before. If the failure had been too late, then the downward acceleration of the building would have slowed: too early, then we would have seen the zone of destruction march up the building. If the floors had failed in some random (rather than sequential) order, then the destruction would have taken on a more random nature, and we would have seen the zone of destruction moving randomly up and down the building. Nothing of this nature was actually observed.

There were forty-seven floors to the building, each with eighty-one attachment points, thus making a total of nearly four thousand in the building as a whole. We have seen that each must have failed at exactly the correct point in time in order for us to be able to make the observations we did. There have only been two hypotheses presented (to the best of our knowledge) for how this might have happened. The first is that some form of controlled demolition was employed, the charges being accurately timed by computer. The second is that the collapse happened on its own as a result of office fires. Followers of *TVism* are obliged to conclude that it is the second of these hypotheses which is the "true" one. Because of this, they are compelled to come up with an explanation for the precise timing of the failures of the attachment points. The most common explanation given is that it was a "coincidence".

The reader is encouraged to try to make an estimate of the odds of this all happening as a result of a random physical process such as a fire. By all accounts, the fire started when the other two towers collapsed, and was put out a few hours later: well before the destruction of WTC7 at 5:21pm EDT. The calculation would need to take into account the likelihood of all the failure events mentioned above occurring in their correct sequence. The reader will soon find that the calculation quickly exceeds the capabilities of a normal scientific calculator, thus allowing us to classify this very clearly as a *coincidence* rather than a coincidence.

If this event had occurred in Biblical times, it would have been termed a "miracle". This is the word that we use to describe an event which is impossible, yet is required to have happened in order to fulfil some part of a belief system. For example, the story of Moses' parting of the Red Sea is something that could **not** have happened, yet is **required** to have happened for a religious purpose. To bridge the cognitive gap, the word "miracle" was used, but, in more recent times, the word has fallen out of use and the vacated ontological slot has been filled by the word "*coincidence*" (as distinct from its poor cousin "coincidence"). To see the parallel between the two words, all we need do is substitute *TVism* with Christianity and the timed failing of the attachment points with the parting of the Red Sea. On doing so, the replacement of the word "*coincidence*" with the word "miracle" seems like a small step.

## Ad Hoc Hypothesis

When neither Erasure nor the claim of *coincidence* (miracle) is suitable, the *believer* may resort to a more devious tactic such as an "*ad hoc* hypothesis". This is an off-the-cuff explanation for which there is no supporting evidence. More often than not, these hypotheses don't hold up too well to questioning. As an example, consider this imaginary conversation between Edward and Barry:

> **Edward** : "If a plane crashed into the Pentagon on 9/11, how come there was little or no visible evidence of wreckage?"
>
> **Barry** : "It's simple: the plane was going so fast that it vaporised on impact."

In this case, Barry's beliefs are under attack as a result of a question that demands a detailed and logical response. Since Barry is employing his *believer* mind, there is no detail to be had, so he resorts to an *ad hoc* hypothesis in order to "sure up" his beliefs. In order for us to establish that this is an *ad hoc* hypothesis as opposed to a normal one, we need to show both that there is no supporting evidence for the idea, and that it readily falls apart under questioning. In this particular example, we must first establish what it is that causes something to vaporise. Barry makes the assertion that it is speed that causes this, but a simple reference to physics or chemistry will tell us that it is in fact temperature. Secondly, we should consider that aluminium (the metal from which aircraft are made) vaporises at 2470° C, yet kerosene (aircraft fuel) only burns at around 800° C. There is no evidence to suggest that a temperature close to the vaporisation point of aluminium was present at the Pentagon. It is clear that Barry's hypothesis does not stand up to questioning, and from this we can conclude that he is employing an *ad hoc* hypothesis.

One of the most common examples of *ad hoc* hypothesis is the claim of "incompetence" which is often levelled at government figures, the armed forces and the media in an attempt to explain away their crimes. For example, in the first few hours after major events such as 9/11, there have been occasions when the mainstream media, in the heat of the moment, behaves with abandon and reports events from the scene as they actually happen, without waiting for the normal editorial controls to be exercised. As a result, the narrative can disagree quite markedly with the narrative offered by the same channel just a few hours later, once the information has been subjected to what's deemed to be the appropriate censorship. When this happens, the *believer* will often advance the *ad hoc* hypothesis of "incompetence" to "explain" the variation in the narrative.

One example of this is CNN's report on 9/11 that there was no sign of a plane at the Pentagon. The clip is easy enough to find on the internet ("the 9/11 video aired once and never aired again"). *Believers* are quick to "explain" this anomaly away as "incompetence". Of course, they offer no evidence to back up their claim and, at the same time, ignore the fact that not one single photo or video from the day shows any significant wreckage of a plane, with the exception of a few tiny fragments.

## Religious Reasoning Chain

When an *ad hoc* hypothesis is attacked to the extent that it looks like it might crumble away, the *believer* may seek to support it with another. If this subsequent hypothesis comes under similar attack, we may elect to continue this process to create a chain of *ad hoc* hypotheses, each one formulated in an attempt to correct the failings of its predecessor. To this iterative process we will give the name *Religious Reasoning Chain:* a process which embodies the flailing attempts of the *believer* to bridge the cognitive gap between their beliefs and reality. Again, an example will help to illustrate this:

> **Edward** : "If a plane crashed into a field in Shanksville, Pennsylvania on 9/11, how come there

was little or no visible wreckage in the crater at the main crash site?"

**Barry** : "Well, the plane came down at such a steep angle that it broke up on impact."

**Edward** : "But, if that happened, wouldn't we still expect to see large parts, for instance the wings, fuselage and engines, on the ground at the site?"

**Barry** : "This one's easy to explain: the plane crashed onto some disused mine workings which meant that the ground was soft, resulting in the wreckage ending up underground."

**Edward** : "So why don't we see the larger pieces of wreckage at the bottom of a deep crater?"

**Barry** : "Err, no, we wouldn't see anything, because the earth closed up once the plane had gone underground."

**Edward** : "But earth is a solid and it is only fluids (liquids and gasses) which can exhibit the behaviour you describe."

**Barry** : "It's obvious <*raises voice in anger*>: the speed of impact and the angle of the plane's path meant the ground acted like a liquid, you fool. Why are you carrying on with these stupid questions?"

As you can see, Barry's Religious Reasoning Chain gets progressively more preposterous during the course of the interaction, culminating in the "appeal to miracle" which presents itself at the end. Accompanying this, we observe an increased level of anger as Edward's questions continue.

As was pointed out at the beginning of this chapter, this list of behaviours is by no means exhaustive, and the reader will, in all probability, be able to find additional examples of their own. However, this simple exploration is sufficient to illustrate the process of Canonical Filtering, the tool which holds a central position in the *believer* world. We will leave this theme for now, but will refer back to it on occasions throughout the course of the book. In the next chapter, we will move on to describe another prominent example from the *believer* toolkit.

# - 10 -
# Authority Filtering

*"They must find it difficult, those who have taken authority as the truth rather than truth as the authority."*

Gerald Massey, English poet

---

Starting with the previous chapter, we have been looking at the tools available in the *believer* kit which can be used to extract meaning from the world. The process of Canonical Filtering, which we have already discussed at length, enables our *believer* mind to remove evidence that would otherwise be an affront to our belief system. In this chapter we will move on to examine the question as to where these beliefs come from in the first place and how it is that the *believer* is able to pick one particular set in preference to any other.

The simple answer is that these beliefs come from a source of authority, a concept which was introduced in chapter 2. For most of us, the authority will take the form of a TV news channel, a newspaper or some highly regarded individual from within the peer group of the *believer*. The problem is, of course, that there are many such sources all around us, so the subject must first filter out the unwanted ones using a process which we will call *Authority Filtering*.

In order to do this, the subject must first construct an Authority Hierarchy, although we are mostly unaware that we are doing so. The exact layout will vary from person to person, but, typically, the *believer* will build it to mirror the hierarchy that has been constructed by his or her peers. This is ascertained by means of careful observation of the speech and behaviour of those around us, paying special attention to that of those who have the greatest influence. A typical hierarchy can be seen in Figure 6.

The hierarchy is kicked into action when the *believer* mind is presented with some kind of stimulus. In theory, this stimulus could be anything you care to imagine, but, typically, it will be a new idea that has been presented to the subject, or a sequence of world events as reported in some media or other. The hierarchy is used in two phases. In the first of these, the subject will determine whether or not the stimulus is to be accepted. In the second, he or she will select a narrative to accompany it. For the hierarchy to work, the subject must be aware of the authority presenting the narrative or stimulus. The nearer the authority to the top of the hierarchy, the more likely it is for the new information and narrative to be accepted and assimilated.

It's important here to note that we are only likely to see a **complete** acceptance or complete rejection. A partial acceptance, or one made conditional to any *caveats*, would not be expected since this would only be possible if there were an analysis of the events, and an analysis of this nature lies out of scope of the *believer* mind, the aim of which is to avoid detail.

Once a hierarchy has been established, the *believer* has no hesitation in using it to filter out unwanted events and their associated narratives. For instance, he or she may maintain that a report aired on CNN is "true" (because it is on CNN) while one available only on YouTube is "false" (because it is on YouTube). Such a process presents a problem, however, in that it is not clear what is to be done in the case where the *believer* first sees a report on YouTube that was originally aired on CNN. The potential paradox presented by this conundrum is a constant threat to the *believer*.

In reality, the idea of a "source" for a news story is often more complicated than we might at first imagine. In the case of CNN, it is as likely for the report to have come from some external source (be it a news feed or a freelancer) as it is to have come from one of their own reporters.

**An Authority Hierarchy**

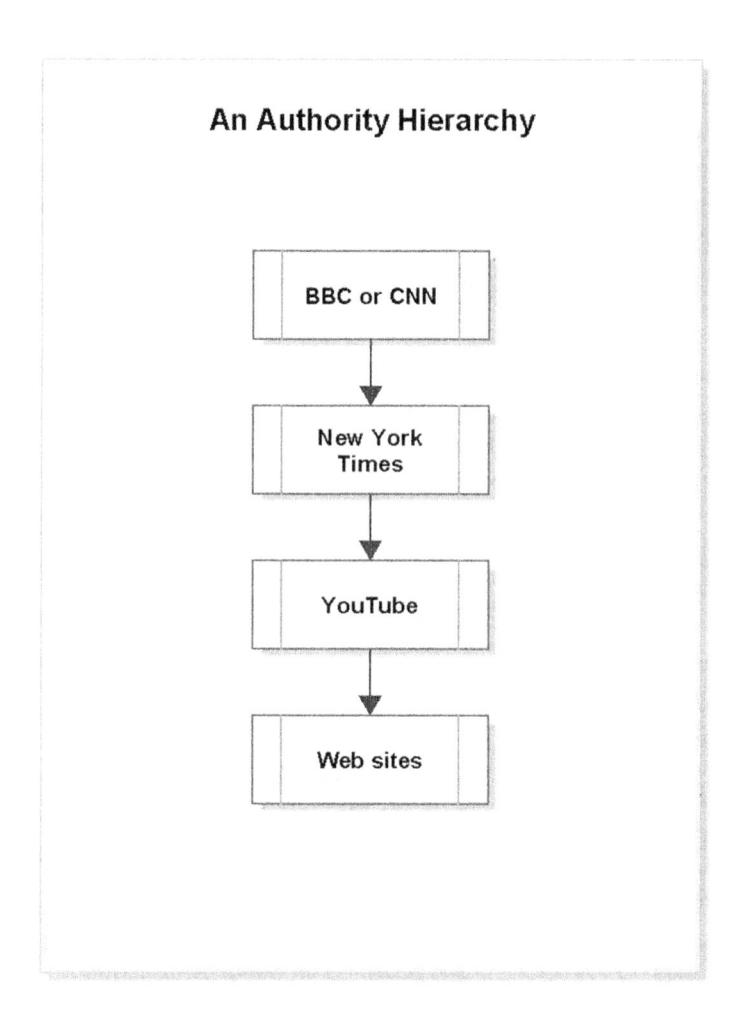

BBC or CNN
↓
New York Times
↓
YouTube
↓
Web sites

Figure 6

In addition, the item may first be broadcast on CNN's own channel, but later be rebroadcast by other channels (TV, cable or online). When looked at from this perspective, we can see that the lines between "source" and "medium of transmission" can often become blurred, and this fact may tempt us to view the *believer's* behaviour as having little merit.

By contrast with the Authority Hierarchy, the *explorer's* analytical process is both detailed and laborious. Although we may take into account the source of the report (because there are many occasions when there may be a motive for fakery), this is only done in conjunction with a careful study of the evidence itself. At no point would we be expected to take into account the medium of transmission, as there is no logical reason to do so.

Up until now, we have looked at some of the practical problems that are associated with Authority Filtering. Now this is out of the way, we can move on to a more formal critique of this kind of thinking. From a logician's point of view, the problem is that the Authority Filter is one example of a broad range of nonsensical arguments knows as the *Logical Fallacies.*

For nearly three thousand years, philosophers and logicians have tried to define a unified framework for logical thought: a set of rules which, if followed, will result in logical ideas and valid deductions. For the most part, this quest has proved unsuccessful, because as soon as one philosopher proposes a theory, ten more pop up to destroy it. One might be forgiven for thinking that all this effort has been in vain, yet there have been some good things to have come from it. Thanks to all the healthy criticism of these theories, we now have a long list of ways of thinking which we know are categorically wrong. Amongst these are the body of pitfalls known as the Logical Fallacies. We know that if someone makes an argument which employs a logical fallacy, then that argument is, by definition, invalid.

Let's look at an example. Consider the following two propositions:

"If it is raining, then I will put on my coat."

"It is raining."

If we assume that these two propositions are true, then we can always make the following deduction:

"I will put on my coat."

This is perhaps the most common example of a valid logical deduction, and is known to logicians under the name of "*modus ponens*" or "sufficient condition". In this example, it has been stated that the presence of rain is all that is required to make the subject put on the coat. Once we know that it **is** raining, the wearing of the coat must follow. Now compare this to the following:

"If it is raining, then there must be clouds in the sky."

"There are clouds in the sky."

If we assume that these two propositions are true, then it is **not** valid to make the following deduction:

"It is raining."

In this case, if the speaker has attempted to make this deduction, then their argument is a fallacious one known as "Affirming the Consequent". To understand why it is given this name, we must first understand the difference between the antecedent and the consequent. In this case, the antecedent (the idea which comes first) is the phrase "If it is raining". The consequent (the idea that is deduced as a consequence) is the phrase "there must be clouds in the sky". When we affirm the consequent, it is erroneous to assert the truth of the antecedent, since to do so would be to turn the sense of the original logic on its head.

Although the above explanation may seem a little confusing, if we were to simply imagine a rainless, yet overcast day, we can easily see that the mere presence of the clouds gives us no guarantee of rain. Before leaving this second example, it's worth remembering that we still don't know whether it is actually raining or not: if we are told that the two propositions are true, it may be that it is raining, but this is not a deduction that we can logically make.

There are in the region of three hundred different logical fallacies, this being just one. Although we will come across some of the others in the following chapters, there's not room to explain them all here. What is interesting to note, however, is that many of these can be (and, indeed, have been) easily exploited by politicians, the mainstream media and others in order to trick the gullible into flawed reasoning. For anyone keen to know more of the remaining two hundred and ninety nine or so logical fallacies, these are covered in Madsen Pirie's "How to Win Every Argument"[xi].

The *explorer* mind sees Authority Filtering as an example of the logical fallacy known as "Appeal to Authority". This particular fallacy fits into a broad category of similar ones known as "logical *non sequitur*": a conclusion that does not relate to its antecedent. To put this more precisely, this means that if we take these two propositions:

> "Charlie is perceived to be an authority on a particular topic."

> "Charlie states that a proposition A (which relates to that topic) is true"

We **cannot** make the following deduction:

> "A is true."

Before we leave the subject of logical fallacies, there is one last thing to think about. When a speaker employs a logical fallacy in lieu of a rational argument, the only thing we can say for sure is that the argument which contains the fallacy is invalid. We cannot make any deduction about the truth or falsity of the original proposition. This means that the fact the *believer* has used the Authority Filter in place of a rational argument does not give us the right to state that the original proposition is false.

As a footnote to this, it's worth pointing out that to make such an erroneous deduction is an example of a logical fallacy all of its own: the fallacy of *Argumentum ad Logicam*. But let's leave it there as far as the practical problems of Authority Filtering are concerned, since I don't know about you, but my head is starting to spin. In the next chapter and the two subsequent ones, we will carry on with our exploration of some of the other tools that comprise the *believer* toolkit.

# - 11 -
# Religious Labelling

*"Labels are for filing. Labels are for clothing. Labels are not for people."*

Martina Navratilova, ex tennis champion

---

Over the last few chapters we have been looking at the tools in the *believer* kit which can be used to derive meaning from the world around us. We have looked at the way in which the belief system is constructed and the mechanisms on hand for avoiding any evidence that may challenge the resulting edifice. But belief is a delicate thing, and steps have to be taken to ensure that challenges are adequately compartmentalised and stripped of all detail. In this chapter, we will look at the process that is used to achieve this: *Religious Labelling*. As this is a somewhat complex area, we must first digress a little and take stock of some background concepts.

In chapter 6 we introduced the notion of an in-group, "us", and an out-group, "them"; and have since seen how this delineation is applied in a whole host of different circumstances. One of the most widely reported examples of this, perhaps, is President George W. Bush's announcement in an address to a joint session of Congress on September 20th 2001, in which he said:

> "Either you are with us, or you are with the terrorists."

But what makes us "us" and them "them" in the first place? In order to understand this, we must first understand what makes me "me".

A suitable place to start the story is with a truism which, though widely accepted at face value when applied to oneself, is often overlooked when it refers to others: the idea that no two individuals are identical. Over the course of our lives, we are all subjected to a unique set of stimuli, originating both from nature and nurture. It is this set of stimuli that has gone to form our personality, our attitudes and our core belief system. Exactly what it is that constitutes a personality has eluded psychologists for nearly a century. Although many theories have been put forward (biological, cognitive, developmental, social, etc.), no concise definition has been agreed upon. Indeed, it's quite likely that none ever will. The different ideas that have been presented over the years are too lengthy and complex to go into here, but the interested reader can follow up the topic in Edwin G. Boring's "History of Experimental Psychology"[xii].

To help us think about this more clearly, we will introduce a simplified model. Imagine your personality could be broken down into a set of qualities or traits. For example, we might consider creativity, common sense, honesty, impulsiveness, conscientiousness and religiosity (the extent to which one is "religious") and so on. Now imagine each of those as a slider on a DJ's mixing desk: we can imagine as many sliders as we can imagine traits. Each slider can be set to any position on its scale from zero to one hundred. If it turns out that a particular trait cannot be represented simply on such a scale, we would just break it apart into as many sub-traits as necessary.

If we consider one of our own sliders and try to imagine its position, we are likely to start by considering the (supposed) position of the same slider in those around us. The human mind is better at making comparisons than it is at judging absolutes. For example, a person who was a practicing, non-fundamentalist Catholic in the UK in the 21st century might regard themselves as being pretty high up on a scale of religiosity. However, take the same person and place them in nineteenth century Eire (Ireland), a far more religious society than most we see today, and we would likely see a re-evaluation of the position relative to those around them.

There is, however, a big problem with all of this. When we examine our own position, we are using what philosophers call "first person privilege". On the other hand, when we examine the position of those around us, we are making a second-hand guess based on our perception of what we can see. This is just a fancy way of saying that we can see into our own mind, but we cannot see into the minds of others.

From our simple starting point, we are led into a sea of complexity when we try to categorise personality and core beliefs. At this point, many would be tempted to give the whole thing up as a bad job. Nevertheless, time and time again, we see attempts to label people based on the position of just one of those sliders, and use the label to divide the world into "us" and "them". When a label is given to a target (a person within a group of people that, supposedly, share a certain trait), they are effectively being told what they should think and what they should be.

Now that we have our broad definition of Religious Labelling, we can move on to think about its consequences. More important, perhaps, than the effect the label has on the target, is the effect it has on the speaker. As soon as the label pops into our mind, no matter where it comes from, a process called *Splitting* occurs. Splitting (sometimes called "black-and-white thinking") is the tendency to take a continuous quality and view it as if it were a binary one. So what's the difference between these two? As always, a simple example, such as the one which follows, will help to clarify this.

Barry can choose whether or not to wear a hat. If he chooses to do so, he is "wearing a hat". If he chooses not to do so, he is "not wearing a hat". Since he can never be "half wearing a hat" we can consider "wearing a hat" to be a binary attribute.

In contrast, Edward may decide to engage in some form of religious behaviour. We might then view this as a slider which could be set at a number of positions of increased intensity:

- Atheism: the subject does not believe in gods.

- Agnosticism: the subject is unsure as to their belief in gods, or does not care enough to think about it.
- Deism: the subject believes that gods created the universe, but that they do not meddle with it.
- Theism: the subject believes that gods created the universe, and that they play an active part in its destiny.
- Fundamentalism: the subject takes the religious scriptures as literal truth, and the resulting confusion renders them unable to distinguish between reality and fiction.

It's clear from this that "religiosity" is better viewed as a continuous rather than a binary quality.

Once we have used the label "religious" to describe a group of people including Edward, we have lost sight of the continuous nature of the quality of religiosity. In our mind, the sample set has been split into two homogenous sub-groups: "non-religious" and "religious".

When we try to understand the concept of Labelling, we can do so from at least three different perspectives. The first of these is the psychological perspective: that's the Splitting we have already discussed. After this comes the logical perspective: where the phenomenon is viewed as a logical fallacy, the Fallacy of the Excluded Middle. Since we'll have a lot more to say about this in due course, we will skip over it for now.

That just leaves us to explain the philosophical perspective. The linguistic philosopher Paul Grice[xiii] helped us to understand the meaning and purpose of many of our modes of speech. According to Grice, the purpose of a statement (as opposed to a question or an order) is to induce a belief. This just means that the listener is being invited to believe that the statement made by the speaker is true. The purpose of both questions and orders, on the other hand, is to induce an intention in the listener. In the case of the order, we have an invitation to an intention to perform an action. In the case of the question, it's an invitation to the intention to think (about the answer). By a similar argument, the purpose of a label must surely be as an invitation for the listener to cease to think. The label tells us that the thinking has already been done for us, and that we should no longer concern ourselves with it.

But where does the impetus for a speaker to assign a label to an individual or group come from? There are two obvious possibilities that spring to mind, so we will consider each in turn.

The first possibility is that both the label and the desire to give it come from the speaker themselves. Given what we now know about first person privilege, this notion makes very little sense. The speaker has no way of knowing what's in the mind of the target and, even if they did, a judgement of the suitability of the applied label would be based on a comparison between themselves and the target. In order to assign the label accurately, the speaker would have to make a comparison between two things. The first of those is well known and understood: their own mental state or attitude. The second, however, can only be indirectly perceived: the state of the target. For this reason, the desire for labelling, if it were to come from the speaker, would tell us more about the state of the speaker (the more well-known of the two reference points) than it would tell us about the state of the target. It's for this reason that this possibility seems unlikely. It goes without saying that, in this analysis, we have glossed over the fact that the label must have originally been created by at least one person: we are not trying to say that it appeared spontaneously.

The second possibility is that the label comes from someone else **other** than the speaker. For people in the West, this source will typically be a combination of the government and the media. For instance, the labels "terrorist", "extremist" and "Islamist" are all coined as part of the agenda of a government, echoed by the mainstream media and reinforced by our peers. In more religious societies (to use the word in its traditional sense), the label, such as "heathen", "infidel" etc., may come from a clerical source. However, the peer-reinforcement component of the process will remain the same.

Take a look at any country, even one without any functioning government, and you will see a power structure. There are those who do the ruling and those who are ruled. Now imagine that you are part of the group that is doing the ruling. At the forefront of your mind would probably be the desire for things to stay the way they are and for you to continue to rule. Secondarily to this, for many people, we might expect to find the desire to make the most of your position as leader by accruing wealth and power. The problem is that, if you concentrate too much on doing the latter, you might find that your ability to do the former is brought to an abrupt end by a revolution, or something similar. In order to avoid this, you could resort to a simple technique for the manipulation of the public as follows:

- Identify something that you don't want the population to think about (for example, a recent attack your forces made against your own people in order to blame some "enemy", an action known as a false-flag attack).
- Identify an idea which people can easily oppose (for example, the idea that the Earth is flat).
- Create a label that encompasses both ("Conspiracy theory").
- Have your controlled media repeat the label many times.

At this point, Splitting is likely to occur in the minds of the population. The undesirable thought patterns will be conflated with the opposable idea, and a confused public, in avoiding thinking about the false-flag attack, will be less likely to form a rebellion. In some respects, we can view this as a weak form of mind control.

This may seem a little complicated as an abstract concept, so we'll take a real example in the hope that it will shed some more light on the matter. For our example, we will take the label "conspiracy theory" and demonstrate how it fits in with the above agenda.

Many people suppose that this term was introduced just after the assassination of John F. Kennedy on November 22nd 1963. In fact, the first recorded use of the term that has so far been found was in a 1909 publication entitled "The American Historical Review", but its origins may be even earlier than this. Regardless of when the term was first coined, it was certainly thrust onto the world stage following the events at Dealey Plaza. The term was introduced by the media, so the story goes, in order to ridicule people who refused to believe the government's "Lone Gunman" narrative.

If we take some examples of things that have been labelled "conspiracy theories", we see a fair mixture of truth and falsehood and a broad range in the degree to which they have been accepted as "true" by the public. Not only that, but we also find many examples where the degree of acceptance has changed quite dramatically over time. A few examples of this will help us to uncover some patterns.

In 1990, it was suggested that the theory of global warming might be false, and that the concept was invented as a conspiracy on the part of the elite to promote a world government. Exactly how it was that this fabrication was supposed to facilitate such a thing has not been explained by the proponents of the theory. At the time, there was no serious evidence presented to back up the claim. When it was first mooted, this "conspiracy theory" was regarded by the majority to be false. At the time of writing, the theory is slowly gaining in popularity, but there is still little or no evidence to support it. Until such evidence is forthcoming, it's probably best to assume that the proposition is false. It is worth noting that this is distinct from the question as to whether or not global warming itself is true or false: that is not the question we are concerned with here. As for the "conspiracy" aspect, we see an example of a "conspiracy theory" that initially was regarded by most to be false and today is still mostly regarded as such.

In the early 2000s, it was announced by the US and UK governments (among others) that Saddam Hussein had conspired with foreign powers to obtain "weapons of mass destruction" (WMD). At the time, this conspiracy theory was so widely believed by those in the West, that it resulted in a war. Even at the time, however, there were a handful of people, such as the UK weapons' expert David Kelly, who spoke out against the conspiracy theory by pointing out that it had no supporting evidence. David Kelly's death, an alleged suicide, shortly after this is regarded by many as an example of state-sponsored murder. After some years, the lack of any evidence of WMD has become so obvious that, today, it is difficult to find anyone who still believes that there ever were any. Here then, we see an example of a conspiracy theory which was initially regarded by most people to be true, but today is widely accepted as false.

In 2012, it was suggested that a group of traders scattered across a number of the world's largest banks conspired with each other to manipulate the LIBOR rate for their own profit. The LIBOR rate underpins the value of some $350 trillion of derivatives around the world. The conspiracy was admitted, first by some senior traders at the Royal Bank of Scotland then, subsequently, by traders in other banks. This "conspiracy theory" was regarded by most to be true at the time, and is still regarded as true today.

In 1964 there was a major event which catapulted an overeager US into the Vietnam War. In the Gulf of Tonkin Incident, the USS Maddox, an Allen M. Sumner-class Destroyer, was said to have been attacked by three North Vietnamese Navy torpedo boats of the 135th Torpedo Squadron. This resulted in the passing of the Gulf of Tonkin Resolution by Lyndon B. Johnson, thus enabling a war spanning almost twenty years which went on to take the lives of approximately 2.5 million Vietnamese, not to mention thousands of US soldiers. To this day, many are still suffering from the devastating effects of the millions of gallons of highly toxic Agent Orange, a chemical defoliant sprayed over around 4.5 million acres of land from 1961 to 1972. For years, the proposition had been advanced that there was no attack in the Gulf of Tonkin and that the event had been staged as a culmination of a conspiracy involving the captain of the Maddox and others. In 2005, following a FOI (freedom of information) request, the NSA revealed that the alleged "attack" had indeed been a staged "false flag" hoax. In this context, a "false flag" is a covert operation whereby an act of aggression is committed by one side against their own servicemen or civilians, but is blamed on enemy forces. So, in this example, this "conspiracy theory" was regarded by most to be false at the time it was said to have happened, but, today, is regarded as true.

As we have seen here, it's easy to find examples of "conspiracy theories" which are:

- at first viewed as true, but subsequently viewed as false;
- at first viewed as false, but subsequently viewed as true;
- at first viewed as true and still viewed as such;
- at first viewed as false and still viewed as such.

It should be immediately obvious that grouping together true propositions with false ones on the basis of an arbitrary label lacks any merit. It should also be apparent that the truth or falsehood of a proposition stands above any label (in this case "conspiracy theory") that we may wish to apply. If we are to group them at all, perhaps a more meaningful way would be to do so using the four categories as shown above. The label of "conspiracy theory" bears all the hallmarks of being a Religious Label formulated by those in power in order to misdirect an unwary public.

Before we move on, it's worth returning briefly to the subject of JFK. On August 14th 1978, a magazine called "The Spotlight" published an article by a former CIA official, Victor Marchetti. Marchetti had revealed that the CIA intended to publicly admit that another CIA agent, E. Howard Hunt, had been involved in the JFK assassination. As a result of the publication, Hunt filed a law suit against The Spotlight and the case was eventually heard by a jury in a court in Miami in 1985. On the February 6th 1985, the jury found that there were no grounds for the case, thus making a legal statement that the CIA had been involved in the assassination. The spokesman for the jury is reported to have said the following:

> "[The defence counsel] was asking us to do something very difficult. He was asking us to believe John Kennedy had been killed by our own government. Yet when we examined the evidence closely, we were compelled to conclude that the CIA had indeed killed President Kennedy."

Needless to say, the case was never reported in the mainstream media.

But this is by no means the only time that a court has confirmed something that had previously been labelled as a "conspiracy theory". On December 8th 1999, a jury in a civil trial in Memphis, Tennessee reached the unanimous verdict that, on April 4th 1968, Dr. Martin Luther King Jr. was assassinated as a result of a conspiracy involving the mafia, and local, state and federal government agencies. Once again, this was not widely reported by the mainstream media.

Of course, the saga that started with The Spotlight's story doesn't "prove" that all "conspiracy theories" are true or that they are all false. However, it is interesting, not to mention somewhat strangely amusing, to find that the very case for which the term was first popularised (for the purpose of stifling dissent) actually turned out to be a genuine "conspiracy".

According to Richard Petty, as described in "Social Psychology"[xiv], if we dismiss the views of others without spending any time thinking about them, then we can be said to have engaged in "superficial processing". Under these conditions, we tend to absorb the label but not the detail. Conversely, if we think in depth about the information presented, consider the evidence (both for and against) and contemplate the ramifications of the idea, then we have engaged in "systematic processing". When the government and the media take an idea that they don't like and repeat the label that they have coined ("conspiracy theory", in our example) they are attempting to coerce us into the practicing of superficial processing in order to stop us thinking about the idea they don't want us to think about.

However, there is also a second level that operates here. If false (or even ridiculous) stories are invented and categorized under the same label as legitimate (though unpalatable) ones, then this will serve to further muddy the waters. There is evidence to suggest that such stories are sometimes introduced by government disinformation agents masquerading as members of the public or part of the alternative media. When the story is "reported" by the mainstream media, they are instructed to use the term "conspiracy theory" in their scorn-laden report. At this point, Splitting will ensure that the ridiculous story is conflated with any other ideas to which the label has been applied. The clever, but devious, use of this technique can often be all that's required to stop people from taking evidence based theories seriously.

As an example, let's say that a disinformation agent introduces the rather comical, yet baseless idea that Hilary Clinton is a lizard impersonating a human. The media and everyone else, with the possible exception of David Icke, will (quite reasonably) be quick to ridicule the idea. A simple application of the label "conspiracy theory", in conjunction with the ridicule, will turn this idea into an instrument of control. Next time an idea comes along that the government would prefer you not to think about, all that is required is to apply the same label again, and the resultant Splitting will encourage superficial processing for the majority.

For a real example of this we could take the idea that the Earth is not a spheroid, but is flat. This idea is called the "Flat Earth Conspiracy Theory", though it is hard to imagine who is supposed to have "conspired". When we apply the scientific method to this theory, we find that there is a huge body of evidence to support the conventional view of the world as a sphere, and none which holds any water (no pun intended) to support the view that it is flat.

As a counterpoint to this, we have the theory of the controlled demolition (or something similar) of the three towers in New York on September 11$^{th}$ 2001. Firstly, there is a mountain of evidence to support this theory. Secondly, the main alternative hypothesis (that the buildings collapsed on their own after some fires) is in direct contravention of the laws of physics. In order for the three towers to have collapsed with acceleration approaching that of free fall, there would need to have been a constant application of energy, at the location of the destruction, throughout the few seconds that spanned the actual collapse. There is no provision for this in the self-collapse model, and it is this lack of energy that makes the theory impossible.

Anyone who puts these two ("Flat Earth" and "Controlled Demolition of the three towers on 9/11") together under the same label, attempting to use the falsehood of the first to deduce the "falsehood" of the second, would seem to have missed the whole point of critical thought itself.

Perhaps a more disturbing example of the government and media's conversion of a label into an instrument of control is to be found in their use of the word "Muslim". It should be obvious by now that the degree to which one adheres to the faith of Islam is a continuous quality, just like we saw at the beginning of this chapter. At the bottom of the scale we have the millions of people who just happen to follow Islam, but more interesting than this is what we find at the top of the scale: the head bogeyman himself. To understand the power that a bogeyman can have, we must take a look into our past.

As a young child, most of us can remember, at one time or another, our fear of non-existent monsters that hide under the bed ready to attack at night. As adults, we are susceptible to some very similar fears, if they are presented to us in a certain way. Just as the child is incapable of a detailed analysis of the bogeymen, an analysis which would quickly debunk it; the media's creation of the Muslim bogeyman encourages a similar disinclination for rational thought in the adult. Just as the child, feeling both afraid and helpless in the imagined presence of the bogeyman, seeks the reassurance of a parent; so the adult, feeling the same thing, seeks the reassurance of authority: the government.

According to the mainstream media at the time of writing, the current bogeyman is Abu Bakr al-Baghdadi, head of "ISIS", and we are encouraged to think of him as a representation of all Islam. It seems as if the mainstream media's drive to demonise Islam and all of its followers (by associating them with the bogeyman) is rampant. With each alleged terrorist attack reported to have been orchestrated by Muslims, the tendency to identify the label as one which corresponds to an out-group has become stronger. This, in turn, forms a divide between Muslims and non-Muslims and creates Splitting in the minds of the followers of *TVism*. Over time, the devotees, increasingly inclined towards superficial processing, form the habit of assuming that Muslims are the perpetrators of all the attacks (whether they are or not). Ultimately, the adherents identify themselves as "good" and the bogeyman, along with everything associated with him, as "evil". Of course, any evidence that comes along to contradict this narrative is rejected, courtesy of a little Canonical Filtering. When such evidence is presented in a more robust fashion, it will be vigorously attacked, and the target of the attack will gradually shift away from the evidence and towards the messenger.

Evidence that this is the real aim of the media's "reporting" is easy to find, simply be conducting a short thought experiment. Let's consider a couple of cases: the alleged Charlie Hebdo attacks in France (as described later in chapter 15) and the alleged attack on the island of Utøya in Norway, purported to have been carried out by Anders Breivik. In the first case, the media was quick to label the supposed attackers as "Muslim Extremists". Some might argue that this was due to the fact that the attackers were alleged to have shouted the words "Allahu Akbar", but this argument has little merit since words are inherently cheap. Anybody can shout these words, or any others for that matter, and doing so is no proof of any religious or ethnic persuasion of the speaker. By contrast, in the second case, Breivik was not labelled as a "Christian Extremist", even though there would seem to be some strong (Christian) religious themes to his beliefs.

Of course, the whole idea of a Christian extremist would not fit the media's agenda at all, as it would dilute the message of "Muslim Extremist" which they push in nearly all other cases. There is no point in going to all the effort of creating a bogeyman, only to have the fear that he induces diluted when our attention is refocused elsewhere.

In this chapter we have seen how our inclination for Religious Labelling can be fuelled by the labels that are formulated by the agenda of our government or others who seek to control us. Once the label has been introduced, the media ensures its uptake through a process of endless repetition. When the *believer* mind encounters the label, Splitting is the inevitable result, and superficial processing in line with the government's agenda is the inevitable consequence. In the next chapter, we will move on to look at the next tool from the *believer* toolkit.

## - 12 -
# Ad Hominem Attack

*"I always cheer up immensely if an attack is particularly wounding because, if they attack one personally, it means they have not a single political argument left."*

Margaret Thatcher

---

In this chapter, the fourth of this sequence of five, we will carry on with our investigation of the tools available in the *believer* toolkit. In the previous chapter, we looked at Religious Labelling, a tool whose purpose is to neutralise threats to the belief system by avoiding the levels of detail that would otherwise become evident as a result of analysis. *Ad Hominem Attack*, the subject of this chapter, is another example of such a tool.

This logical fallacy, also known as "*Argumentum ad Hominem*", translates as "Attack to the Man", and is one of the cruder tools in the *believer*'s arsenal. In it, the *believer* seeks to focus on the character of the speaker in order to avoid the details of the debate.

This can be illustrated in the following simple example. Once again, since it's only the behaviour we are interested in, we should focus just on this and ignore any ideas we have as to which (if either) of the two speakers is "right", regardless of our temptation to do so:

> **Edward:** "On September 11th 2001, three buildings in New York were destroyed by some process resembling controlled demolition. This event was

most likely orchestrated by rogue elements within the US government, perhaps with the help of MOSSAD."

**Barry:** "You would say that because you are a conspiracy theorist".

It is clear here that Barry is not interested in considering any evidence that might support (or otherwise) Edward's claim. Instead, he avoids the matter entirely and focuses on attacking Edward's character. We could explain this simply as a desire to avoid losing the argument, but it is more likely to be a fear-response resulting from the threat to his beliefs.

Since we are on the subject of conspiracy theories once again, we should probably pause to work out a dictionary definition for the term. As we have seen before, it is often the simple questions that go unanswered and our failure to address them which can cause us to set off on the wrong foot.

In an attempt to proffer a definition, we could try something like this:

> A conspiracy theory is a hypothesis suggesting that an unfavourable event, normally considered to be caused by a particular agent, is in fact the result of the premeditated actions of two or more persons other than that agent.

To show the falsity of this definition, we might consider a simple counter-example, such as the Manhattan Project which was conducted in the US during World War II. This was led by an American physicist, J. Robert Oppenheimer, and resulted in the production of the first atomic bomb. Starting as a small research program in 1939, the project eventually employed more than 130,000 people. It resulted in the creation of multiple production and research sites that operated in secret. Participants were organised in "cells", each unaware of the existence of the others, in order that very few people were able to piece together the goal of the project. Given its size and structure, it is widely considered to be one of the largest conspiracies in history. The government never admitted to it, the media never reported on it and, as a result, the public had no idea of its existence for over twenty-five years. This fascinating story is disclosed in Richard Rhodes's "The Making of the Atomic Bomb"[xv].

Although this project could not have succeeded without the conspiracy of a huge number of people, nobody would ever refer to it as a "conspiracy theory". Clearly it is not the act of conspiring that makes a "conspiracy theory". Even though it may be a necessary condition, it is not a sufficient one.

One of the things about the Manhattan Project is that it has lots of supporting evidence for its existence, not the least of which is the dropping of two atomic bombs on the already defeated Japanese. So maybe this is our clue as to what is missing in the definition above? Building on this, we might try again with a modified definition such as the following:

> A conspiracy theory is a hypothesis suggesting that an unfavourable event, normally considered to be caused by a particular agent, is in fact the result of the premeditated actions of two or more persons other than that agent; even though there is no evidence to support the hypothesis.

Again, a simple counter-example is all we need to dispel any credibility this new definition may seem to offer. For a suitable example, we need look no further than the events in New York on September 11th 2001, where we find at least two hypotheses concerning the identity of the perpetrators.

The first of these is that two of the buildings were brought down using airplanes by nineteen men under the command of one with a beard in a cave, with the third falling down on its own (as a result of a fire).

The second hypothesis is that the controlled demolition (or something similar) of the three buildings was instigated by rogue elements within the US government, perhaps with the aid of the security forces of a foreign power.

The latter hypothesis happens to have a mountain of evidence to support it, but what evidence do we have to support the first? It turns out that there are two things. The first of these is the telephone calls that were alleged to have been made by the passengers on the flights. A lot of investigation and analysis has gone into these, with one of the best reference sources being Elias Davidsson's, "Hijacking America's Mind on 9/11"[xvi]. Davidsson's detailed investigation leads us to the inevitable conclusion that it was impossible for these calls to have originated from on board the planes in the manner that was claimed in the government's narrative. The second piece of evidence is the "Bin Laden videos" which allegedly show "Bin Laden" taking the credit for the events. Critical analysis of these videos has shown that they depict multiple individuals purporting to be Bin Laden. It is nearly impossible to confirm the identity of any of them, so this "evidence" must be described as flimsy at best.

Now, going back to the two hypotheses, it is clear that the term "conspiracy theory" can be applied to the second hypothesis (controlled demolition), but not the first (man in the cave). Both hypotheses involve a conspiracy of a group of individuals, yet, oddly, it seems that it is acceptable to apply the term to the one supported by a strong weight of evidence, but unacceptable to apply it to the one which lacks such evidence. Clearly then, it is not a lack of evidence that is the crux of a "conspiracy theory", so we need to try a little harder if we are to arrive at an accurate definition for our term.

If we pause to think about these two 9/11 hypotheses for a moment, it becomes apparent that there is another key difference. The first theory (man in the cave) has been endorsed repeatedly by the TV, whereas the second (controlled demolition) has not. With this in mind, we are in a position to attempt our third definition:

> A conspiracy theory is a hypothesis suggesting that an unfavourable event, normally considered to be caused by a particular agent, is in fact the result of the premeditated actions of two or more persons other than that agent; but only when the hypothesis

has not been canonised into lore by the religion of *TVism*.

Now we clearly understand that the phrase's roots lie in its contradiction of doctrine, we can see that the term "conspiracy theorist" plays the same role within *TVism* as the term "heathen" or "infidel" does within mainstream religions. These are all pejorative terms which are used to label members of the religion's out-group. In this respect, using the term "conspiracy theorist" is a form of Religious Labelling as we saw in chapter 11.

Armed with our corrected definition, we could go back to Edward and Barry's conversation and replace the terms used with our more accurate versions:

> **Edward:** "On September 11th 2001, three buildings in New York were destroyed by some process resembling controlled demolition. This event was most likely orchestrated by rogue elements within the US government, perhaps with the help of MOSSAD."
>
> **Barry** (in a fit of honesty): "You would say that because you are a person who bases their views on evidence rather than accepting the religious canon offered by the TV."
>
> **Edward:** "Exactly! How about we discuss this further over a beer, Barry?"

Before we put *Ad Hominem* Attack to bed, there is one final point to consider: it doesn't always have to be an individual who is the target of the attack. In many cases, it can be an organisation, a website or a group of researchers. When applied in this way, the *Ad Hominem* Attack can work in partnership with the Authority Hierarchy in that it provides a way for this to be communicated. By employing *Ad Hominem* Attack against non-canonised sources, the subject is sending signals to their peer group, and perhaps also to themselves, in order to indicate, wittingly or unwittingly, the structure of the hierarchy they have constructed. By exchanging signals in this way, the herd can ensure that the hierarchy remains the same across the various individuals which comprise it.

With these thoughts in mind, we will leave this topic and move on to our final example of the offerings from the *believer* toolkit.

# - 13 -
# Religious Inferencing

*"You can't convince a believer of anything; for their belief is not based on evidence, but on a deep seated need to believe."*

Carl Sagan, American cosmologist

---

Over the course of the last few chapters, we have been looking at a number of tools which are to be found in the *believer* toolkit which can be used to make sense of the world around us. We shall round off our investigation in this chapter with a look at *Religious Inferencing*: the ability to make deductions about the real world based on reference to a belief set. Under normal circumstances, when we hear the term "belief set", we think of beliefs associated with traditional religion, but the phrase actually has a much wider meaning. Now, we will get a glimpse of this breadth and see how there is a certain uniformity that applies to all belief sets, regardless of whether they are of a religious nature or otherwise.

Whenever we are faced with something new, it is our natural instinct to try and make sense of it: to come up with an answer. So strong is this desire that we are sometimes even tempted to provide an answer when we have little or nothing to go on. The new stimulus may take the form of an observation, a world event or even just an idea; but the inclination to reconcile it remains the same. If the stimulus is entirely new, this desire presents us with a problem since, having no directly relevant experience with which to compare it, we may find ourselves at a bit of a loss. In this situation, we are forced to resort to some other mechanism to achieve our goal.

Assuming that the stimulus takes the form of a world event, the *explorer* mind's first step is a careful analysis of the facts surrounding the event, taking great care to avoid conjecture and opinion. After this, the subject will normally call upon their life experience to answer a sequence of questions. Have I seen an event similar to this before? If so, what are the key differences and similarities between this new event and the previous ones which are comparable? Other questions, more specific to the details of the event in question will, no doubt, also arise. For all of us, our life experience acts as a reference source for our interpretation of new events.

For the *believer* mind, since we have access to an additional reference source in the form of our belief system, things often follow a different course. In many cases this takes precedence over our perceptual experience and, as such, can be a powerful instrument for shaping our interpretation of the world. The ease of use of this tool means that it gets a good deal of exercise, but instances of its application are often concealed from view. More often than not, the language used by the subject to describe their reasoning consists of simple everyday phrases, and the fact that they are so commonplace means that we rarely stop to think about their underlying meaning. The result of this is that their true nature is often overlooked, not least by the subject themselves, and the only way to reveal the meaning is by a detailed analysis of their vocalisations.

As usual, the best way to see this in action is with an example such as the following:

> **Edward:** "Many of the planes you think are passenger jets are actually tankers carrying metal oxide aerosols which are being sprayed into the air. The purpose of this activity is unknown, but you can easily spot the persistent trails they leave if you simply look up."
>
> **Barry:** "That's not true. They would never do that."

As always, our aim here is not to concern ourselves with which of the two participants is correct, but, instead, to analyse the psychological processes at work. To do this, we will start by studying Barry's words very carefully.

The first clue we have is the word "they". When he uses this word, we have to assume that Barry is referring to the group of people who are doing the spraying (if that's what it is). The problem with this is that we do not yet know who "they" are. In his proposition, Edward has not specified "their" identity and, furthermore, from the words that Edward has used, we cannot reliably conclude that he is even aware of it. Not only that but, if Barry is right and the spraying is not happening, there can be no "they" to be the subject of his counter-thesis.

What is clear is that the identity of the group does not constitute the main point of Edwards's argument: the fact that (in his view) the spraying is taking place. In substituting the central theme of the discussion with a new one that is centred on belief, Barry has attempted to avoid the topic.

But, as is often the case, there is yet an even deeper level to the problem, in that Barry's response encapsulates another example of a logical fallacy. It is reasonable to assume that any identification of the perpetrators we might make would be as a result (or output) of the discussion. Yet, in Barry's response, we see a presupposition of the identity deployed as a premise (or input) into the same discussion. This kind of circular argument is an example of the logical fallacy known as *Petitio Principii* (also called "Begging the Question"). Any argument that requires the assertion of its own conclusion in order to prove the same argument is not an argument at all.

When we hold a belief based on a false assumption, we often find a logical fallacy lurking at the root of the story that's told to justify the belief. It can often be difficult to get the subject to admit that this is the case, possibly because, somewhere deep down, he or she is aware that there is "something wrong" with both the belief and the justification that surrounds it. As the *believer* is questioned in an increasingly more robust fashion, we would expect to see a corresponding increase in the emotional nature of the response. In many cases this will take the form of anger, but, on occasions, we can expect to see other irrational responses such as childishness, scorn or mockery. In the unlikely event that the fallacy actually is vocalised, either wittingly or unwittingly, the *believer* will usually refuse to discuss matters any further.

So much for the word "they", but what can we say about Barry's use of the words "would never"? When he utters this phrase, Barry is telling us that he imagines there is a moral code that forbids such an activity (the spraying) and that the group of people previously identified as "they" adhere strictly to this moral code. At this point we must ask ourselves exactly how it is that we can ascertain someone's moral code. Whether it's a friend or a public figure, such as a politician, the only way we can do this is by means of a careful observation of that person's speech and behaviour. As we have seen before, an accurate appraisal of a person's motivation for their speech and actions is a complex task, and is certainly not something that one can do in an instant. The observation would have to take place over the course of some months or years, and even this may only result in an incomplete answer. The problem with Barry's assertion is that, as we have already seen, the identity of the group of people referred to as "they" has not yet been ascertained, so a process of observation is therefore impossible.

Some might say that, when Barry says the word "they", he means "the government". If we accept this explanation, we would still need to know which member or members of the government we would need to monitor. Would it be someone from the national government, the civil service, the local government or from one of the many alphabet agencies which seem to have taken on an ever increasing portion of our governance? Without something specific, we would have to accept the idea that **all** of these people somehow conform to the same moral code, a concept which seems unlikely, to say the least.

Others might say that, although Barry does not know "their" identity, he is using this word as a dummy pronoun, similar in sense to the word "it" in the sentence "It is raining". For many people in Barry's situation, this explanation may be nearer the mark. For followers of traditional religion, the notion of the creator is there to provide the comfort of a benevolent force that is in some way watching out for us. For a follower of *TVism*, it may well be that the source of benevolence has shifted in such a way that it is no longer synonymous with a "creator", but is now synonymous with the state. Barry lives in a world presided over by a benevolent force, and a world such as this has no place for the spraying of poisonous aerosols (if that's what's going on) by the people who are supposed to be watching our backs. For this reason, Barry must reject Edward's proposition.

Now that we have understood the meaning of Barry's words, we are in a position to take a more balanced view of his interaction with Edward. The observation that leaps out at us is that, even though they appear to be having a conversation on one particular subject, they are actually talking about two different ones. Edward is making a statement about his observations of what seems to him to be the spraying, while Barry is simply making an expression of his faith in the state.

In many ways, this is similar to the situation we examined at the beginning of chapter 4 where we saw the problems that could arise when we had a mismatch between *explorer* and *believer*. Just as before, the only way Barry and Edward can have a fruitful (no pun intended) interaction is if one of them changes his choice as to which "mind" he is prepared to use. *Believer* versus *believer* may lead to feelings of comfort and social advantage, whereas *explorer* versus *explorer* may lead to a better insight into the workings of the world, perhaps something along these lines:

> **Edward:** "Many of the planes you think are passenger jets are actually tankers carrying metal oxide aerosols which are being sprayed into the air. The purpose of this activity is unknown, but you can easily spot the trails they leave if you simply look up."

**Barry:** "I've seen trails like the ones you describe ever since I was a child. They are a normal consequence of the fuel's combustion products' being injected into cold air. What leads you to believe that these trails are different?"

**Edward:** "Trails of water and ice crystals like the ones you describe would be expected to disappear after a few seconds, as a consequence of Brownian motion. When the trails persist for hours, spreading out and becoming bigger, science tells us that this cannot be the result of ice alone."

It goes without saying that this would probably be just the start of the conversation. As the questioning and analysis proceeded, each participant would, without doubt, learn more about the physics and chemistry that underlie the concepts.

This analysis of Religious Inferencing has enabled us to focus once again on the behavioural characteristics that can be observed when a *believer* and an *explorer* mind attempt to engage in dialogue. This seems a fitting point at which to leave the discussion of the *believer* toolkit, and turn our attention in more detail to the psychological forces which are at play during interactions such as this. But before we do so, it is worth summarising what we have covered so far.

The table in Figure 7 lists some stimuli and the behavioural responses we can expect when the *believer* and *explorer* minds, respectively, are running the show. This can be used as a quick guide to ascertain which of the two minds is dominant in a subject at any given moment. In the same way, it can also be used to determine what is going on within one's own head. The cross-reference to the Structure axis of the Myers-Briggs Type Indicator[xvii] is included for those who are familiar with this method of psychological profiling.

| Stimulus | Believer | Explorer |
|---|---|---|
| Reacts to information contradicting belief by | ignoring it | analysing it |
| Identifies impossible narratives as | coincidences | untruths |
| Reconciles outlying facts with | ad hoc hypothesis | re-evaluation of knowledge |
| Responds to new events by seeking | explanation from authority | an exploration of detail |
| Reacts to divergent ideas by | labelling | listening |
| Responds to a new message by | judging the messenger | analysing the message |
| Understands new situations by | reference to belief | reference to observation |
| Treats the narrative of authority as | absolute conclusion | opinion |
| Greets military actions of home nation with | patriotic support | balance using "reversal" |
| Myers-Briggs type indicator, Structure axis : | judging | perceiving |

**Figure 7**

## - 14 -
# Protect the Religion

*"All truth passes through three stages. First, it is ridiculed. Second, it is violently opposed. Third, it is accepted as being self-evident."*

Arthur Schopenhauer, German philosopher

---

For the *explorer* mind, the world is a source of evidence waiting to be discovered. For the *believer*, on the other hand, the world is a construction which emanates from our cultural beliefs. Maintaining this construct is no mean feat, and the *believer* mind, whether it is aware of it or not, must go to great lengths to protect it from harm. This constant effort gives rise to a set of behaviours which we will call "Protect the Religion".

In psychological terms, it can be viewed as a game in the sense described by Eric Berne in "Games People Play"[xviii]. Berne describes complex human social interactions in terms of the consequence of behaviour deriving from three separate "ego states" as follows:

- "Parent" (P) represents the set of behaviours that one might associate with a parent figure. When a subject exhibits behaviour from this category, they are mimicking the behaviour that was exhibited by their own parents during their childhood.
- "Adult" (A) is the behaviour we might expect to see when a subject is making an objective appraisal of reality.
- "Child" (C) represents the set of archaic behaviours that became fixed during the subject's childhood.

When the subject exhibits behaviour from this category, they are mimicking their own behaviour which was exhibited while interacting with their parents during childhood.

When two people interact in conversation, a stimulus comes from one of these three ego states in the first individual and a response is elicited from one of the three in the second. In its simplest form, a "Game", to use Berne's terminology, is an interaction between two people. At the social level, the interaction can be viewed as taking place between one of the three ego states (P, A, C) in the first person and one in the second. In most cases, this will be the "Adult" of each person. But the twist is that, at the psychological level, the interaction takes place between a different pair of ego states. Exactly which two are exercised depends on the "Game" being played. For instance, in the game of "Alcoholic", the "Child" state in the alcoholic may be deployed to interact with the "Parent" in a long-suffering partner.

"Protect the Religion" is a Game for two players, the first of whom is required to think in an *explorer* way, while the second must adopt a *believer* stance. For simplicity's sake, following the interaction diagram as shown in Figure 8, we will refer to the two players throughout this chapter as the *explorer* and the *believer*.

The game starts with the *explorer's* presenting some evidence or argument to the *believer*. As before, we will call this "the proposition" and we will not concern ourselves with whether it is true or false. In general terms, it will contain a central thesis, some supporting premises, some background material (to explain the context of the thesis) and will be couched in a certain language or turn of phrase. After the presentation of the proposition, the two players will engage in some form of dialogue.

As we have already said, the Game of Protect the Religion operates on two different levels of interaction. The **social** interaction (shown as a dotted arrow) occurs between the Adult *ego* states of each participant. The **psychological**

**Protect the Religion**

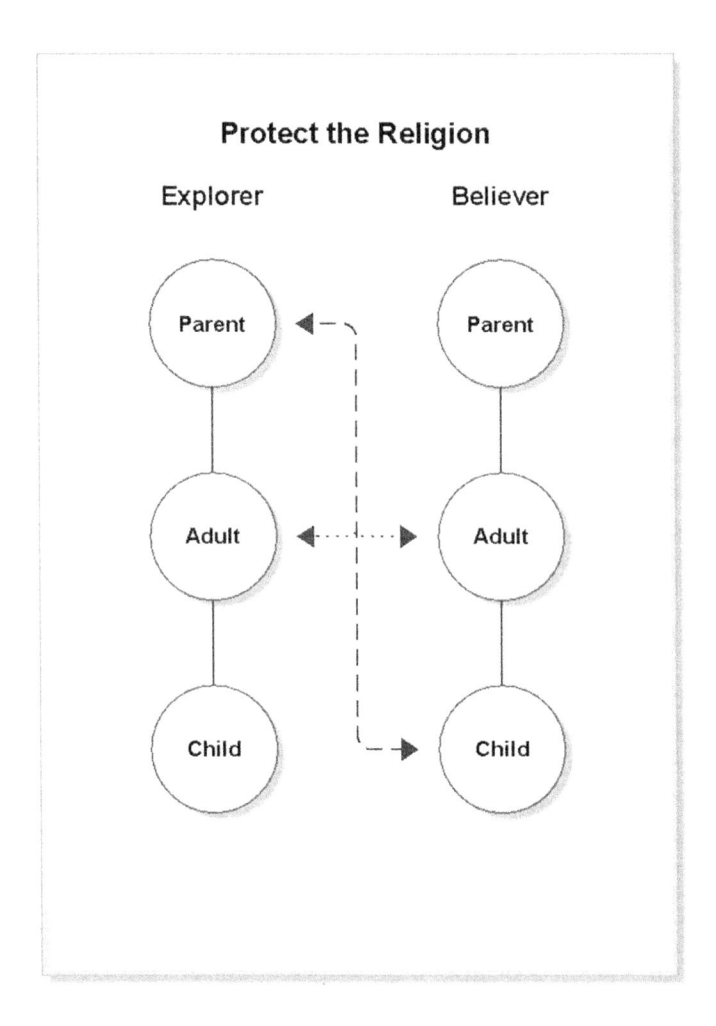

Explorer / Believer

Parent — Parent
Adult ↔ Adult
Child    Child

(with dashed arrow from Explorer's Parent to Believer's Child)

**Figure 8**

interaction (dashed), however, occurs between the Parent of the *explorer* and the Child of the *believer*. It is tempting to put the "blame" for this kind of interaction on the Child, but we must remember that for any Game to proceed, at least two participants are required. If either were to cease to participate, the Game would quickly come to an end.

The object of the Game is for the *believer* to engineer ways to protect their "religion", or belief set, from the damage that would otherwise ensue if they were to accept the proposition presented by the *explorer*. After all, since the *believer* is likely to have invested a lifetime in their beliefs, they are not just going to give them up because a little bit of evidence gets in the way. The object of the game from the perspective of the *explorer* is to educate the *believer* in the same way that a parent educates a child.

Similar Games have been observed between Christian Fundamentalists and researchers who have examined the Bible from a logical perspective. Typically, the researcher will identify two passages in the Bible which contradict each other, and the fundamentalist will be invited to put together some narrative that "explains" the contradiction. To illustrate this, we could take the book of "Genesis" and consider an example of a dialog:

> **Edward:** "In the first creation story, it is stated that animals were created on day five, while humans were created on day six. However, in the second creation story, it is stated that Adam and Eve were created before the animals. How can the animals have been created both before **and** after the creation of man?"
>
> **Barry:** "Actually, in the second story, it is stated that the 'beasts of the field' were created after man. The other animals were already in existence at the time, so it was just those in the **fields** which were created after man."

Of course, it's not important whether or not you believe in either of these stories. What is important is Barry's move in the Game of Protect the Religion.

When analysing a Game, one factor that Berne considers is how "hard" it is played. In mild forms, a Game can take the form of light hearted banter. In harder forms, it can end up with one or more of the participants in hospital or jail. The "hardness" of the game will depend on the extent to which the *believer* identifies themselves with the belief set that is under attack. If the subject feels that he or she has nothing much going for them in life, other than their beliefs, then it is likely that a harder version of the game will be played. This may arise in situations where the subject has low self-esteem or has strong feelings of inadequacy or self-doubt. Under these circumstances, we would expect to see a low engagement with the proposition presented by the *explorer* and, as a result, the subject will tend to be dismissive or confrontational. If, on the other hand, the subject were more self-confident, we may expect to see a greater level of engagement, because he or she would have less to lose in the event that the belief system were to be unravelled.

This gradation of degree of engagement will result in a hierarchy of behaviour such as that shown in Figure 9. At the bottom of the hierarchy we see low levels of engagement and a hard Game. Towards the top, we see more engagement and a milder Game. Over the next few paragraphs, we will take a look at each level in a little more detail.

Right at the bottom of the hierarchy, we see *Name Calling*. Step on a dog's tail and you get a bark and maybe a bite: step on the religion of a follower of *TVism* and you can expect a similar reaction. As we have already said, a response like this is more likely in cases where the subject has a feeling of low self-worth. The greater the subject's dependence on their beliefs, the more they have to fear from the prospect of the destruction of those beliefs. It's this fear which leads to a more highly emotionally charged response. At this level, the subject is unwilling even to consider the proposition, let alone the central thesis or supporting premises.

Only a little better than this is *Ad Hominem Attack*. At this level of response, just as with the previous one, the subject's attack is directed specifically at the *explorer* presenting the proposition. As this has already been described at length in chapter 12, we won't have much more to say about it here

## Argument Hierarchy

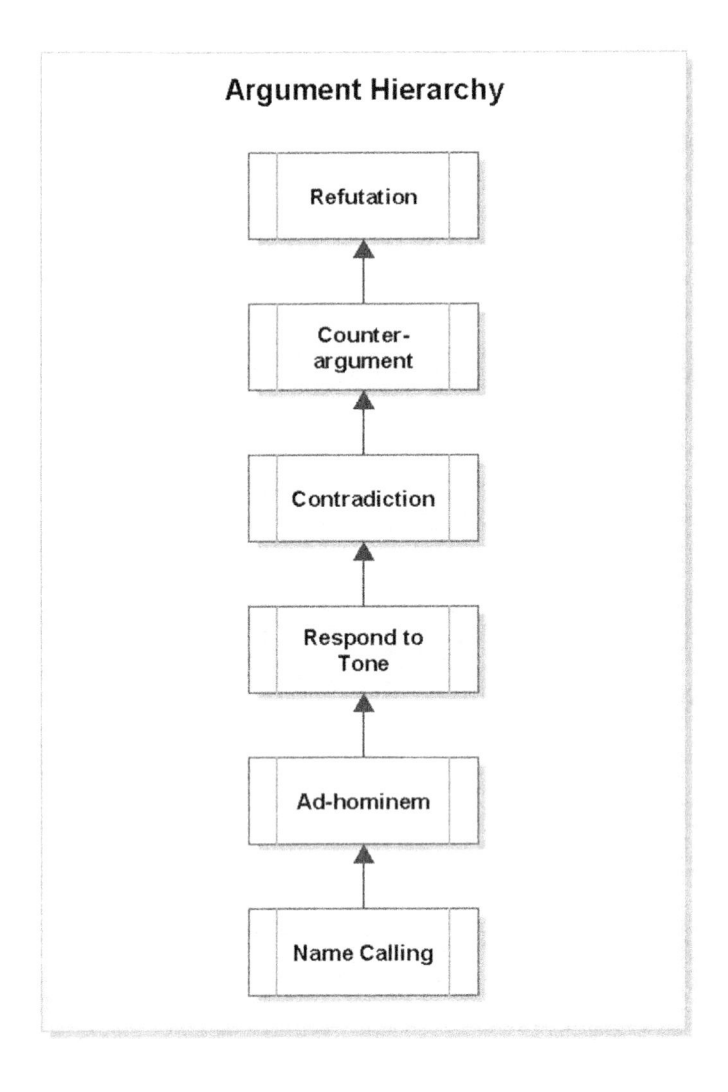

- Refutation
- Counter-argument
- Contradiction
- Respond to Tone
- Ad-hominem
- Name Calling

**Figure 9**

except to point out that, just as with the previous level, we find a total lack of willingness to engage with the proposition.

The next level, *Responding to Tone*, is interesting in that it is the first level in which there are any signs of involvement with the proposition. The goal for the subject, when behaving at this level, is to seek to neutralise the proposition by objecting to the way in which it has been written or spoken. In some respects, this can be viewed as a form of *Ad Hominem Attack* which is aimed not at the messenger, but at the tone of the message or the medium of its transmission. Even though the involvement here is of a cursory nature, it is, nevertheless, **an** involvement. It shows that the subject has listened to or read at least part of the proposition.

A variant of this occurs when the subject claims to be "offended" by the content. In this case, the subject's focus on their own construed "offence" is designed to avoid a focus on the proposition. In contrast with this, the *explorer's* method leaves little room for taking offence, since the focus is on the evidence and the reasoning that can be made on it. The *explorer* accepts that any emotion they feel can have no bearing on the evidence, so refuses to let offence form part of the proceedings. Facts are simply facts, after all.

For a *believer*, offence occurs when their beliefs come under attack from facts, and an emotional response like this is only possible when the subject has some corner to defend: a standpoint taken by the *believer* that will remain fixed regardless of any evidence that is presented. The *believer's* strong emotional tie to their belief system forces them to live within a distorted narrative which is in discord with the factual world. They are unwilling to acknowledge the possibility that they may be wrong because of the emotional harm that this would cause.

The act of taking offence can help the *believer* to avoid a potentially more embarrassing response. As we have already seen, their insistence on living in a fictional world necessitates the disposal of any inconvenient, contradictory facts. To do this based on a simple refusal or denial can often seem childish, whereas to claim "offence" seems to have developed an air of social acceptability. Choosing this route can often allow the *believer* to save face to some degree. In psychological terms, we might say that taking offence acts as a "permission-slip" for the subject to go ahead and ignore the facts.

While we are on the topic of "offence", we cannot ignore the growing tendency, here in the West, for the right not to be offended to take precedence over the right to free speech. The real danger we face as a result of this trend is that it might ultimately lead to the silencing of free speech completely, since whenever an unpalatable truth is presented, it can always be silenced by an allegation of "offence". It goes without saying that there is a fine line to be had here, as we can show with a couple of examples.

For the first of these, let's imagine a scenario in which a person engages in racist name-calling directed at some specific victim. In this case, most of us would agree that the right of the victim not to be offended outweighs the aggressor's right to free speech.

In the second, we could take the example of James Tracy, a former Florida Atlantic University professor, who was fired from his tenured position after asserting on his public blog that the alleged Sandy Hook Elementary School massacre was a hoax. As with all the examples in this book, our beliefs as to the nature of the event are not important here. Instead we should concentrate on the question as to the balance between Tracy's right to free speech and the rights of the families of the alleged "victims" not to be offended. In this case, the assertion of the families' rights over those of Tracy would seem to be a more dubious decision, as will be seen later.

One mechanism we might use to define the line between the two is the metric of Popper-compliance which we have used a few times already. The first of our examples is non-Popper-compliant, since no mechanism has been presented by the aggressor to disprove the racial epithets, and it is difficult to see how such a thing could be possible. The second example, on the other hand, is Popper-compliant, since Tracy has presented a mountain of compelling evidence to support his claims. In order to disprove Tracy's hypothesis, one need only consider his evidence and demonstrate how it is fallacious.

With this is mind, perhaps we might offer the suggestion that, in the case of Popper-compliant propositions, the right to free speech should outweigh the right for observers not to be offended.

Returning once again to the diagram, we find the next level: *Contradiction*. Here, we see the *believer* simply asserting the negation of the central thesis, without offering any logical analysis or counterargument. Most of us can remember this kind of thing from the school playground when one kid would shout "No it isn't" (or words to that effect) when presented with a new and perhaps unsavoury fact. So what do we really mean when we say something like this? What we are actually trying to say is **not** "No it isn't", but "No, that's not how I want it to be".

The next level, *Counterargument*, sees the *believer* offering a counter-thesis, adjunct to the original one, in the hope that this will distract attention from it. By means of this tactic, the subject can give the impression that they are engaging with the proposition, whilst deflecting the conversation away from the central thesis threatening their beliefs. From a practical perspective, there are many variations that can be observed with this tactic. Typically, the *believer* will focus on a supporting premise or some aspect of the background material, taking care to pick a point that is lacking in clarity or detail. Once this is pointed out, the *believer* will argue that this weakness in the supporting premise must imply that the central thesis is false, and that the default official canonised narrative must therefore be true.

In formal terms, it will come as no surprise to the reader that what we see here is another example of a logical fallacy. This one is known as *Argumentum Ad Ignorantium*, which translates as: "Argument from Ignorance". Perhaps the best way to see how it works is with an example:

> **Edward:** "All three of the buildings that came down in New York on September 11$^{th}$ 2001 descended at free fall acceleration during the final destruction phase. Since such a thing is impossible without the

> constant application of energy during the progress of the descent, we know for sure that it couldn't have been caused by the planes which hit two of the buildings around an hour before. This conclusion is corroborated by the fact that there were three buildings which were destroyed, yet only two planes."
>
> **Barry:** "If it wasn't the planes, then where did those planes go? If you can't tell me what happened to the planes, it means that your argument doesn't hold water. Therefore it must have been the two planes that caused the destruction of the three towers."

Once again, our purpose here is not to discuss the details behind Edward's hypothesis. For that, the reader should consult some of the many references we have listed. What is important here is the *Argumentum Ad Ignorantium*: the focus on the doubt that exists as to the fate of the planes that Edward says existed. Barry has pointed out that Edward is not aware of this detail, and we are forced to agree that Edward has not made this clear. However, Edward's lack of ability to answer this question is not a sufficient cause for Barry to discount the central thesis of Edward's argument, his appeal to the laws of physics.

In many ways, this example is similar to the following conversation that Edward and Barry might have had at the age of six:

> **Edward:** "When you put a tooth under your pillow at night and wake up to find it's been replaced by a coin, it's not the Tooth Fairy but your mother who makes the switch."
>
> **Barry:** "Which side of the pillow does your mother lift in order to take the tooth, the right or the left?"
>
> **Edward:** "I don't know because I am asleep at the time."

> **Barry:** "Because you can't answer the question, it means that your theory is wrong. Therefore, we have to assume that it's the Tooth Fairy who replaces the tooth with the coin."

Returning once again to Figure 9, we see at the top of the hierarchy the final level, *Refutation*. At this level, the subject is fully engaged with the central thesis. If the refutation is successful, then we can assume that the central thesis was false. If, however, the *believer* engages with the central thesis yet is unable to refute it, we might come to the conclusion that the central thesis was true, at least in terms of the evidence and hypotheses available to the participants at the time.

Let's assume for a minute that the *believer* has been forced to accept the central thesis. At this point we have reached the end of the road for Protect the Religion, but not the end of the psychological journey for the subject. If the thesis that has been conceded is a difficult one to stomach, the *believer* will, in all probability, have a tough job reconciling it with their world view. In many ways, we might compare the experience with that of facing up to the inevitability of the death of a loved one or family member. In her book, "On Death and Dying"[xix], Elisabeth Kübler-Ross tells us about the five stages that people typically go through when faced with the prospect of death such as this. If we take a few moments to look at these stages, we will see many similarities between this emotional journey and the path that the *believer* will inevitably follow under the circumstances we have described.

The first stage is *Denial*. During this phase, the subject will try to pretend that the event has not happened or that it will somehow go away. In some ways, this is analogous to the process of Erasure as discussed in chapter 9. After this comes *Anger*: something for which we saw evidence in the stages of Name Calling and *Ad Hominem* Attack from earlier. The next stage, according to Kübler-Ross, is *Bargaining*, a behavioural sequence which we might view as an "acceptance ladder" in that it consists of a sequence of acceptance and denial.

Let's look to Barry and Edward again for an example:

> **Edward:** "On 9/11, a passenger jet couldn't have crashed into the Pentagon because, if it had, there would have been some large chunks of wreckage left behind, such as fuselage, engines, wings and tailplane."
>
> **Barry:** "Oh, I've always thought there was something dodgy about that. It was probably a truck bomb, but they were too embarrassed to admit to the breach in security that let it get through. All the other events happened though, just like in the official story."

In this example, Barry's *believer* mind has allowed a sacrifice to be made in the hope that this might prevent further damage. A bargaining stance is offered to try to reach agreement with his *explorer* mind. The *believer* allows the *explorer* to win the fight, on this one point, in the hope that this will bring an early end to the battle.

At some point later, the conversation might continue:

> **Edward:** "In New York, on 9/11, the three towers could not have been destroyed by air liners because there were only two planes."
>
> **Barry:** "Oh yes, I thought there was something dodgy going on with that third building. Perhaps explosives were used. But the Twin Towers definitely came down as described in the official story."

Here, we see Barry's *believer* mind still holding out hope that the central thesis of the religion, "we're OK: they're not OK," can be maintained, but being forced to concede another point in order to save face.

Going back to Kübler-Ross's model once again, we find that the next stage is *Depression*. This can be a very real problem for the subject once the *believer* mind has given up the battle. Yet it is a necessary stage that everyone must go through if they are to reach the final stage of *Acceptance*.

Over the course this sequence of chapters, we've looked at the tools and techniques that are used by the *believer* to build and maintain the fictional construct they take to be reality. In this chapter our focus has been on the perpetual game the *believer* must play and how those tools are used as the game proceeds. That's probably enough about the *believer*, for the time being at least. In the next chapter we will change the topic a little and look in more detail at the *explorer* mind.

# - 15 -
# A Madness in Paris

*"Who is so gross that cannot see this palpable device? But who's so bold but says he sees it not?"*

William Shakespeare (from Richard III)

---

In chapter 1 we looked at the differences between the Correspondence and the Constructivist Theories of Truth by applying each to a simple, fictional example. In this chapter we will show how each of these paradigms can be used to analyse a more complex, real-world event. Since the example we will use is a somewhat emotive and controversial one, it would be easy for our emotions to sway us from the task at hand. For this reason, it is important that we take care to adopt the same methodical process as that which we employed previously.

This chapter's story concerns the alleged attack on the offices of Charlie Hebdo, a French satirical magazine, which occurred on January 7$^{th}$ 2015 at around 11:30AM CET. For those unfamiliar with the events, there follows a summary of the known facts and evidence we have so far, leaving out any presupposition of the identities of the assailants or their motives.

On the morning in question, it is alleged that two attackers entered the magazine's offices, killing eleven people and injuring twelve others. They are said to have made their getaway in a car driven by an accomplice, but, before doing so, it is claimed that they killed a French National Police officer outside the building by shooting him in the head. A manhunt conducted by the police led to the discovery of the alleged suspects in the offices of a company in Dammartin-en-Goële on January 9th. According to reports, they were shot dead on emerging from the building later that day. It is also alleged that, at around the same time, a further accomplice, not present at the original attack, took hostages in a kosher supermarket at Porte de Vincennes in Paris. This individual, according to reports, was also later killed by the police.

In the following analysis we will study these events in some detail, focusing in particular on the three specific observations listed below. The first of these is an element of the narrative from the TV, while the other two can be directly observed in video footage shown on the TV on the day in question, copies of which can still be found on the internet. Of course, these are not the only observations which can give us clues as to the nature of the events, and we are certain that the astute reader will be able to find plenty of others. On the other hand, they do serve our purpose well, as we hope will become clear as the chapter proceeds. The observations are described in full in the text which follows, but can be summarised thus:

A. The ID cards left behind in the getaway car which was abandoned close to the scene.
B. The blocked road outside the magazine's offices.
C. The apparent missed shot to the head of the police officer who was alleged to have been shot.

We will start the analysis by applying the model dictated by the Correspondence Theory, and leave the Constructivist one until a little later. To do this, we must refer back to the flow diagram as shown in Figure 1. At the top of the flow, we see the first step, Observation. This has already been completed, at least in part, in the outline of events as summarised above. In an ideal world, we would like to be able to observe the events first-hand but, needless to say, this luxury is not one we would expect to find too often in the real world. For the most part, we are forced to rely on recorded evidence and eyewitness testimony. Although we face the possibility that these may be unreliable, we can seek to mitigate this by looking for corroboration between various sources. In the event that we arrive at a contradiction, this will lead us to suspect that one or more of the sources we used are in error.

Now our observations have been made, we are now in a position to move on to the next phase of the flow: Hypotheses. As we saw in chapter 2, it's important at this stage not to let ourselves be swayed by what we think we already know about the case. The Correspondence model requires that we formulate a broad range of hypotheses, even if we think that they sound unbelievable or the prospect of their being true makes us uncomfortable. If a hypothesis we put forward fails to fit the facts, the Correspondence model will soon allow us to identify and eliminate it. After all, a theory which cannot produce results that fit with our observations is a worthless one, and will not score highly in the Evaluation Phase.

It goes without saying that, once we have established the facts, our goal is to determine the identity of the attackers. In the interests of brevity, we will limit ourselves to just four hypotheses. We feel that these represent a broad range of potential narratives, but it goes without saying that the reader should add to the list, should he or she feel the inclination to do so.

1. The attackers were Islamic Fundamentalist terrorists.
2. The attackers were members of the French, British, American or Israeli security services.
3. The attackers were aliens from Mars.
4. The "attackers" were actors in a staged event.

Now we have a number of hypotheses to work with, we can move on to the next phase: Evaluation. This is the part where we consider the evidence at our disposal in order to determine how well it fits with each hypothesis. In the paragraphs which follow we will take our observations (A, B and C) in turn and discuss them in the context of each of our four hypotheses (1, 2, 3 and 4).

Given that we were told that the "attackers" successfully fled the scene, the first question we should probably ask ourselves is: how were the authorities able to identify and locate the suspects? The answer for this, as provided by the TV, was that the "attackers" left their ID cards behind in the getaway car which was abandoned close to the scene. We will start by taking a critical look at this idea.

Common sense tells us that one of the goals of any criminal is to escape detection for their crimes. Some may argue that, while this is true for most categories of criminal, it is not true for those who might "want" to get caught (for some unspecified reason). If this were true of the suspects in this example, then leaving the ID cards at the scene might be explained by such a desire. In tandem with this, we need to consider the fact that the "attackers" were seen attempting to flee the scene in a getaway vehicle, an act which would seem to suggest a desire to evade capture. When considered together, these two ideas lead us to an obvious contradiction. As we pointed out in our opening comments, reaching an impasse such as this in the course of our reasoning can often indicate that one of our starting points is invalid. In this instance, we will make the tentative assumption that it is the idea that the cards were dropped in an attempt to ensure capture which is the more likely to be flawed.

Some have argued that another possible explanation is that the act of bringing the cards was a random event, a mistake; and that the act of dropping the cards was a second random event. One way to calculate the probability of these two events' happening in tandem would be to multiply together the probabilities of each happening alone, but coming up with a figure for the probability of each is a difficult task in itself. Common sense tells us that the probability of this coincidence is low, but that doesn't mean we can ignore it. We will deal with this idea in due course.

Now, to summarise all of this, logic tells us that these "attackers" were attempting to escape detection, so it would seem very unlikely they would deliberately leave their ID cards in the getaway car. Similarly, the probability of such a sequence of events occurring by accident seems very low. For these reasons, we should consider the first of our hypotheses to be a poor fit with the observations.

If we accept that the ID cards were found at the scene as described, another possible explanation for their presence is that they were fakes planted by the perpetrators in order to frame someone else. This explanation would fit with any of the first three of our four hypotheses, but, leaving aside the question as to who might have put them there, how likely is it for someone to do this as part of a frame?

The techniques typically employed to frame an individual or group are subtle and carefully thought out, the goal being to maintain the credibility of the illusion so as to allow the real perpetrators to escape detection. As we have seen in the above scenario, both subtlety and credibility are lacking, making it unlikely that it has been constructed as part of a "frame". So, while the second hypothesis may seem, at first sight, to represent a close fit for the observations, there are still some major flaws with it.

Now we can move on to our third hypothesis: the aliens. Everyone knows that these guys use holographic retinal scanning for ID checks, so wouldn't be seen dead with something as old fashioned as a plastic ID card. Not only that, but if they felt the need to frame someone for the crime, then surely they would have a more technologically advanced way of doing it than this? For this reason, the hypothesis is another which offers us a poor fit for the observations.

Joking aside, it's worth pausing here to make a point about our reasons for including the aliens. We have done so purely to show that we should have nothing to fear from any hypothesis, no matter how ridiculous, since our paradigm will soon eliminate it if and when its predictions fail to match the observations. In the real world, however, we should treat all the presented hypotheses with respect and give them a fair trial, no matter what we may think of them.

There is, however, one scenario where criminals **do** leave their ID cards behind at the scene: in the movies. We've all seen those Hollywood blockbusters where this kind of thing is commonplace. At first it appears that the perfect crime has been committed, but, lo and behold, left behind at the scene is the assailant's earring, library card, false eye or whatever it takes to make a good story. This is the idea that we are alluding to in the fourth hypothesis: the one in which the "attackers" are actors in a staged event. At first sight, it does seem as if this hypothesis represents the best fit for the observations we've looked at so far.

A little earlier, we discussed the possibility that the ID cards were brought along and dropped by the "attackers" by accident. Although we said that this explanation was an unlikely one, the Correspondence Theory does not allow us to use this excuse to ignore the idea. After all, it's sometimes the unlikely links that are the key to solving a puzzle. So how can we determine whether or not the suggestion is reasonable? Perhaps a short thought experiment will help as follows.

Terrorism, contrary to what the mainstream media would have us believe, is not a commonplace crime. For instance, in the US, you are far more likely to be killed by the police than you are to be killed by a terrorist. One thousand US citizens were shot (on home soil) in 2015, of which around two hundred were unarmed. This compares with around twenty who were reported to have been killed in acts of terrorism (worldwide) in the same year.

It goes without saying that there are other categories of crime that are much more common than either of these. In 2004 in the UK alone, for instance, there were more than 50,000 robberies. In the same year there were around 200 arrests for suspected terrorist activities. The ratio between these two figures is about 250:1, so that means that if the dropping of ID cards at the scene of the crime were an occurrence spread evenly over all crimes, then in each year, for every terrorist that dropped their ID card, we would expect 250 robbers to follow suit. If this were to happen, we might expect the following (fictional) news article to be commonplace:

> "Police, today, are investigating a hold up at a supermarket in Birmingham, England in which two masked men demanded cash from a checkout assistant, before driving off on a stolen motorbike.

Fortunately, the suspects dropped their ID cards at the scene of the crime so the police were quickly able to apprehend them."

Yet announcements such as these are, in fact, extremely rare. Could it be that we are just not being told about these cases or is it that they simply don't exist?

For terrorists, however, we are told that the dropping of ID cards is commonplace. ABC News, for instance, reported that a passport belonging to alleged 9/11 hijacker Satam Al Suqami was found in Vesey Street, near the North Tower by a passer-by of unknown identity, before the towers "collapsed". Suqami's name did not appear on the manifest, so we can assume that he used a different ID to board the flight before taking care to make sure the correct one flew out of the plane's window after it had been smashed, yet before the plane was engulfed by the fireball.

But this was not the only example of a hijacker's passport being found on 9/11. The FBI told us that the charred remains of the passports of two of the alleged hijackers, Ziad Jarrah and Saeed al-Ghamdi, were found at the UA93 crash site at Shanksville, Pennsylvania. Curiously enough, Ghamdi was interviewed by a London-based Arabic daily newspaper, Asharq Al Awsat, a few days after the alleged attacks, this being reported by the BBC on September 23$^{rd}$ 2001. If this is true, it leaves us with a big problem when it comes to explaining how his passport came to be found in the wreckage. One or more of the following must surely be true:

- His passport boarded the plane on its own.
- The "terrorists" walked away from the "crash" unscathed.
- His passport was taken onto the plane (or placed directly at the "crash" scene) as part of a deliberate attempt to deceive.
- His passport somehow got onto the plane by "accident" and that it was all just one big "coincidence".

Of course, a person on a plane is much more likely to be carrying a passport than a person committing a robbery, but we must still account for how the passports were able to escape the fireball that (so we are told) consumed the planes on impact. With all these doubts in mind, we are obliged to consider alternative hypotheses to explain the "discovery" of the passports, and ask ourselves if the one presented by the TV really provides the best fit for the observations.

Similar narratives to these are to be noted in many other terrorist incidents around the world. For instance, three of the four alleged suicide bombers in the London tube bombings of July 7th 2005 were reported to have been identified by ID cards found at the scene: Mohammad Sidique Khan (on the tube at Edgware), Shezad Tanweer (on the tube at Aldgate) and Hasib Hussain (on the bus at Tavistock Square). Later on, the police changed their story to say that Khan's ID had not been found at Edgware, but, instead had been found both on the bus **and** at Aldgate. They also claimed that Tanweer's ID was not only found at Aldgate but also on the bus: the bus which exploded almost an hour after he was supposed to have died. For further details on this, the reader should refer to Nick Kollerstrom's definitive work, "Terror on the Tube"[xx].

At this point, the *believer* might point out that this does not prove anything. And they would be right, because the Correspondence Theory does not provide us with "proof". It just allows us to select the best possible hypothesis from the limited set we have at our disposal, given the evidence that is available at the time. As explained in chapter 2, we must remain open to the possibility that new evidence and new hypotheses might arrive at some point in the future. In contrast with this approach, the Constructivist will **start** with the single conclusion that has been given to them by their chosen source of authority and respond to any challenge with the demand that it first be disproven before they will agree to engage in any further thought.

Our findings so far can now be summarised as shown in Figure 10. The degree to which the evidence supports each of the provided hypotheses has been indicated with a tick to indicate a strong positive correlation, a cross to indicate a weak negative correlation and a bold cross to indicate a strong negative correlation.

| Observation | 1. Muslims | 2. Security Services | 3. Aliens | 4. Staged Event |
|---|---|---|---|---|
| A. Dropped ID cards | ✘ | x | ✘ | ✓ |

Figure 10

This event was quite unusual in that video footage of the proceedings outside the offices of the magazine (seemingly taken from a vantage point at an upper floor window) was shown on the TV. The clip, taken by an amateur, can be found on the internet (at the time of writing) with a simple search ("Paris shooting Charlie Hebdo") and the reader is encouraged to find and watch it if he or she has not already done so. The footage purports to show the "attackers" coming out of the building, shooting the aforementioned police officer and then making their getaway in an awaiting vehicle. During the course of these events, no other vehicles or pedestrians can be observed moving up or down the street.

Without further evidence, we might posit a number of hypotheses to explain this:

a. The events took place at a time of day when there happened to be no traffic.
b. The street was temporarily closed to traffic by the police.
c. The street was permanently closed to road traffic, by means of gates or bollards.

In order to find out which, if any, of these hypotheses are true, we have to take a step back and look for more evidence. This is exactly the same procedure that we adopted in chapter

1 when, in order to distinguish between the two hypotheses, we walked a kilometre and checked for damp ground.

For our current analysis, it doesn't take much searching online to discover further footage of the same events, this time from street level. Again, the reader is encouraged to go and view the clips ("Charlie Hebdo new video false flag"). This second piece of footage shows that the police appear to have blocked off the road before the "attackers" leave the building. At this point, we could make an educated guess as to the elapsed time between the attackers' arrival and their departure, and make a similar guess as to the time it would take for the police to arrive and set up a road block after receiving an emergency call. In an ideal world, the timeline of events would have been accurately reported by the media, but, to the best of our knowledge, this was not the case. For instance, the Guardian reported that the "attackers" were in the building for a period of five minutes, but, in the case of the BBC, the page that would have provided the details seems to have been removed.

If we take the Guardian's view that the period of time from the attackers' arrival to their departure was around five minutes, then it would be reasonable to assume that this would be too short a period of time for the police to be called, to arrive and to set up the road block. Given this, and assuming that the timing we have been given is correct, we might conclude that the police had some element of foreknowledge of the event. If this were the case, we would have to view this evidence as being a poor fit for the first hypothesis. If we took the opposite view, then we might say that it was a good fit. In the absence of any further evidence, this will have to remain a value judgement on the part of the reader.

Another factor to muddy the waters is the possibility that the police received an advance tipoff, even though no such event was reported in the media. There is also a chance that a tipoff came from a witness who observed the attackers before they were able to gain entry to the building. Again, even though there was no report of this in the media, we cannot simply rule out this possibility.

Given what we now know about the police road-block, we must revisit our four hypotheses to check the extent to which they fit this piece of evidence. As we have already seen, it's difficult to say with any degree of certainty whether or not there is a fit with the first hypothesis. For this reason, it has been left as a blank on the correlation diagram.

At this point, it makes sense to consider the second and fourth hypotheses together, since both of these would imply the possibility of foreknowledge on the part of the police. If the events were staged, or if they were conducted by the security services, it is very likely that the police would have been informed of the proceedings in advance in order that they could be on the scene to prevent any unwitting interference in the proceedings on the part of the public. For this reason, we must note a positive correlation between the evidence and these two hypotheses.

Before we move on to the next piece of evidence, we should make sure that we don't get ahead of ourselves by forgetting about the aliens. In this case, our third hypothesis, it should be obvious that there is a strong negative correlation with respect to the observations. This is because the Martian's language is completely alien to any language spoken on Earth, even French. This means that the aliens would be unable to communicate the foreknowledge of the events to the police, even if they had a desire to do so.

Adding our latest findings to the results obtained so far, we can see a tentative picture beginning to develop as shown in Figure 11.

| Observation | 1. Muslims | 2. Security Services | 3. Aliens | 4. Staged Event |
|---|---|---|---|---|
| A. Dropped ID cards | ✘ | x | ✘ | ✓ |
| B. Blocked road |  | ✓ | ✘ | ✓ |

**Figure 11**

Now, going back to the original footage we discussed earlier, there is a further point of interest to note. If we observe closely the part of the clip where the police officer, who is lying on the ground, is "shot" in the head, we notice a few strange things. Firstly, no appreciable reaction can be seen from the "victim" at the moment when he is supposed to have been struck. Secondly, one can make out a small puff of white smoke on the ground approximately 30cm in front of his head where, one might assume, the bullet actually struck. Thirdly, no blood can be seen as a result of the "injuries". These visual clues strongly suggest that the officer may not have actually been shot at all, and that it is possible that this particular portion of the proceedings was staged.

But there is more to this. The first time this clip appeared on the TV, it was shown in its entirety, but, on subsequent airings, a short section in the middle (the segment that contained the actual moment of the "shooting") was omitted. Since then, the original has been uploaded to YouTube many times, and, on many occasions, it has been removed.

If we consider the first hypothesis, the Muslims, it would seem that it offers a poor fit with the observations. However, there is one possibility that we should consider. It could be that the footage somehow does not accurately represent the event, and that the victim **was** in fact shot, even though this appears not to have been the case. The censoring of the clip (if that's what it was) might then be explained by YouTube's rules about not showing violence. This argument is substantially weakened, however, by the fact that uncensored acts of violence on YouTube are easy to find (for instance: "Collateral Murder Wikileaks Iraq").

So is there any further evidence we can examine which may help us to ascertain whether or not the officer, Ahmed Merabet, was shot in the head? Fortunately, we have some eyewitness testimony from one Djamel Adane, who worked in a bar across the street from where the police officer was said to have been shot. In an interview conducted by Public Radio International Adane told the interviewer:

"We heard the shots being fired". "We looked up and saw the policeman on the ground, and the assailants get back in their car and speed away. I ran across the street and the policeman was on his side, face down. When I turned him over, I recognized [Merabet]. He had a wound in his leg. I pressed on the wound with a paper towel that people brought me."

Adane went on to say that Merabet seemed relieved to see a familiar face, that he managed to make a tourniquet with the policeman's belt and that he kept talking to Merabet as they waited for an ambulance to arrive. He said:

"It took a long time. I was alone with him until his colleagues arrived and we waited for the first responders. I have no idea why it took so long, but it seemed like an eternity."

From this testimony, we can note that:
- Adane mentions the wound on the officer's leg and his attempt to stem the bleeding, but makes no mention of what would be the far more significant wound to the head.
- According to Adane, Merabet was still alive and able to respond, even though he had, supposedly, been shot at point blank range in the head.
- The ambulance took a long time to arrive, despite the fact that police were already at the scene.

Putting all this together, it seems unlikely that the policeman was actually shot in the head, as the narrative of the first hypothesis, the Muslims, requires, so we have good reason to suggest a weak negative correlation at this point on our diagram.

Once again, it makes sense to take the second and fourth hypotheses together with respect to this observation, as they both show the same degree of correlation. In neither of these two scenarios would the objective be to actually kill the "victim", so we would expect to see a missed shot and a number of stories that don't correlate with each other.

Of course, we cannot move on without remembering to consider the Martians. In this case, it should be apparent that, with their superior alien technology, they would never miss a shot from close range. This gives us, once again, a strong negative correlation.

There is a lot more evidence we could consider for this event, and we could certainly extend our analysis to cover it all. In the interests of brevity, however, we will leave it there. The reader is encouraged to continue the process on his or her own. Perhaps a good place to start would be the "suicide" of the Limoges police chief, Helric Fredou, who was given the task of investigating the event.

The important point to take away from all of this is that any event can be broken down into its constituent parts, and each of these can be made the subject of scrutiny, both independently and with respect to the other parts. The more we do this, the greater our ability to distinguish between a real story and a false narrative. With a true story, the scrutiny will yield a concordant picture of the whole, while a false narrative will result in many contradictions and impossibilities.

At this point, we will leave the Evaluation phase and move on to the final step: Qualified Conclusion. To do this, we just need to glance once again at the completed correspondence diagram as shown in Figure 12 and add up the ticks and crosses against each hypothesis. On doing this it becomes apparent that, from the set of hypotheses we started with and the evidence currently at our disposal, the most likely candidate is the "staged event" hypothesis. A close second is the hypothesis that the acts were carried out by our own security forces. A fair way back, in third place, come the Muslims. Trailing in last place and putting in what, quite frankly, amounts to a pretty poor show, we have those pesky men from Mars.

Now that we have dealt with the Correspondence approach, all that remains is to look at the Constructivist equivalent.

This is a much simpler matter, as all we have to do is to turn on the TV or open a newspaper then search for the official narrative. On doing this, we find that the "Muslim" hypothesis is the only one to be canonised, so we are forced to conclude that this is the "true" version of events.

| Observation | 1. Muslims | 2. Security Services | 3. Aliens | 4. Staged Event |
|---|---|---|---|---|
| A. Dropped ID cards | ✘ | x | ✘ | ✓ |
| B. Blocked road |  | ✓ | ✘ | ✓ |
| C. Missed shot | x | ✓ | ✘ | ✓ |

**Figure 12**

Although, for this example, we have shown that the narrative provided by the TV is likely to be inaccurate, we should remember that our aim is not to say definitively which narrative is "true". If there is one thing we have learned so far, it's that truth can be both subjective and malleable. It is our hope that the reader will take the opportunity to conduct their own investigation and formulate their own conclusion based on what they find.

## - 16 -
# Belief

*"It's easier to fool people than to convince them that they have been fooled."*

Mark Twain

---

In chapters 6 and 7 we looked at two parallel belief systems, one based on a view of a fundamentalist or extremist religion, the other based on the teachings of *TVism*. In this chapter and the two which follow, we will take a broad look at some aspects of psychology, specifically those which relate to belief. For many of us, our belief system is so well entrenched that we are all but oblivious to the fact that we are enchained by it. When we attempt to analyse the articles of our faith, we are inclined to view them as a collection of axioms or "truisms" which are not candidates for question. It's for this reason that we often find it hard to make our beliefs the subject of critical analysis. In this chapter we will take a closer look at the origins of our beliefs and the factors which make us adhere to them.

Perhaps a good place to start our investigation would be to consider the extent to which we are able to exercise control over what we believe in the first place. There are two schools of thought on this. Voluntarists are those who argue that belief is a matter of will alone in that we have the same control over what we believe as we do over our actions. Involuntarists, on the other hand, argue that we cannot choose our beliefs in the same way that we cannot choose to make our heart stop, as we discussed in the Introduction. Also worthy of note is the fact that some beliefs are based on observation and evidence and, as such, are likely to be Popper-compliant as we discussed in chapter 4. Other beliefs (such as religious beliefs, for instance) do not fall into this category.

This comparison demonstrates an obvious contrast in the way beliefs are formed, and leads us to deduce that Popper-compliant belief might be involuntary, while the religious kind of belief is more likely to be voluntary. For example, if you look out of your window, see two cars coming together and hear a crashing sound, you may form the belief that there has been a road crash. At no point have you made a **decision** to believe this, since the conclusion flows directly from the observations. At the same time, the belief is Popper-compliant because a careful analysis of the evidence might provide a means to disprove it. In contrast with this, in a non-Popper-compliant case such as the belief in a god, we see clear evidence of voluntary belief since at some point we must have made an active decision to believe.

To harbour a belief may not necessarily result in an action on the part of the believer, however it is normally the **result** of some action or sequence of actions, for example reading a book or newspaper, watching the TV, engaging in dialogue or using social media. Beliefs thus formed may go on to have an influence over our future actions. When we consider that some of these actions may be the selection of further books, newspapers and websites, it is easy to see how a positive feedback loop might be set up. Such a thing is likely to cause our beliefs to be amplified, resulting in our becoming entrenched within them, possibly without our being aware of it.

Research has shown (see, for instance, "Principles of Neural Science"[xxi]) that our minds consist of a vast network of pathways. A pathway is built as the result of a new experience, and is strengthened as a result of the repetition of that same experience. Think back to when you first learned to ride a bicycle. That first time was probably a real struggle, and perhaps you felt that you'd never get the hang of it. As soon as the pathways had begun to form in your mind, however, things started to get a bit easier, though it would still have taken many repetitions to get you to the state where you were competent in all situations. Once those pathways had been fully formed and strengthened through repetition, riding a bike had become second nature, and you no longer had to think about the mechanics of it.

The pathways responsible for knowing how to perform operations like this are stored in what Endel Tulving, an Estonian-Canadian experimental psychologist, termed the Procedural Memory. Tulving has described[xxii] this mechanism as being part of the long term memory. These memories can be recalled automatically, and this is why, once we have learned to ride a bicycle, we never forget how to do so.

The spiral of belief reinforcement follows a similar pattern. By the end of it, we may find ourselves selecting only those sources of information which concur with our pre-existing beliefs. As already discussed, it's this repetition that results in the physical entrenchment of those beliefs within our mind. Of course, it's no accident that it works in this way. A human brain in its untrained state is an incredibly flexible instrument. For instance, a person living in a city in the West might not relish the prospect of switching places with a tribesman living in a jungle. They might view such a life as being a hardship they couldn't tolerate. Yet, if forced to make the switch, although they might find the change hard to adjust to at first, it probably wouldn't take too long before they grew used to their new way of life. The point is that the mind forms strong pathways as a result of repetition in order to make day-to-day tasks effortless. At the same time, skills (with the exception of the procedural ones we have already looked at) that have become disused grow "rusty" and become more difficult to perform.

It's hardly surprising that those who have become fixed within a belief system are more likely to show a tendency to deliberately ignore facts and evidence that contradict it. This process, which we have previously termed Canonical Filtering, is described in detail in chapter 9. The motivation to do this stems from our desire to avoid the uncomfortable feelings that arise from the holding of two contradictory beliefs (also known as cognitive dissonance) as described in chapter 8.

Another way to categorise belief is to describe it as either rational or irrational with reference to the sequence of events prior to its adoption by the subject. A person who uses the scientific method, rejecting all propositions which are not supported by evidence, can be said to have formed a rational belief. The key facet of such a belief is that it does not involve a **decision** to believe: the evidence alone leads us to the conclusion without the necessity of any additional "choice". Some have suggested that the term "belief" might be somewhat misleading when used in this context.

Conversely, an irrational belief is formed when the subject **wants** something to be true, even though all the available evidence may point in the opposite direction. In this case, the subject has made an active choice to hold the belief. For example, if a relative or friend has lied to us, we may feel that we want to believe that they have told the truth, even though we know this not to have been the case. When we make an active choice to believe them, we are using an irrational belief as an instrument of self-deception.

We can see another example of this when we consider the behaviour of the US government over the last fifty or so years as explored in chapter 9. We may be aware to some degree of their wrong-doings, but we would prefer a world in which this wasn't so. As a result, we are prepared to make an active choice to deceive ourselves, ignoring the uncomfortable facts and continuing to look upon them as the bringers of peace and democracy.

This willingness to ignore the wrong-doings of others has been termed *Wilful Blindness* (or *Wilful Ignorance*). The use of the word "wilful" reflects the choice we have actively made when we indulge ourselves in the irrational belief that there is no wrong-doing. The term itself comes from common law where it refers to the act of engaging in some part of an activity whilst deliberately avoiding any question of the broader scope of that (criminal) activity. This evasion is done in an attempt to escape the complicity that would result as a consequence of such knowledge. In legal terms, criminality is assumed regardless of whether the subject is ignorant by accident or by design.

A simple example of this is a person who is caught transporting packages containing illegal drugs. In their defence, the subject might claim that they weren't aware of the packages' contents, and hence lacked the requisite intent to break the law. In this case, however, the law would say that the defendant should have exercised due diligence by finding out what was in the packages before agreeing to transport them. By failing to do so, the defendant has exercised criminal recklessness and is thus legally culpable.

The concept of Wilful Blindness also applies in situations where the subject is not directly involved in the criminal act, yet is, nevertheless, in a position where they can (and should, from a legal perspective) report it or address it in some way. For example, if an MP, congressman or member of the police force (or anyone else, for that matter) finds that they are party to evidence concerning individuals' participating in paedophile activities, then they are obliged to act on this knowledge. Yet, in many cases, we have seen officials turn a blind eye to such evidence. For example, in 2004 it came to light in the UK that Jimmy Savile, a TV presenter and household name, was the perpetrator of a horrific catalogue of sexual abuse conducted over many decades, affecting hundreds of victims. It turned out that many people in positions of power knew about his activities, yet kept quiet about them. And this is by no means an isolated case.

With just a little research, it is easy to find evidence to suggest that the same thing has been going on for years inside the UK government. It has become the norm for information concerning specific individuals to come to light only after their deaths. In the cases where information does come to light before this, it seems that the victim suddenly develops some incapacity which renders them unable to stand trial. In the rare cases where the claim of incapacity is overturned, we often find that the individual meets with an unexpected death.

A detailed examination of this topic could quite easily result in a whole book, not to mention a law suit, so further research into this matter will be left as an exercise for the reader.

It is this Wilful Blindness, of course, which plays directly into the hands of the authorities that rule us, and allows them to take advantage. Like it or not, our MPs, congressmen, regulators, teachers, priests, newspapers and TV channels (along with the corporations that control them) all have their own agenda. If we take a moment to consider this, it becomes apparent that this agenda is unlikely to be compatible with our own. Where their interests and ours diverge, it doesn't take a genius to work out which path they will follow. We, however, persist in our belief that our leaders, along with their appointed "experts", have our best interests at heart, that newspapers and TV channels are there just to inform us and that corporations exist merely to supply us with the products we genuinely want and need. In persisting with such beliefs, we are all engaging in Wilful Blindness on a daily basis.

There are occasions when we indulge ourselves in Wilful Blindness because we are unwilling to jettison our wished-for world in favour of the harsh reality of the real one. But there are other instances where we are forced down this route by our fear of retribution for our actions. For instance, a worker who uncovers a case of fraud committed by their employer or colleague may quite legitimately fear losing their job. Equally, the thought of being ostracised by their peers and branded with the label of "whistle-blower" can act as a deterrent to doing the right thing. In cases like this, we can see that our desire for inclusion and our inclination to "look out for ourselves" is likely to override our sense of morality. Readers who wish to look into this subject in more detail might want to start with Margaret Heffernan's book, "Wilful Blindness"[xxiii].

Yet another motivation for Wilful Blindness is the realisation of futility we get when we feel that our actions would have little consequence. This effect is known as Learned Helplessness.

This psychological condition was first documented in the 1960s by Martin Seligman[xxiv] when he performed a series of brutal experiments on dogs. On the first day of his experiment, Seligman subjected around one hundred and fifty restrained dogs to a series of sixty-four painful and inescapable electric shocks. It didn't take long for the dogs to learn that they could not evade the torture. At this point, they gave up trying to escape and passively succumbed to the pain, whining and rolling over in a submissive posture.

Twenty-four hours later, the next stage of the trial began with the dogs' each being put into a box with a jumpable barrier through the middle. As before, shocks were administered but, this time, as soon as the dog jumped over the barrier, the shock was disabled. In addition, a light was placed in the box which, when dimmed, acted as a signal that the next shock was just a few seconds away. This meant that the dogs could learn to associate the two stimuli and escape the shocks by jumping the barrier as soon as the light was dimmed.

Seligman also did the same day-two experiment on a control set of "naïve" dogs that had not undergone the first day of the trial. They were also presented with the opportunity of learning to avoid the shocks altogether by jumping when they saw the dimming of the light.

When placed in the box, the dogs from both groups ran around frantically for the first thirty seconds or so after the shocks started. After that, some deviation in behaviour was observed between the two groups. Instead of discovering that they could jump to safety, around two thirds of the first group (those that had been previously subjected to the inescapable shocks) just gave up, lay down and whined while the shocks continued. They maintained this behaviour until the end of the experiment. By contrast, the other third of this group along with nearly all of the second set (the naïve dogs) were able to learn that they could avoid the shocks by jumping the barrier.

The day-two experiment was repeated a number of times, and it was discovered that all of the dogs that passively submitted continued to display this behaviour from that point onwards. Seligman concluded that they had learned to feel helpless and hopeless. We could surmise that these dogs generalised their initial inescapable trauma and proceeded to experience a feeling of being trapped in all future traumatic situations, even those that were escapable.

But what about the other third of the pre-conditioned dogs: the ones who acted like their naïve counterparts? How were they able to avoid Learned Helplessness? Other experiments have shown that individuals who have experienced trauma previously in their lives but have managed to free themselves from it, or somehow overcome it, are less likely to give up in the face of subsequent trauma, even if it is of the inescapable kind. Maybe these animals had had such an experience early in life?

In this chapter we have seen how our beliefs are formed, are reinforced and can ultimately become so pervasive that we erect a wall of Wilful Blindness to protect them. We have also seen how the condition of Learned Helplessness can stifle our attempts to liberate ourselves from these beliefs. On the other hand, we have seen that, if the chains of Learned Helplessness can be broken at least once, then our chances of escaping it get better when faced with traumatic events in the future. In the next two chapters, we will develop these ideas further by looking more closely at how our beliefs relate to the society we live in.

# - 17 -
# Conformity

*"People don't want to hear the truth because they don't want their illusions destroyed."*

Friedrich Nietzsche, German philosopher

---

If it were possible to have a nation of individuals with no government, then perhaps there would be no need for conformity, but, living in an organised society as we do, we are surrounded by numerous sources of authority. These include the ones that are imposed upon us, such as government, the police and the legal system; and those which we construct for ourselves by virtue of our Authority Hierarchy. As an inevitable consequence of authority, we must expect to find either conflict, conformity or a combination of the two.

Within the narrative of psychology which we began to look at in the previous chapter, conformity is a crucial factor because it dictates the extent to which our thoughts and beliefs can be said to be our own. Over the years, there have been a number of ground breaking experiments which have opened our eyes to the significance of this factor. It's these experiments that are the subject of this chapter.

A good place to start is with the grandfather of them all: the Milgram experiment which we mentioned briefly in the Introduction. In this experiment, a volunteer is invited by an authority figure, who in this case is a "scientist" wearing a white lab-coat, to act as a "teacher" in an "experiment", ostensibly to study the extent to which a physical inducement can aid learning. The "learner" is placed in an adjacent room and hooked up to a machine which can deliver electric shocks of varying severity. The "teacher" is asked to help the "learner" to remember some pairs of words and then to test their memory by selecting a pair of words at random, reading out one of the words and inviting the "learner" to recall the matching word.

Each time the "learner" gets a word wrong, the "teacher" is told to use the machine to administer a shock, starting with a small one and building up the severity gradually with each wrong answer. Before the start of the "experiment", the "scientist" makes it clear to the "teacher" the point on the scale at which the shocks are likely to be fatal.

Unbeknown to the "teacher", the machine is actually a fake, and the "learner" is an actor who has been told to scream ever more loudly at each increasing "shock". The actual subject of the experiment is the "teacher".

The Milgram experiment presents the subject with a situation in which there are two opposing drivers for their actions. The first is the impulse to obey instructions from an authority figure, while the second is the desire not to harm the "learner". Using this experiment, Milgram was able to show that, although many of his subjects questioned both the experiment and the authority of the "scientist", sixty-five percent went on to administer a fatal electric "shock", despite the screams coming from the "learner". It's a great illustration of the powerful effect that authority can have over our thoughts and behaviour.

Aside from authority, social influences can also affect our beliefs and behaviour. The desire for conformity, popularity and even notoriety can all have an impact on the beliefs we hold and the ones we reject. We all seek to fit in with our respective peer groups, and it is our sharing of a common belief system that helps us to achieve this goal. Just as we saw earlier, the desire to conform can result in our selecting the same books, magazines and TV shows as our peers. At the same time, the same desire leads us to reject other sources for the simple reason that they are rejected by our peers.

The extent to which we are controlled by the effect of social influence was first demonstrated around 1952 in the conformity experiments of Solomon Asch[xxv]. Asch's work was similar, in some respects, to Milgram's, in that it involved actors who pretended to be subjects in an experiment. A subject was placed in a room with a number of other "subjects" (who were actually actors). The participants (the subject and the actors) were first shown a card with a sample line drawn on it, and then a second card depicting three lines, one short (A), one medium length (B) and one long (C), as shown in Figure 13.

Participants were then asked to say aloud which line (A, B, or C) was the closest match (in length) to the sample line. Care was taken to ensure that the match was free of ambiguity. Each experiment consisted of one such pair of cards and one question. This process, termed a "trial", was repeated a number of times to form the experiment as a whole.

Prior to the set of trials, the actors were given specific instructions on how they should respond to each question. Specifically, they were told to give the correct response for the first few trials, and then to all give the same, incorrect response in the others. The participants (the subject and the actors) were positioned in such a way that the subject was always the second to last to answer the question. The trials in which the actors gave the incorrect answer were termed "critical trials".

What Asch discovered was that seventy-five percent of subjects gave at least one wrong answer in the critical trials and, where this incorrect answer was given, it matched the incorrect answer given by the actors in nearly all cases.

So, what was it that made the subjects conform with the group so readily? When Asch interviewed them, most said that, although they didn't believe their answers, they gave them because they feared ridicule from the group if they failed to go along with the majority. This particular conformative pressure is known as "normative influence", since it plays on our desire to appear as "normal" within our peer group. On

**Solomon Asch Experiment**

Sample

A    B    C

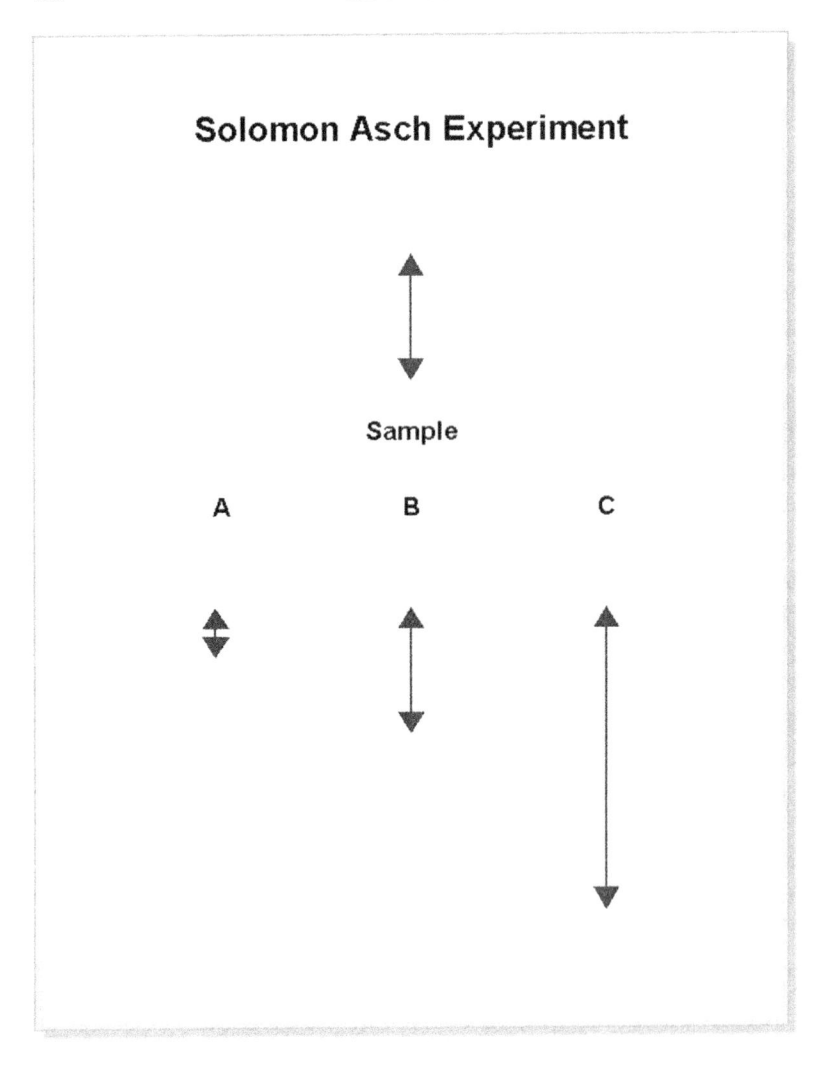

Figure 13

the other hand, a few of Asch's subjects said that they actually believed that the group's answers had been correct. This has been termed "informative influence", the belief that the majority are better informed than us, even if this directly contradicts the evidence of our senses.

For an example of this at work in the real world, we need look no further than our relationship to the TV. When we falsely assume that the TV news channels are independent from each other, we get the impression that there is a large group of people who have adopted the same narrative, and this plays on our tendency to succumb to informative influence. This effect is further enhanced when the TV tells us that a certain opinion comes from a body of "experts". Our inclination towards critical thinking diminishes, and we show a strong tendency to give up our own authority.

When the TV offers us role models, for instance celebrities and prominent sportspersons, we naturally tend to aspire to be like them. This has changed our attitude towards the TV in that we have begun to think of it not just as a source of entertainment, but also as a mentor or life coach. In effect, the TV is telling us what we need to do and what we should be like if we are to be accepted and liked by our peers. In this way, we tend to fall prey to normative influence, and this causes our own authority to diminish further. Given all of this, it's easy to understand the TV's powerful ability to create and reinforce conformity in its viewers.

As Asch increased the number of actors in the group from one to three, the tendency for the subject to conform to his or her "peers", by delivering the wrong answer, was increased. Although Asch used as many as nine actors in some of the trials, increasing the number of actors to four or more was observed to have little or no additional effect.

Interestingly, Asch found that if one or more of the actors were told to give the correct answer in one of the critical trials, then the power of the group to influence the subject was vastly diminished. Specifically, if just one collaborator answered correctly, taking their turn before the subject, this was sufficient to reduce the conformity of the subject by as much as eighty percent. This would lead us to conclude that, in a broader context, a small, yet vocal, dissenting minority could have a significant impact on the majority.

Asch also investigated what happened when the medium of delivery of the decisions was altered. When the subject was instructed to write down the decisions instead of delivering them verbally, conformity fell. Furthermore, if the whole group submitted their written decisions anonymously, the rate of conformity fell to zero.

Asch's experiments show us how conformity works in unambiguous situations, since the sample line was always drawn to the same length as one of the reference lines, A, B or C. Muzafer Sherif's Autokinetic Experiment[xxvi], however, takes a different approach by showing us what happens when there is ambiguity involved in the test.

Sherif conducted his experiment in a totally dark room in which a small dot of light was shone on one wall. A complete lack of any frame of reference such as this (as a consequence of the darkness of the room) means that, for any subject, some movement of the light will be observed, even though no such movement exists. This Autokinetic Effect, as it is called, will manifest itself for any observer under similar conditions.

Participants in groups of three were invited to enter the room and watch the light. They were then asked, as a group, to confer and come to an estimate as to how far the dot of light moved, with the estimates being made out loud. With repeated trials, each group of three was found to converge on an estimate, with some groups converging on a high estimate, some low, and some in-between. The critical finding was that, in all cases, each group converged to a "social norm": the agreed estimate of the group which was ratified by all participants. And all of this without the dot moving at all.

These and other conformity experiments illustrate the power of suggestibility: something to which we all fall victim. We all have a strong, instinctive inclination to agree with and act on the suggestions of others, accepting what they say consciously and uncritically. To put it another way, we tend to exhibit behavioural conformity with the suggestion of others in preference to the behaviour that would otherwise be orchestrated by our conscious minds.

It's easy to see Sherif's experiment as an exposition of the same kind of conformity as can be seen in the other experiments, but there is one very important difference. With the experiments of both Milgram and Asch, we see a form of conformity which only persists for the duration of the experiment. When it is concluded, the subject's behaviour will return to normal. What this shows us is that the subject has not changed their view of the world, but has merely given the impression of doing so when they are within a certain social context. In Sherif's experiment, on the other hand, we see an internalisation of this conformity in that the subject's view of the world is changed permanently. This was demonstrated by the fact that, when the subjects were interviewed after the experiment, they stuck to the decision they made as a group. Given all of this, it is clear that if a peer group were to contain one or more people whose intention it was to deliberately deceive, then the subject would show a tendency to internalise this disinformation and may even become convinced that it is their own, unbiased opinion.

In the 1950s, when Milgram and Asch were conducting their experiments, the authority of someone in a position of responsibility (such as a scientist) and the surrogate authority of one's peer group had a big part to play in shaping our thoughts and beliefs. Since then, however, the rapid rise in popularity of the TV and the corresponding increase in its power to exert authority have meant that its influence over our beliefs and behaviour can hardly be ignored.

When we watch the TV or read a newspaper, the extent to which we are inclined to accept and potentially act on the suggestions and ideas portrayed is termed "suggestibility". The degree to which we respond to this varies not only from individual to individual, but also varies according to the context of the suggestion.

For instance, an idea that is presented during the course of a TV advert may cause an individual to exhibit low suggestibility, while the same idea presented in the TV news may lead the same individual to show a greater response. This is why an advertisement presented as a news item can present a far higher value to the vendor than a similar one presented in a standard advertising slot.

Individuals who exhibit high suggestibility are more likely to uncritically (but consciously) accept what they are told, even though there might be an abundance of evidence to contradict the message. In a variant of this, the subject may exhibit behavioural conformity rather than acceptance. In this case, they will tend to follow the instructions given to them even though they don't necessarily accept them. We could describe this by saying that the subject displays suggestibility without gullibility.

Various hypnotists have advanced the theory that a subject's suggestibility is a key factor in their susceptibility to the induction of useful hypnotic states. John Kappas[xxvii] went as far as to identify three different types of suggestibility: emotional, physical and intellectual. However, his is not the only analysis, and there is still much dispute about what suggestibility actually is, how it is materialised and what factors control it. One factor agreed by all, however, is the idea of repetition. Indeed, the repeating of misinformation can greatly affect one's recollection of an event, especially for an individual who exhibits a high degree of suggestibility. The effect is amplified when the repetition comes from multiple sources which are assumed by the subject (rightly or wrongly) to be independent and trustworthy. When the repetitions are frequent and the sources are multiple, the suggestible individual's memory of events will soon be replaced with those of the supplied false narrative.

In the 1970s Elizabeth Loftus, an American cognitive psychologist, published a highly influential series of studies on eyewitness suggestibility[xxviii]. Her studies provided clear evidence of the existence of the "misinformation effect", to use her terminology, which indicated that suggestive interviews can lead to profound errors in eyewitness testimony. In particular, she found that exposing witnesses to misleading information after an event can lead them to report items and events which they never actually saw. When the event to which the eyewitnesses are exposed is a traumatic one, this is thought to further increase their susceptibility to suggestion.

It's not hard to imagine how this could take place on a much larger scale. If a whole nation or group of nations were to be exposed to a traumatic sequence of events, such as those of 9/11, and were then subjected to misleading information repeated over and over again, it is more than conceivable that the senses and instincts of the majority might be overturned and replaced with the false narrative.

As a closer-to-home example of this kind of suggestibility, we might consider the little known, yet fairly common phenomenon called "Medical Students' Disease". As its name might suggest, this condition is one which is reported by medical students who imagine that they are experiencing the symptoms of one of the diseases they are studying. It is thought that the condition is brought on by the combination of a fear of contracting the disease and a preoccupation with the symptoms studied. This leads them to a more heightened awareness of any casual physiological and psychological indications which are consistent with the symptoms under study. These are then erroneously attributed to the disease. Moss-Morris and Petrie[xxix] studied the condition and described it as "a normal perceptual process", rather than a form of hypochondriasis. They outline how, after a mental schema of the illness and the symptoms is formed by the subject, any sensations consistent with the schema are more likely to be noticed, while those that don't fit are more likely to be ignored.

Irving Janis[xxx] made further advances in the study of suggestibility with his theory, Groupthink. In his study, he suggests that irrational or dysfunctional decision-making is likely to be the outcome within groups in which harmony or conformity is seen as a priority. The minimisation of conflict is sought in order to reach consensus, with the result that critical evaluation of alternative points of view is avoided. In order for the group to be protected from destabilising outside influences, such viewpoints are often actively supressed by the majority. Individuals in the group who raised controversial issues would be considered disloyal and would be ousted from the group if they persisted in vocalising those issues. This is the point at which an "in-group" and an "out-group" are created, and it's this that leads to the religious entrenchment we saw in chapter 6. Conformity to the group norms can be orchestrated by subtle, unconscious influences or by direct, blatant social pressures. It can occur in small social groups, within whole countries, or even globally.

Taking a closer look at the notion of repetition in conjunction with suggestibility leads us on to a discussion of conditioning. This comes in two flavours: classical and operant.

Classical Conditioning is the process that was brought to light thanks to the well-known experiment by Pavlov[xxxi], in which he conditioned his unsuspecting dog to salivate on hearing the ring of a bell. This form of conditioned learning involves two pairs of elements: an unconditioned stimulus (UCS) coupled with an unconditioned response (UCR) and a neutral stimulus (NS) coupled with a conditioned response (CR).

To see how this works, imagine that you are walking blindfolded and barefoot on a soft carpet. Now imagine a UCS, such as the stepping on the prongs of an upturned (UK) plug. This leads to a UCR which, in this case would be the swift removal of your foot away from the plug. Now we must add an NS, such as the sounding of a buzzer, and place it just before the UCS. You could imagine the buzzer's being actuated by an experimenter just prior to your footfall on the upturned plug. Next comes the most important part: the repetition of the two stimuli. Once the NS and the UCS have been repeated in sequence a sufficient number of times, we can move on to the last stage. Here we present the NS (the buzzer) on its own, without the presence of the UCS. Now the sound of the buzzer will cause you to abort your step before your foot drops down onto the imagined plug. Now this conditioned response, the CR, will follow the NS every time it is presented, regardless of whether the upturned plug (UCS) is present or not.

An obvious example of Classical Conditioning is the attempt by advertisers to try to influence our attitudes in favour of their products. For instance, a TV commercial in which actors are used to promote a sports drink may portray imagery of young attractive people having fun on a beach while drinking the product. The advertiser's goal here is to encourage the viewer to develop an association between the product and the beach activities, to tap into their positive thoughts and emotions, and, ultimately, to sell a larger volume of their product. Similarly, if a celebrity is featured in the scene, the viewer will quickly come to associate the celebrity with the product. Now, whenever we see the celebrity, the product will be brought to mind, and this will reinforce the message. The more liked and well-known the celebrity, the more successful this form of conditioning or advertising is likely to be.

The use of Classical Conditioning and other psychological tricks in advertising is what enables successful brand formation. If you were asked to quickly list ten popular brands, it's more likely that you would visualise a sequence of symbols, celebrities, logos, images, tastes, smells and sounds that you have associated with popular brands, rather than simply thinking of a list of names. It's the close association of this imagery with a particular product or company that can make or break a brand. Branding and advertising has developed into a very precise science which takes advantage of our psychological vulnerabilities in order to influence the choices we make, while allowing us to retain the illusion that we act with free will.

This form of conditioning is virtually inescapable, since we are exposed to advertising not only on billboards, radio, magazines, internet and television, but also as a result of the product placement we see in films and TV programs. The celebrity plays the part of the UCS, and our positive feelings towards them are the UCR. The product being endorsed is the NS. So, just as in the case of Pavlov's dog, the association of the UCS and NS leads us to associate our feelings towards the celebrity with the product or service. Studies have shown that the more frequently the commercial is shown (at least initially), the stronger is our conditioned response. However, perhaps surprisingly, over-exposure can reduce the desire for the product or even eliminate it altogether. The response is also made stronger when the viewer is not consciously aware that the association is being made. This means that product placement in films is often more effective than a basic commercial, but by far the most effective is when the commercial masquerades as a news item.

In the 1930s, this idea was taken further by B. F. Skinner in his study of Operant Conditioning[xxxii]. He believed that a better way to understand behaviour was to look at the causes and consequences of an action rather than to try and theorise about what was going on inside the subject's head. Building on Thorndike's theory of "Law of Effect", Skinner focused his attention on the idea of reinforcement, arguing that behaviour that is reinforced by its consequence is more likely to be repeated, while that which is not reinforced tends to diminish and die out. Three different types of operant were identified by Skinner: reinforcers, punishers and neutral operants. Reinforcers are responses from the environment which are appealing to the subject and so increase the probability of the behaviour's being repeated. Punishers are responses that are unappealing and so decrease the probability of repeat behaviour. Neutral operants are responses that do neither of these two things.

To illustrate the point, let's imagine a child at school who tries smoking a cigarette for the first time. If, as a consequence, he or she ends up being accepted by some in-group, then the behaviour has been reinforced and is more likely to be repeated. Further repetition and reinforcement may well lead to the child's taking up smoking on a permanent basis. If, on the other hand, the child were caught, reprimanded and punished by a teacher and perhaps his or her parents, then the behaviour can be said to have resulted in a punisher. Under these circumstances, the behaviour is less likely to be repeated.

This may all seem pretty obvious, but, of course, this kind of conditioning is going on all the time, whether we are aware of it or not. Reinforcing and punishing operants appear from the environment whenever we act or speak, and it is inevitable that these will modify our thoughts and behaviour to a greater or lesser degree. In the next chapter we will conclude our look at psychology by looking at one final mechanism of conformity.

# - 18 -
# Prison Break

*"The man who lies to himself and listens to his own lie comes to a point that he cannot distinguish the truth within him, or around him, and so loses all respect for himself and for others."*

Fyodor Dostoyevsky

---

In the previous chapter we looked at how our conformity to authority could play a big part in shaping our thoughts and behaviour. Yet there is one facet of conformity that we still need to examine: the extent to which the prevailing conditions within society can play their part in this process. A perfect illustration of this can be found in the Stanford Prison Experiment[xxxiii], conducted by Philip Zimbardo in 1971.

In this experiment Zimbardo started by recruiting a group of twenty-four male college-student volunteers from in and around Stanford University, Palo Alto, California. He advertised for students to participate in a study of prison life, enticing them with the prospect of earning $15 per day if they were chosen. The individuals selected were those deemed to be the most psychologically stable and healthy. The group was divided at random into two halves, the first assigned to be prison guards, the rest to be prisoners. With the help of experienced consultants, a mock prison was constructed in the basement of Stanford's Psychology Department building, complete with prison cells, solitary confinement rooms and a corridor that was used as a prison "yard".

No specific training was given to the guards, although prior to the start of the experiment Zimbardo said to them:

"You can create in the prisoners feelings of boredom, a sense of fear to some degree, you can create a notion of arbitrariness that their life is totally controlled by us, by the system, you, me, and they'll have no privacy ... We're going to take away their individuality in various ways. In general what all this leads to is a sense of powerlessness. That is, in this situation we'll have all the power and they'll have none."

He instructed them not to physically harm the prisoners but, instead, encouraged them to implement their own ideas to maintain order in the prison and to command the respect of the prisoners. They were warned, however, of the potential dangers of the situation into which they were about to enter, just as real guards would be in the real world.

After the guards had divided themselves into shifts to cover each twenty-four hour period, their next action was to set up a system of "counts" which took place several times on each of these shifts. In these exercises, each prisoner would have his number called and be forced to respond to confirm his presence. In order to break down their sense of personal identity, the prisoners were only allowed to refer to themselves or other prisoners by the number they had been assigned. The counts provided a regular opportunity for the guards to exercise control over the prisoners. Light-hearted at first, these counts led gradually to a series of direct confrontations between guards and prisoners. If the prisoners stepped out of line, the guards would demand push-ups from the prisoners as a form of punishment. It's interesting to note that this form of control has been and still is common practice in prison camps across the world and throughout history.

It was on day two of the experiment that both the guards and the prisoners began to step up to their new roles. That which had previously been treated by both sides as a light-hearted role-play now began to take on an edge of realism. Day two was also the day of the prisoners' rebellion which saw them barricade themselves into their cells by putting their beds against their cell doors.

The problem the guards faced was what they were going to do in response. When the morning shift of guards arrived for duty, they were upset at the night shift, whom they suspected of having been too lenient. As a result, they felt motivated to deal with the situation more forcefully themselves. They called up reinforcements, used a fire extinguisher to force the prisoners away from the doors, broke into each cell, stripped the prisoners naked and forced the rebellion's ringleaders into solitary confinement. These measures were swiftly followed with the guards' setting up various new techniques of control based on what can only be described as psychological torture. For instance, certain privileges were granted to some prisoners yet not others, the aim being to create resentment in their ranks. Attempts were made to break prisoner alliances by tricking the ringleaders of the rebellion into believing that those who had been the least involved were actually informants. By dividing and conquering in this way, disharmony among the inmates was promoted, thereby deflecting any potential aggression away from the guards. It is interesting to note that, in a real prison, the greatest threat to any prisoner's life comes from their fellow prisoners.

The first psychological casualty of the experiment occurred after less than thirty-six hours, when one of the prisoners began suffering from emotional disturbance, uncontrollable crying and rage. Initially, his behaviour was met with scepticism, but, after some negotiation, he was begrudgingly released.

After this, things began to follow a downward spiral, culminating in a rumour of a mass escape plot. According to the rumour, the prisoner who had been released was going to enlist the help of some friends on the outside to organise a breakout of the remaining prisoners. At this point, one might have expected the experimenters (who were neither guards nor prisoners) to prepare themselves for the escape by making sure they were well placed to record the supposed events as part of the research. But this was not the case. Instead, they became deeply concerned over the security of the prison and elected to conduct a strategy session with the guards to plan how to foil the escape. They even went as far as to seek the help of the local police. Although the escape plot turned out to be no more than a rumour, it was to be a pivotal point in the experiment, as it was the point at which the boundaries between the experiment, the experimenters and the outside world (the police) were transgressed.

Some critics have suggested that the experiment was marred to a certain extent by the failure of the experimenters to maintain their position outside of the experiment, but the fact remains that their own involvement makes a powerful statement about how people might behave in such circumstances. For what had started as make-believe role-play for the participants soon grew to become their reality. The participants' behaviour was gradually modified as their delusion took hold and spread, with that of the guards taking on an increasingly sadistic character and that of the prisoners indicating their increasing feelings of helplessness.

Perhaps more important than this, however, was the fact that this same drift from role-play to reality was extant in the behaviour of the experimenters. The way they allied themselves with the guards in an attempt to thwart the supposed escape plot was testament to this. At this point they had become part of the experiment and were no longer simply observers of the proceedings.

It wasn't long after these events, just six days into the planned two week period in fact, that the whole experiment was brought to an abrupt end. On being informed of the termination, a number of prisoners suspected that a cruel trick was being played and, in disbelief, continued acting the role of prisoner. In addition, many of the guards were disappointed that their sadism had been cut short and questioned whether or not they would still be paid.

Zimbardo's experiment demonstrates how quickly and dramatically people's behaviour can be transformed when they are assigned a role to play, and how readily those conducting such an experiment can end up becoming part of it. If conditions are right, a role-play can be so powerful that it becomes part of "reality" for all those close to it. It doesn't take much imagination to see that, under slightly different circumstances, a similar "experiment", if it involved enough people and were to continue for long enough, could quite easily spill over into society at large. If that were to happen, it's not difficult to envisage the possibility that we could all be wrapped up in the delusion. In such an eventuality, the consequences for society at large could be so dire that it would probably take some cataclysmic event, such as a world war, to dispel the illusion.

We all love a good story. We like to be told them now and again, and we sometimes even tell them to ourselves. Sometimes they can take on the guise of religious mantra, and the resulting self-hypnosis can make them appear to us as if they were reality. Once the story has been taken up by others and has become their reality too, it increases in power like a snowball rolling down a mountain which becomes an avalanche. We live in a world that is spun out of these stories: our cultural history is full of them. Sometimes it takes a gargantuan effort on the part of the minority to be able to see through them.

For a real example of this, we might consider the Nazi Germany of the 1930s. Here we saw a racist and brutal set of ideas which formed in the minds of a few "spill over" into society at large. Eventually, half of Europe fell under its spell, many people playing their part in the performance, after having become convinced of its reality.

But perhaps an even better example can be found here, today in the West. For the last fifteen years, the Western powers have been engaged in a seemingly constant war in the Middle East. Yet many still believe that the purpose of this is to bring the "gift" of democracy to the victims, and that these wars can somehow be thought of as "humanitarian". In reality, a close look at the evidence shows that the motivation for these wars is the same as it has always been throughout history: resources, greed, power and oppression. On a broader scale, we might view the whole of human history as the result of the ebb and flow of the delusional stories that we choose to believe. This is a topic which we will revisit in chapter 25, so we will leave it here for now and return, in the next chapter, to tune in on the TV.

## - 19 -
# An Instrument of Control

*"The media's the most powerful entity on earth. They have the power to make the innocent guilty and to make the guilty innocent, and that's power. Because they control the minds of the masses."*

Malcolm X

---

Back in chapter 7, we looked at the TV in its role as the "holy book", for want of a better phrase, within *TVism*. Having been with us for less than a hundred years, it is evident that there must have been some sequence of events to take it from its infancy to the central role it now occupies. In this chapter we will examine some of the landmarks on this journey and take some time to think about how it is able to maintain its position of dominance in our lives.

Before the TV's development in the 1920s and subsequent rise to the height of popularity we see today, it won't come as much of a surprise to learn that the most popular form of media for the masses was the radio. The Radio Corporation of America (RCA), one of the largest and most influential electronics companies during the 20th century, was instrumental in the rise of radio in the early 1900s, and went on to invest millions of dollars in the development of the television.

By 1939, television was broadcasting short segments of sporting events with occasional forays into politics, such as the broadcast of a speech made by President Roosevelt in the late 1930s. World War II delayed the rise in popularity of TV, with just a few thousand American homes owning a TV set during this time. By 1952 however, this number had rocketed to 12 million homes and, by 1955, over half (around 48 million) of all American homes owned one. Today the TV's omnipresence is all but complete, as over ninety-nine percent of American homes have not one but two or more TV sets per household.

During its growth in popularity, CBS and Rutgers University conducted a study where they surveyed families with televisions. They discovered that the TV was overwhelmingly perceived as a very positive addition to the family home, with some even describing their new sets as members of the family. By the 1950s, sitcoms had become very popular, with many people starting to schedule their day around their favourite programs. Children's television soon emerged as a new and lucrative market, with shows like "The Mickey Mouse Club" gaining mass following. In the 50s and 60s, television began to change the way the masses perceived the news and the nation's leaders, carving out a significant and powerful role for itself in politics as well as entertainment. Radio was adapted to fit a new niche that complemented, rather than competed with, the TV. People continued to listen to the radio while out and about, even though the preferred medium for the home had become the TV.

From the 1960s to the present day, TV has mutated in terms of its sociological position within the family. Whereas at first, it was looked upon simply as a source of entertainment, we now regard the TV as the source of truth, and imagine that its goal is to educate us as well as to entertain us. It has become not only our portal onto the world, but even a substitute for it. Many people take a similar view of the broadsheet newspapers, and some even the tabloids. This positive image of the TV we have acquired is one which we have been conditioned to accept after many years of propaganda from the corporations who control it. Once we take a step back and pause to remind ourselves that nothing in life comes for free, it's easier to see that this naïve view of the TV as our benefactor is far from the truth. The main goal of the TV, of course, is to generate a substantial and consistent revenue stream for those who pull the strings. On a simplistic level, we could look at this revenue stream in terms of the money we spend on buying the products we see promoted on the TV, yet this represents just one small part of the whole story. The reality, even though most are likely at first to reject the notion, is that the TV has become an instrument of control whose goal is the manipulation of the masses for the financial benefit of the few. Later on we will look at some examples which might lead us to suspect that this is indeed the case.

The repetition of official narratives from seemingly independent sources, along with the use of clever propaganda and psychological techniques, has created a distorted worldview that has grown ever more divergent from the truth. This fact, in tandem with the ever increasing pervasiveness of the TV, has resulted in our becoming a nation of believers, decreasingly capable, so it would seem, of critical thinking. And, as if this were not enough, we are fed a stream of programs that discredit and ridicule those that question the veracity of the canon of the TV, often by using religious labels such as "conspiracy theorists", just as we saw in chapter 11. This has had the effect of stifling dissent in a manner reminiscent of the totalitarian state depicted by Orwell in his novel, "Nineteen eighty-four"[xxxiv]. Logic tells us that those who are attempting to control and manipulate us in this way do so with the intention of coercing us into the placid acceptance of their narratives in the hope that we won't interfere with their agenda.

We are all affected by this manipulation, even though we might think we are not. After all, much of what is going on is quite subtle and is not obviously apparent until it is analysed in detail. Yet it is exactly such a detailed analysis of the world around us that is discouraged by the TV. Central to the TV's evolution in this respect was a man called Edward Bernays, and no study of the TV as an instrument of control would be complete without an appreciation of his work.

Bernays was a public relations expert, holding the self-titled role of "public relations counsellor" from 1913 to 1917 in the US. This saw him participating in government led campaigns with the intention of making them seem more accessible and appealing to the public. He acted in the interests of the US government as a kind of facilitator to get people on board with whatever campaign or policy they wanted to promote. Bernays was one of the first to use psychology to persuade, sway and fundamentally control public opinion. The techniques he used were derived from a synthesis of the discoveries in mass psychology which had been made by several theorists and psychologists including his uncle, Sigmund Freud.

An early example of this was the substantial cultural shift that Bernays and his colleagues orchestrated by means of a historic women's smoking campaign in 1929. He helped the cigarette industry overcome the taboo of women's smoking in public by organising an Easter parade in which he paid models to hold lit cigarettes. To these cigarettes he gave the label "torches of freedom", with the intention that this slogan would become associated with the contemporaneous issue of women's rights. The Easter parade itself was a sham, yet Bernays saw to it that it was presented on the TV as if it were a news item. The success of this technique was manifest by the fact that more and more women were lighting up in public, but, more importantly, by the fact that revenue figures for the cigarette industry were booming.

Success followed success when Bernays's skills were called upon again, this time with the idea of water fluoridation, selling it to the public with claims of its benefits to health. He understood that citizens had an often unconscious trust in medical authority, so he correctly surmised that an endorsement from the American Dental Association would result in a successful campaign. Prior to his efforts, fluoride was largely known in the public mind as the chief ingredient of bug and rat poison. As a result of the campaign, however, spearheaded by the endorsement, it became widely hailed as a safe provider of healthy teeth and gleaming smiles. The subsequent approval from authorities such as the Center for Disease Control and Prevention, which named community water fluoridation as one of the ten greatest public health achievements of the 20th century, further reinforced the change in public perception. Fluoride's remarkable transformation from rat-poison to health product, with no strong evidence to support its safety or benefit, was one of Bernays's most stunning and enduring "successes", the results of which are still very much with us today.

As a result of his endeavours, industries became convinced that it was the news, as opposed to advertising, that was the better medium to carry their message to an unsuspecting public. Although Bernays was perhaps best known as being the inventor of consumerism, this was really just the tip of the iceberg in his dark and influential career.

Believing that his work was an important necessity in order to address the behaviour of the masses, which he considered to be irrational and misguided, Bernays argued that the manipulation of public opinion was a necessary part of democracy. In his book "Propaganda"[xxxv], first published in 1928, he wrote:

> "Those who manipulate this unseen mechanism of society constitute the invisible government, which is the true ruling power of our country. We are governed, minds are moulded, tastes are formed, our ideas suggested, largely by men we have never heard of."

It's interesting to note that, despite his significant role in the orchestration of mass mind control, Bernays writes in a way that distances himself from his actions, using such words as "those" and "we" as if to imply that he is one of the masses who are to be manipulated, rather than one of those pulling the strings. He was convinced that his techniques were a benefit to a society whose smooth running could only be assured if everything were simplified. Only then, he surmised, could the masses make an "informed" decision. In this way, he hoped that the confusion he imagined would otherwise ensue, which he referred to as the "jamming of economic life", would be avoided. His procedures for informing and directing the public to make the "best" choices were termed "The Engineering of Consent", and were set out in an essay of the same name, published in 1947.

The impact of Bernays' methods on an unsuspecting public, however, was not only economic but also political. Starting in 1952, Bernays was involved in a covert CIA operation named "Operation PBSUCCESS". This was documented by historian Nicholas Cullather, who was hired by the CIA to produce a detailed, secret document outlining the operation. The results of his work can be found in his book, "Secret History"[xxxvi]. The goal was to facilitate the overthrow of the democratically elected president of Guatemala, Jacobo Árbenz Guzmán, and replace him with a US-backed dictator, Carlos Castillo Armas.

Prior to this, in 1931, Jorge Ubico had been elected president of Guatemala. Under his subsequent dictatorship, the American owned United Fruit Company profited greatly from investments it had made in Guatemala. The company, mostly owned by members of the Eisenhower administration, gained control of forty-two percent of Guatemala's land, and was exempted from paying both taxes and import duties. Ubico was later replaced by Guatemala's first democratically elected president, Juan Jose Arevalo, as a result of the Guatemalan Revolution which began in 1944.

Arevalo was a liberal politician and educator who wanted Guatemala to be a liberal capitalist society. He began implementing social reforms such as increases in funding for education, making improvements to healthcare and introducing a minimum wage. His replacement, Árbenz, elected president in 1950, continued with the social reforms which Arevalo had started and took things one step further by introducing land reform policies, granting land to peasants in order to free them from debt slavery. It was reforms like these which adversely affected the huge profits made by the United Fruit Company, who were no longer able to exploit the workers in the manner in which they had become accustomed.

As a result of this, the company began a massive anti-communist propaganda effort against Guatemala in the US press. Bernays's expertise was sought, and many of his techniques in psychological manipulation were put to use. While the public's image of communism was being manipulated by the promotion of an air of fear, the CIA armed, funded and trained an army led by Armas.

Central to the propaganda campaign was a radio station called "Voice of Liberation", which began broadcasting on May 1$^{st}$ 1954. Its anti-communist message was clear: resist the Árbenz government and achieve liberation through the support of Armas. Claiming to be broadcasting from a location within the Guatemalan jungle, the broadcasts were actually recorded in Miami by Guatemalan exiles, before being flown in to be broadcast from a mobile transmitter. The station made an initial broadcast that was repeated four times, after which it took to transmitting two-hour bulletins twice a day. The radio broadcasts have been credited by historians for the success of the *coup* that ensued, thanks to the unrest they created. The transmissions continued throughout the conflict, broadcasting false news of rebel troops' converging on the capital. This disinformation ultimately led to the Guatemalan army's refusing to fight, and soon Árbenz was faced with little choice but to resign.

Thanks to this campaign of psychological warfare, Armas and his army of just four hundred and eighty men were able to take control of the whole country. This shows how much more powerful manipulation of this sort can be, as compared to the more conventional course of warfare which can drag on for years or even decades.

Moving on to the early 1960s, we see Bernays coming up with the idea of targeting people's self-image in order to create a consumerist culture, ultimately to the benefit of the large corporations which profited as a result of the newly formed revenue stream. By targeting the psychological drive that we all have which gives us the desire to fit in with our peer group, and the use of widespread advertising, he was able to instil in his targets' minds the idea of a want, then to turn that want into a need. Advertisements started to change from being simple descriptions of the product to being vehicles for the making of claims well beyond its intended use. For instance, washing-up liquid was no longer just described as something "to help you wash up", but also as something that "will moisturise your hands". Bernays described the process as an attempt to change the public's mode of thinking in order to make a product appear more attractive in their eyes. Of course, such a persuasive message as his probably would never have been as effectively conveyed had it not been for the omnipresence of the TV, the perfect platform for its dissemination.

In Bernays's mind, the belief that propaganda and purposely created "news" were legitimate tools of his business set him apart from his peers. In his paper, "The Business of Propaganda" he noted that:

> "Propaganda is the executive arm of the invisible government."

A number of scientists and psychologists, such as Trotter, Le Bon, Graham Wallas and Walter Lippmann, went to great lengths to study mass psychology, and came to the conclusion that this new science was quite distinct from that of individual psychology that already existed. Trotter and Le Bon went as far as to suggest the existence of a "group mind" that has impulses, habits and emotions, even though it does not "think" in the traditional sense of the word.

The first impulse for an individual is often to follow the example of a trusted leader. Bernays said:

> "If you can influence the leaders, either with or without their conscious co-operation, you automatically influence the group which they sway. But men do not need to be actually gathered together in a public meeting or in a street riot, to be subject to the influences of mass psychology. Because man is by nature gregarious he feels himself to be member of a herd, even when he is alone in his room with the curtains drawn. His mind retains the patterns which have been stamped on it by the group influences."

When a situation lacks an obvious leader, the tendency for the group is to use clichés, pat words or images that bring about recollection of previous experiences in order to arrive at a decision. For instance, if some authority figure had labelled a politician with a negative word such as "rat", the association may be strong enough that people would vote against them. Playing on a word or image that is associated with corruption can be sufficient to significantly influence the masses.

These studies have led us to a better understanding of how the public can be controlled while, at the same time, having no knowledge that this is happening to them. Propaganda has been so effectively developed and tuned to group psychology that millions of people are conditioned from an early age to believe that all they see on TV is reality and all that they hear is the truth. This mechanism of control, coupled with the fear of condemnation from our peers should we show dissent, has left us unwilling, or even unable, to question authority or to think outside of the box, if you will excuse the pun.

The power of the TV to sell opinions and products has been greatly exploited by America's politicians, journalists and business leaders. At the time of the first televised political debate in 1960, John F Kennedy used it to speak directly to voters, gaining a wider audience and appeal than any debates in the preceding years. Kennedy's tragic assassination in 1963 became a watershed in the history of the TV, further propelling it into the spotlight. Four days of non-stop coverage of the events and the unfolding aftermath were broadcast on all of the channels that were available at the time. The news spread fast, and people gathered around their TV sets to receive the latest on the story. Bulletins where the news anchors presented the story with obvious emotion became most popular. For the first time, the news had mass appeal and began to achieve the size of audience that would be expected of a popular family soap opera.

In 1965, the Vietnam War became the first to be televised, with footage of the brutality broadcast nightly. When this fuelled the country's largest anti-war movement which diminished the public's support for the war, there followed a backlash against the press on the part of the military, who believed that it had been responsible for losing the war by the creation of public opposition. This subsequently fuelled the increasing drive for the use of political propaganda on TV as a way to control public opinion to suit the desired political agenda of the time.

Apart from the creation of false news that we have already seen, the principal way in which this was done was to show only those parts of the story which would rally public opinion towards military action. For example, in the 1980s, the Pentagon adopted a policy of using press pools which gave the military control over the troops who were allowed to talk to the press and the conditions under which this could be done. In this way, it was ensured that only the military's version of events was reported. This policy was implemented during the US invasion of Grenada in 1983, of Panama in 1989 and in the two recent Gulf wars against Iraq. The control over what is broadcast on TV has continued to this day, manipulating public opinion further towards the interests of the large corporations that control the media. Although war may seem undesirable and even objectionable to the average person, we cannot escape the fact that it is very lucrative for both the arms industry and banks who lend money to both sides. Because of this, it should come as no surprise to learn that the selling of war to the masses is part of their agenda. The grand scale of this manipulation is something which very few people seem to be aware of. More disturbing than this, however, is the upsetting fact that even fewer seem to care.

The idea of propaganda in the media is not an alien one. We all take it for granted that, in the communist world, prior to the 1989 fall of the Berlin Wall, propaganda both on the TV and in newspapers was commonplace. The idea that "they" (the communists) had propaganda while "we" (in the West) did not is, of course, yet another manifestation of the religious life position of "we're OK: they're not OK" that we have seen so often. Of course, most of the Russians were well aware that they were being bombarded with propaganda and lies, and interestingly, they were also aware that we in the West were being treated similarly. Perhaps it was the more obvious nature of their own propaganda that enabled them to spot the crucial difference: the fact that, whereas we believed the lies we were fed, they most certainly did not.

This brings to a conclusion our examination of the TV's journey from a source of entertainment to an instrument of control. In the next chapter we will examine the nature of its success from a different, more sinister, angle.

# - 20 -
# Brain Waves

*"My schooling not only failed to teach me what it professed to be teaching, but prevented me from being educated to an extent which infuriates me when I think of all I might have learned at home by myself."*

George Bernard Shaw

---

In the previous chapter we looked at the techniques that are used by the TV to control the way we think. But perhaps a more disturbing facet of this is the physiological effect the TV has on us, a possible consequence of the way in which the images are propagated from the screen to our eyes.

As early as 1924, researchers were attempting to monitor cerebral activity by placing electrodes on the scalp and measuring the weak electrical signals that were detected. The oscillating signals that were found were termed "Neural Oscillations", but are colloquially known today as "Brain Waves".

These signals consist of the small electrical impulses which occur as the result of the communication between adjacent neurons (nerve cells) inside our brains. For the most part, they have a broad spectral range, which means to say that they are comprised of signals of many different frequencies, all superimposed on top of one another. However, activity has been observed to be concentrated within particular frequency bands, and, furthermore, that the prevalent bands change depending on the type of activity the brain is performing. The different bands are summarised in Figure 14. For the purpose of our discussion, we are only interested in the alpha and the beta waves.

| Name | Frequency Hz | Activity |
|---|---|---|
| Alpha | 7.5 to 12.5 | Wakeful relaxation with closed eyes. |
| Beta | 12.5 to 30 | Normal waking consciousness. |
| Gamma | 30 to 100 | Unknown. |
| Delta | 0 to 4 | Deep, non-REM sleep. |
| Theta | 4 to 10 | Motor activity. |

**Figure 14**

When we are awake and alert, our brain produces beta waves which are associated with rational thought. This kind of activity can be loosely associated with the *explorer* mind in that it occurs when we are engaged in analysis or problem solving activities.

In comparison with this, when we are awake but in a state of deep relaxation, alpha waves are produced and become the dominant frequency to be monitored. Not only are these indicative of this condition, but research has shown that they have the effect of disabling our analytic faculties and inducing a sleepy or dreamlike state.

It has been observed that, while watching the TV, our brains very rapidly change their activity pattern from one in which predominantly beta waves are produced to one which favours alpha waves. This lower level of activity has the effect of inhibiting our process of critical thinking. As a consequence, the messages we receive from the TV are more likely to enter our subconscious minds without being subjected to the normal filtering process we habitually impose in order to distinguish fact from fiction. Under these conditions, it's easy to imagine how disinformation might be implanted without difficulty, making us susceptible to conditioning, predictive programing and subliminal messaging.

Nobody has been able to deduce for certain the nature of the mechanism that causes this dramatic change in activity. It has been theorised that it has something to do with the rate at which the TV screen's image is modified. Each half-frame is updated at the rate of twenty-five images per second (US: thirty), and the two half-frames are interlaced with the odd numbered horizontal lines coming from the first half-frame and the even numbered ones coming from the second. This somewhat unusual arrangement was devised in order to minimise the appearance of flicker, whilst simultaneously minimising the bandwidth required for transmission. The result is a refresh rate that is just high enough to avoid most people being able to perceive any flicker. Some have theorised that it is this feature that somehow leads to the brain's switching from the production of beta to alpha waves.

Researchers have shown that the alpha waves our brains produce when we are watching TV are not a phenomenon that occurs normally when our eyes are open, but rather are associated with a reduced state of consciousness such as that which occurs just before sleeping or just after waking. The alpha state is often known as the "hypnogogic state" and can be considered to be the gateway to meditation and the like. It's this state which hypnotherapists try to induce in their subjects or patients. As an example of this, we might consider the case of an individual who has a fear of spiders and who goes to a hypnotherapist in an attempt to cure themselves. The therapist will usually start by getting the subject to relax in order to induce slow alpha wave activity before they begin the therapy. Once this is achieved, the therapist will attempt to implant positive suggestions into the subject's mind with the goal of reducing their irrational fear. The idea is that, by first inducing the alpha state, there is a greater chance of sidestepping the conscious mind which, so it is surmised, is the cause of the problem. At this point, supposedly, the positive suggestions are more likely to enter the subconscious mind of the hypnotised subject. Its success is highlighted by the fact that hypnosis has become a widely accepted alternative therapy, used as an effective treatment for a variety of conditions.

Various people have conducted studies to find out what happens, from a physiological perspective, in the brain of a person watching TV. In November 1969, one of these researchers, Herbert Krugman, conducted an experiment on his secretary, monitoring her brain waves using an electrode taped to the back of her head while she alternately watched TV and read a magazine. After repeat trials, he discovered that every time she watched the TV, her brain waves switched within thirty seconds from predominantly beta to predominantly alpha wave activity. However, when her attention was taken away from the TV screen and she began to read the magazine once again, the beta waves quickly reappeared. This indicates that her brain activity had returned to a state of alert consciousness, replacing the prior hypnotic dreamlike alpha state that had been induced by the TV.

In further research, Krugman confirmed that the left hemisphere of our brain, the one which is responsible for logic and rational thought, tends to be inhibited while we watch TV, leaving the right hemisphere of the brain, which processes information emotionally and non-critically, to function unimpeded.

Krugman's results were replicated by physiologist Thomas Mulholland, whose experiments also showed that, after just 30 seconds of watching TV, the brain begins to produce alpha waves indicative of a near comatose state. Alpha waves are associated with an unfocused and overly receptive state of consciousness in which the brain is virtually incapable of critical analysis. Mulholland deduced from his research that watching TV is neurologically analogous to staring at a blank wall.

Mulholland's research was of great interest to the television industry, especially the marketing and advertising sectors.

When they realized that viewers entered a trance-like state while watching TV, marketers began screening commercials whose aim was not to appeal to the rational mind, but to induce an unconscious emotional state in the minds of the viewers.

At this point, we should question why a flicker rate (if it's the flicker that does it) consistent with inducing an alpha state was chosen in the first place. Was it chosen deliberately, or was it just a coincidence, a fortunate (or unfortunate, if you are on the receiving end) accident? The rate is set at half the frequency of the alternating current of the mains supply, and this frequency was decided when the first supplies of mains electricity were rolled out in the 1890s. For this reason, the effect of the flicker rate is more likely to be an accident than not. One interesting avenue of research might be to investigate the strength of the effect against different flicker rates. If there were any significant difference to be observed across the range of 25Hz (UK) to 30Hz (US), it would be interesting to see if this were related to the cultural differences we see between these two countries in their approach to the TV.

The constant flow of what the majority of us consider to be entertainment and news has grown to shape our perception of the "reality" in which we now live. The carefully shaped messages from the TV guide us to predetermined conclusions, enabling those that control the information's dissemination to control the people who view it. Here in the West, we have been reduced to a situation where so many have now become addicted to the screen that we have lost our ability as a society to differentiate between the fictional world of the TV and reality. The TV dictates when we should laugh and when we should cry: it tells us when to love and when to hate. Without it, we would be lost.

Of course, if this was all made obvious to us, many things may well be different. But the fact is that we are imprinted with the illusion that we are free to make our own choices, when, in reality, many of the "choices" we think we make are actually pre-engineered to move society in a particular direction, a direction beneficial to those who exercise the control. In the moments when we are not staring at the screen, our conversations with our families, friends and colleagues are increasingly filled with our feelings about what we've been watching on screen. The result of this is the reinforcement of the stranglehold the TV has over our lives and, with it, the magnification of the TV Delusion.

This is probably a suitable place to leave the discussion of the TV. In the next few chapters we will turn our attention to some different ways of thinking that lie outside of its straitjacket.

# - 21 -

# Hitler: Epitome of Evil?

*"He who controls the past controls the future. He who controls the present controls the past."*

George Orwell

---

In chapter 19 we looked at the concept of propaganda and the events which led to the TV's becoming its principal conduit. When disinformation of this nature appears on the TV for the first time, many of us are able to recognise it as such, especially if its true nature is brought to our attention by some indirect means. This can lead to a false sense of security in which we believe that no deception can get past us without our being able to detect it. This, in turn, can leave us more exposed to a far greater danger.

Propaganda created in the distant past and repeated by many over the course of the years has been categorised by some as "brainwashing". Whatever label we choose to apply, it is clear that certain narratives have become so woven into the fabric of society, that they often have the power to evade all our efforts to detect them. Under these circumstances, our urge to cling to the narrative and support it can be very strong, and, as we saw in chapter 14, we should expect to see a strong emotional response if such propaganda is criticised. In this chapter we will look at one such example, and consider a rational procedure for approaching the truth which, we hope, will enable us to avoid this kind of response.

"Hitler was evil", the subject of this chapter, is a thesis we hear often repeated, so much so that it has become a truism throughout the Western world. On occasion, from a minority, we might hear the antithesis "Hitler was not evil". When confronted with this form of polarised thesis and antithesis, it can often be difficult to work out how to proceed towards a balanced synthesis.

A couple of things stand out as soon as we look at the words which comprise the thesis. The first is that it bears all the hallmarks of Religious Labelling, as described in chapter 11. The second is that it is completely devoid of all detail. These two observations are sufficient for us to suspect that it is Constructivist in nature.

Knowing what's wrong with the statement puts us in a much better position to be able to work out how to correct it. One demonstrably effective technique to escape the clutches of Constructivism and strive towards Correspondence truth is to try to add detail, but this can often seem a daunting prospect in cases like this when we are presented with a seemingly indivisible truism. Perhaps the only way forward is to scrutinize each word in turn.

An analysis of the first two words doesn't get us very far. Pretty well everyone understands who we mean when we use the proper noun "Hitler", and most will also understand that the word "was" is just a part of the verb "to be", in this case used in its attributive sense.

The real fun starts when we look at the adjective "evil". To work out what it means, we might choose to start with the dictionary definition of the word, here taken from the Oxford English:

> "Profoundly immoral and wicked."

Now we start to see a glimmer of hope in the word "immoral". The word insinuates the existence of a moral code that the subject, the person who utters the word "evil", is inclined to follow. Furthermore, it suggests that when the subject categorises something as "evil", they are identifying it as falling outside of this code. This is a big step forward in our analysis, because it allows us to see that the word "evil" has at least as much to do with the subject, the follower of the moral code, as it does with the person at whom the word is directed. The German philosopher, Friedrich Nietzsche, put it rather succinctly in his work "Beyond Good and Evil"[xxxvii] when he said:

> "There is no such thing as moral phenomena, but only a moral interpretation of phenomena."

We can now see that the categorisation of an act as "evil" is a consequence of the disapproval of the subject who makes the categorisation. In chapter 11 we looked at the idea of Religious Labelling and the closely related psychological concept of Splitting (black-and-white thinking). This is the very trap which awaits us whenever we encounter this word. It entices us to divide the world into two, the good and the evil, whilst avoiding any consideration of the middle ground. When we shift our focus away from the word "evil" itself and, instead, consider the idea of our disapproval of the various actions of the person to whom the label is applied, we find that the trap loosens its hold a little. The liberation leaves us free to see the middle ground more clearly, perhaps because the sensation of varying degrees of disapproval is one which is familiar to us.

Knowing that the individual's disapproval is the key to our analysis, and cognisant of the fact that value judgements are unique to the person making the judgement, we might have cause for concern that it will never be possible to reach a definitive conclusion. However, the fact that the ethics of individuals within a society tend to follow the same trend should be sufficient to buoy our hopes. For instance, in most Western countries, the **concept** of murder, if not its actuality, tends to meet with strong disapproval. Although there will always be some who disagree, the vast majority will tend to exhibit similar attitudes.

Now we have some ideas as to how we might proceed, we are in a better position to formulate a method to analyse the extent to which the original premise is true. A good starting point would be to make a list of Hitler's actions and assign to each a "disapproval coefficient" based on some arbitrary scale. Here we have chosen 100 to represent maximum disapproval, 0 to represent indifference and -100 to represent maximum approval. These are shown against some sample actions in Figure 15.

| Hitler | |
|---|---|
| Action | Disapproval Coefficient |
| Perpetrated holocaust | 99 |
| Created strong economy with low unemployment | -30 |
| Ate muesli for breakfast | 0 |

**Figure 15**

So what's wrong with this approach? There are a couple of obvious flaws which should leap out at us.

The first is that, if we were to list all of Hitler's actions, we would end up with a huge table and find ourselves having to collate an enormous amount of data, most of it utterly irrelevant. It should be obvious that we can simplify matters by leaving out all his actions that we perceive as having had little or no effect on anyone else's lives.

The second problem is a little more subtle. For most of us, when we consider individuals who have engaged in activities that meet with our extreme disapproval, our feelings are unlikely to be mitigated by examples of one or two good deeds. For instance, many people have claimed that Hitler's supposed love of animals or his alleged vegetarianism go to "prove" that he was a nice guy, but statements like this, be they true or false, will never have any real bearing on our judgement of the man. As the table stands, it's begging someone to come along and total up the right hand column so as to come up with some overall figure. If this were to happen, we would end up with a result that was wholly misleading.

Taking these objections into account, we might have a second attempt at presenting our data. This time we will include only those actions which affect others, and we will leave out all actions unlikely to meet with disapproval. The updated table with some new sample actions is shown in Figure 16.

| Hitler | |
| --- | --- |
| Action | Disapproval Coefficient |
| Perpetrated holocaust | 99 |
| Invaded Poland | 50 |
| Bombed London | 60 |

**Figure 16**

To most people, this new analysis will seem a lot closer to the mark, but there is still one important factor that we have overlooked.

When we consider our disapproval of an individual's actions, it becomes apparent that we are looking at a relative measure rather than an absolute one. For instance, if we were to examine ten candidate actions and were to be invited to identify those which could be categorised as "evil", it would be of little merit to apply the label to the acts that attract the least disapproval. Or, to put it more simply, if evil exists at all, then it can only exist in reference to something less evil.

What all this tells us is that, in order to be in a position to judge the extent to which our initial premise is true, we would have to pick some people with whom we might compare

Hitler, and then repeat our procedure accordingly. The obvious candidates for this would be some of the other world leaders of the time such as Franklin D. Roosevelt, Joseph Stalin and Winston Churchill.

If we were developing our procedure in a business or engineering context, it would be normal to subject it to a risk analysis. In doing this, we might hope to identify the possible pitfalls with our method and the corresponding hazards these present to the results of our analysis. With the risks identified, we might be able to identify the steps we should take in order to mitigate them. Since we are trying to be professional, it makes sense for us to give this idea some consideration.

So what could go wrong? In order to answer this question, we might start by considering the often-quoted words of Winston Churchill:

> "History is written by the victors."

If we think about what Churchill said for a moment, it's easy to see the truth in his words. A country decimated and conquered after a long war is hardly in any position to be able to contribute their side of the story to the history books. Furthermore, the winning power will have both the opportunity and the motive to play down the parts of the story which reflect negatively on them. What reason would they have to publicise their own wrongdoings? At the same time, it is reasonable to assume that they would go out of their way to exaggerate the negative aspects of the enemy's behaviour, in order to ensure that their war against an "evil" foe be seen as a just one.

One of the key themes running through this book has been the idea that, in order to reach a balanced view on a particular subject, it's necessary to seek out and understand the narrative from all sides, and in examples like that of Hitler, we might have to do some considerable digging to achieve this. With this in mind, a number of possible risks with our procedure become apparent.

The first is the possibility that some of the items on Hitler's list may have been misrepresented. This might well apply to any or all of the items on the list, but since the holocaust is the one which, for most people, attracts the greatest disapproval, it makes sense to focus our attention there. The central premise of this event, agreed on by many the world over, is the following statement:

> "Six million people of Jewish descent were murdered in gas chambers."

There are two main drivers for our disapproval of this event. The first is the actual number of people affected. If the number were to change, to 6.1m or 5.9m for example, then we would expect our disapproval to change accordingly, at least to some extent.

The second driver is the mode of death. For some reason, death by gas chamber seems to attract a greater degree of disapproval than pretty much anything else. As an illustration of this, it has been estimated that more than 0.1m people of all ethnicities died in the camps as a result of Typhus Fever, yet this fact is virtually unknown to all but the most studious of researchers. This unpleasant, though eminently treatable, disease has a fatality rate of around twenty percent (estimates vary considerably) and is caused by a bacterium, *Rickettsia Prowazekii*, transmitted by the human body louse, *Pediculus Humanus Humanus*. The only way to curb the spread of the disease is to attack the louse by means of the fumigation of the clothing, hair and body of those thought to be at risk. The fumigant used by the Germans in the camps was a pesticide containing cyanide and marketed by IG Farben under the name "Zyklon B".

Another big killer in the camps was the confusingly, similarly named Typhoid Fever. This, too, has a mortality rate of around twenty percent, but is caused by a different bacterium, *Salmonella Typhi*, acquired by the ingestion of contaminated water. Figures for deaths from this disease are a lot harder to come by, perhaps because numbers were not recorded as accurately.

Of course, malnutrition played a part too, but this didn't take its toll until near the end of the war when, as has been documented by many historians, the "allies" had all but cut off food supplies to the camps. During the greater part of the war, evidence suggests that the prisoners were adequately fed. After all, the labour camps had been set up to produce raw materials and goods for the war effort, and it is reasonable to assume that starving the work force would not have been the best way to harvest their labour.

For many years, there was a notice on the gate of what was once the *Auschwitz-Birkenau* labour camp, the largest of its kind, situated in the modern day state of Poland. The notice told us that four million people were killed there during the war. In the early 90s, Franciszek Piper, director of the Auschwitz museum, following new evidence that came to light as a result of the newfound availability of Russians' records, famously reduced this number to 1.1 million. The notice was promptly replaced with a new one. It's worth pointing out at this point, that we, the authors, are not attempting to put a figure on the number of deaths at the camp, but are merely discussing Piper's decision to change his own statement of that number.

Under normal circumstances we would expect that the 6 million would be reduced to 3.1 million to represent the deficit caused by this correction. The problem is, of course, that the figure is protected by law in Germany and so cannot be changed. This has given rise to the new academic study of Religiothematics (Religious Mathematics). The thing that distinguishes this study from its more scientific progenitor is the difference in its treatment of basic algebra. Whereas in mathematics we might see the following:

$a - b = c$

In religiothematics we get the following:

$a - b = 6$

Of course, this holds for all values of *a* and *b*. The mechanics of the operation are decided by conventional algebra, but the result of the calculation is decided by religion. In Germany, any attempt to face up to the cognitive dissonance that arises is punishable by a prison sentence, and the same is true in many other countries too.

While researching any subject, there are a few golden rules which exist to help us on our way. One of these states that when we start to see anomalies, it should be taken as a sure sign that the matter requires further investigation. In this case, an easy thing to do would be to pick another camp and check to see how the figure denoting the number of deaths has changed over time there. In Figure 17, you can see the results

| Deaths at Majdanek Through the Ages | | |
|---|---|---|
| Date | Source | Deaths |
| July 1944 | Soviet Union, on liberation of camp | 1,700,000 |
| November 1945 | Soviet Union, Nuremberg trials | 1,500,000 |
| 1948 | Commission for Investigation of Nazi Crimes | 360,000 |
| 1960 | Soviet Union movie | 350,000 |
| 1998 | Majdanek Museum handbook | 234,000 |
| December 2005 | Tomasz Kranz, Majdanek Museum | 78,000 |
| March 2007 | Majdanek Museum website | 80,000 |

**Figure 17**

of such an exercise conducted for the Majdanek camp, situated, once again, in what is now Poland. This table shows the total number of deceased, regardless of the cause of death or ethnicity of the victim. Once again, the reader is reminded that we are not attempting to revise any of the figures here or to claim that any of them are accurate. We are merely reporting the figures that have been officially documented over time.

It is interesting to note that the biggest drop in claimed deaths occurred as a result of the research conducted by the Commission for Investigation of Nazi Crimes in 1948. It's difficult to say exactly why this was, but perhaps it was the first time anyone thought to conduct an actual investigation.

Now we have looked at a couple of camps, it's time to put it all together and look at the big picture. In Figure 18 we can see the totals across all the major camps and some of the smaller ones. At the risk of repetition, we would like to remind the reader that we are not trying to claim that these numbers are accurate and we are not reproducing figures from so-called revisionists, but are merely stating the **official** version of the figures. We trust that the reader will have patience and understand our need to issue this reminder at each and every stage.

The primary source for these figures is Jewish Virtual Library, an online resource that is part of the American-Israeli Co-operative Enterprise. If the figures are skewed or misrepresented, then we invite the reader to make up their own mind as to the direction of any such bias. Here is an excerpt from their mission statement:

> "The American-Israeli Cooperative Enterprise was established in 1993 as a non-profit and nonpartisan organization to strengthen the US-Israel relationship by emphasizing ... the values our nations share."

The information they provide is pretty light on deaths of people of non-Jewish ethnicity. Wherever possible, we have augmented the data using Wikipedia as the source, and used the opportunity to cross-check all the figures. Looking at the table, what stands out immediately is the fact that the official

| Concentration Camp Deaths |||||||
|---|---|---|---|---|---|
| Camp | Country | Jews Gassed | Jews Shot | Others Gassed | Others Died |
| Chełmno | Poland | 150,000 | | 5,000 | |
| Bełżec | Poland | 600,000 | | | |
| Sobibór | Poland | 200,000 | | | |
| Treblinka | Poland | 700,000 | | 2,000 | |
| Majdanek | Poland | 50,000 | 24,000 | 20,000 | |
| Auschwitz-Birkenau | Poland | 960,000 | | 140,000 | |
| Mauthausen-Gusen | Austria | 4,000 | | 51,000 | |
| Bergen-Belsen | Germany | 0 | | | 35,000 |
| Neuengamme | Germany | 450 | | | 43,000 |
| Sachsenhausen | Germany | 150 | 3,850 | | 30,000 |
| Natzweiler-Struthof | France | 200 | | | 22,000 |
| Stutthof | Poland | 1,000 | | | 85,000 |
| Ravensbrück | Germany | 2,300 | | 2,200 | 50,000 |
| Dachau | Germany | 0 | | | 32,000 |
| Total | | 2,668,100 | 27,850 | 220,200 | 297,000 |

**Figure 18**

total, 2.7 million, is less than half of the normally quoted figure, even if we assume a possible error of up to ten percent.

Interestingly, it also equates to just three quarters of the number who have been needlessly murdered in the West's phoney and illegal "War on Terror" to date (May 2016).

On a personal note, the most shocking revelation of this study has been the case of Bergen-Belsen. For those of us who grew up in the UK in the late 1970s, and no doubt for many others, this camp epitomised the horrors of this chapter of WW2 history. Perhaps this was because the camp featured in so many war documentaries, films, books, essays and poems, even cropping up in popular culture such as the music of the Sex Pistols, a UK punk rock band from the 1970s. To find out from official sources, all these years later, that this camp had no gas chambers, no death machine, no ovens, and that nearly half of the people who were said to have died there did so after the camp's "liberation" came as a bit of a bombshell, to say the least. It would seem that the more insidious is a piece of propaganda, the greater its opportunity to embed itself into our culture, and the more challenging it is to rid ourselves of it.

So, after all this, we are still faced with the concept of the six million, a number which doesn't seem to match the officially accepted figure, and which seems to possess a certain religious quality in its imperviousness to the laws of mathematics. This may be a good point to ask ourselves where exactly this figure does come from.

In studying the origins and spread of words, etymologists will often start by looking at historical records to find the first appearance of a term in newspapers and books. We include here, deliberately without comment, an incomplete list of such usages, some of them verging on the prophetic in character. These are taken from newspapers and other publications in the years leading up to the war. It is left to the reader to judge what he or she is to make of these findings.

> Encyclopaedia Britannica 10$^{th}$ Edition page 482, 1902, "While there are in Russia and Rumania six millions of Jews who are being systematically degraded ..."

> The Jewish Criterion, September 18$^{th}$ 1903, "... six million downtrodden brethren."

Deseret Evening News, March 17th 1908, "... poverty, starvation and disease are the afflictions which now beset the six million Jews in that country and Roumania. (*sic*)"

The Zionist Congress, 1911, "... complete annihilation for six million people ..."

The New York Times, January 14th 1915, "... of whom more than 6,000,000 are in the heart of the war zone; Jews whose lives are at stake and who today are subjected to every manner of suffering and sorrow ..."

The Mercury, December 4th 1915, "... six millions of Russian and Polish Jews are to-day the most pitiable victims of that race hatred and that race fanaticism which have been the creed of Germany ..."

The Tacoma Times, February 28th 1916, "... there were 6,000,000 Jews in Europe absolutely without food or resources."

El Paso Herald, April 7th 1919, "... to save from starvation six million Jews who are the helpless victims of the German Terror."

The New York Times, May 2nd 1920, "... six million human beings, without food, shelter, clothing or medical treatment."

The Montreal Gazette, December 28th 1931, "... fears crisis at hand. ... six million Jews in Eastern Europe face starvation, and even worse, during the coming winter."

The New York Times, March 29th 1933, "It is now active in relief and reconstructive work in Eastern Europe where 6,000,000 Jews are involved."

The London Times, November 26th 1936, "... Jews ... in Eastern Europe there were 6,000,000 unwanted unfortunates who were condemned to be penned up ... the presence of these 6,000,000 people without a future whose condition was a threat to Europe."

The New York Times, January 9th 1938, "persecuted Jews seen on increase. 6,000,000 victims noted. [...] all are today the victims of governmental anti-Semitism ..."

The Jewish Western Bulletin, March 3rd 1939, "six million Jews overseas facing persecution, discrimination and economic ruin ..."

The Jewish Criterion, April 14th 1939, "... whether our 6,000,000 fellow countrymen will live or die [...] More than a million refugees, starving, tortured, fear-dazed, have been dragged from their homes, separated from their families, expelled from their countries. Five million more, await with horror the moment this misery will strike them ..."

The Southern Israelite, November 28th 1939, "... the coming war would be the annihilation of the six million Jews in East and Central Europe."

New York Times, June 25th 1940, "Six million Jews in Europe are doomed to destruction, if the victory of Nazis should be final. [...] The chances for mass emigration and resettlement of European Jewry seems to be remote, and European Jews face the danger of physical annihilation."

The London Times, January 25th 1943, "... the extermination already carried out is part of the carrying into effect of Hitler's oft-repeated intention to exterminate the Jewish people in Europe, which means in effect the extermination of some 6,000,000 ..."

At this point, we will leave the topic of the camps in order to return to the main theme of this chapter. But before we do so, it is worth pointing out that, although we have taken care to avoid all so-called revisionist ideas, there are some who have investigated this disturbing portion of history from such an angle. If the reader is inclined to continue their investigation of this unsettling, yet compelling topic, perhaps a good place to start might be Nicholas Kollerstrom's book "Breaking the Spell"[xxxviii].

Now, returning once more to our risk analysis, we can move on to the second big problem with our procedure: the fact that we may be inclined to omit certain key items when considering the likes of Roosevelt, Churchill and Stalin. To illustrate this, we will look at some such examples for each of them.

The first event for consideration is that of Eisenhower's Death Camps, sometimes called the Rheinwiesenlager or Rhine Meadow Camps, a network of internment camps set up after the end of the war by General Dwight D. Eisenhower, under the presidency of Roosevelt. The stated purpose of these camps, in operation between 1945 and 1953, was to house both surrendered German troops and German civilians alike.

Unlike Hitler's camps, evidence suggests that these were somewhat disorganised arrangements, lacking as they did in any buildings for the shelter of the inmates. Instead, they consisted of areas of bare land that soon turned into quagmire, surrounded by a barbed wire fence. The reason for the disparity was a simple one: these camps had a different purpose. Whereas Hitler's had been designed as labour camps, the function of the American ones was that of simple internment. All the available evidence indicates that the inmates were very poorly fed, had little access to clean water and no medical supplies. The result of all this was that, even though there were no gas chambers, huge numbers needlessly died of Typhus Fever, dysentery and starvation.

The number of people who died in Eisenhower's Death Camps is very difficult to ascertain with any degree of accuracy, partly because the information appears to have been supressed and partly, some might say rather conveniently, due to the poor record keeping on the part of the American captors. Estimates for the number of people targeted by this peacetime holocaust range from as few as 10,000 to as many as 15 million, but, weighing up the evidence available to us, it is likely that a figure of around 1.7 million is close to the mark. Other than the fact that Eisenhower, by his own admission, did not like Germans, there was no reason for their deaths: they were not the targets of any particular ideology and, for the most part, their only crime was the fact that they were German and had just lost a war.

Until very recently, the details of the atrocities committed by the "Allies" had been so successfully supressed that very few researchers were aware of them; but this began to change with the release of Thomas Goodrich's well researched and chilling book, "Hellstorm"[xxxix]. As an accompaniment to the book, there was also a movie. Shortly after release, this was made available on YouTube, but has subsequently been subjected to censorship in many countries, including the US and the UK. It is clear that this is a touchy subject which some would prefer never to see the light of day. We can only speculate as to who might benefit from burying it.

Moving on, the next event worthy of consideration is the bombing, by the "allies", of the German city of Dresden which took place in a series of four raids over the course of three days, starting on February 13th 1945. Nearly four thousand tons of high explosives and incendiaries were dropped by the USAF and RAF, resulting in a deadly firestorm in which thousands of civilians were burned alive.

Estimates for the total number of deaths range from 275,000 to as many as 400,000, the vast majority of them being innocent civilians. The killing machine was particularly effective because people made homeless in the initial raids gathered together on open land where they were deliberately targeted by machine gun fire during subsequent attacks. Although knowledge of the attacks on Dresden is fairly widespread, perhaps due to the staggeringly high death toll, less well known is the fact that the same treatment was dished out to many other German cities during the closing months of the war: Hamburg, München, Stuttgart, Köln, Berlin and others all suffered similar fates. The number of deaths in these additional cities is not included in the above figure.

Some have suggested that the terror that was inflicted on Dresden can be justified by the fact that Britain was fighting for its survival, rather than fighting for some strategic or economic goal. At the time of the Battle of Britain, between July 10$^{th}$ 1940 and October 31$^{st}$ 1940, there was certainly some truth to be found in this narrative, though some would argue that this could have been avoided if Britain had simply not declared war on Germany in the first place. But the fact is that the Dresden firestorm bombings, like the atomic bomb attacks on Japan which happened at about the same time, are events which happened long after the tide of war had turned in Britain's favour. By 1945 an "allied" victory was pretty certain, and the only countries fighting for their lives were Germany and Japan.

By now, British readers may have formed the opinion that a necessary precursor for their nation's involvement in purposeless mass-murder is a partnership with the US. But, on the contrary, it would seem that they are perfectly capable of doing this all on their own. Around three million, for instance, are estimated to have died in 1943 in India in what has been dubbed "The Bengal Holocaust" or "The Bengal Famine". Admittedly, there were some factors for which the British cannot be held responsible, but the fact remains that the food crop that would have otherwise fed the starving population was syphoned off to feed British troops in war-torn Europe, and it was this that ultimately led to the demise of all those Bengali civilians.

All this begs the question as to whether this atrocity can truly be judged to be any less evil than what we refer to as "the holocaust." If we think it can, what gives us the moral high ground to say that the lives of one race are more important than the lives of another? Could it be that we have been conditioned to recognise "evil" only when we are on the receiving end, and ignore it when those inflicting the death and suffering are our own leaders?

Then we come to the USSR under Stalin between 1932 and 1937, where it has been estimated that as many as six million lost their lives. Some of these were the victims of a deliberate policy of slaughter in Ukraine based on nationality and social class. Others starved to death in a famine in Kazakhstan that later spread to Russia and, again, to Ukraine. But it didn't stop there: by 1937 the killing entered a much more sinister phase under the "Great Terror". This saw the large-scale purge of the Communist Party, the repression of both the peasants and of the army leadership, with imprisonment and arbitrary executions being the norm.

This is by no means a complete list of the atrocities carried out by the "allies" during WW2, and, with a little investigation, the reader will be able to identify many others. But even without doing so, we probably have a sufficient weight of evidence to balance the scales. Whatever way you look at it, the loss of human life on a scale such as that which was seen in WW2, affecting as it did so many on both sides in so many countries, is a tragedy. In order to understand its complexities one must get a firm grasp on all the events, take into account the views of both sides and try to understand people's motives in as balanced a way as possible. Whatever process we use to try and discern the truth, it's probably fair to say that applying the Religious Label of "evil" to the actions of one side, while ignoring the very similar actions of the other is probably not the best way to go about it.

In this chapter we have looked at a simple procedure that can be used to analyse a sensitive part of the narrative that constitutes our history. By applying these techniques, we are able to move away from the simplicity of "good and evil" and proceed towards a more adult world of detail and balance. In the next chapter we will build on this idea and take a look at a similar procedure that can be used to analyse society throughout the ages.

# - 22 -
# A Health Check

*"The ruling class in every age have tried to impose a false view of the world on their followers."*

George Orwell

---

When we look at various examples of societies around the globe and over the course of the centuries, it is our tendency to try to judge them as good or bad. As we have seen before, a binary categorisation like this offers us little in our quest to understand the world. Nevertheless, there are some techniques we can use to measure the health, or lack thereof, of these societies. In this chapter we'll explore an example of such a metric.

Around 1780, during the Carolingian Renaissance, the word *Trivium* was coined to describe a formal framework for critical thinking based on the evidence of our senses along with the formal study of grammar, logic and rhetoric. This school of thought (the name of which translates as: "the place where three roads meet") was based on earlier bodies of knowledge going back to antiquity on a journey of more than a thousand years. It is still in use today.

When we are faced with some new event, the *Trivium* provides us with a set of formal rules which can be used to help us make sense of it in a way that is most likely to lead to our obtaining an accurate understanding. In particular, it tells us what questions we should ask and in what order we should ask them:

- **What?** – How can we describe the event in terms of our senses? What did we see and hear?

- **Where?** – Whereabouts did the event take place?
- **When?** – At what time did the event take place?
- **How?** – What mechanism underlies the event?
- **Who?** – Who was or were the perpetrator(s)?
- **Why?** – What motivated them to do it?
- **Explain?** – How can we explain our reasoning for arriving at our conclusions?

This will seem like common sense to older readers since, up until the 1990s, there were many examples of this paradigm in use all around us. It is less common today, as we will see in due course.

Let's imagine for a moment that a crime, perhaps a murder, has been committed. What events might we expect to occur between the discovery of the body and the punishment of the guilty party?

The first thing that typically happens when the police arrive is that they ask **what** happened: that's how they work out whether they are dealing with a murder, a robbery, fraud, etc. Once it has been ascertained that there has been a suspicious death, say, we can then move on to the next set of questions: **where** was the crime committed? Where is the body now? Was the victim killed at that position, or has the body been moved after death? At the same time, the police will ask **when** the body was discovered and when was the victim last seen alive.

These are the fundamental questions we must ask in order to establish the basic facts of the situation. In answering them, the police will combine various different types of evidence such as scientific, physical, testimonial etc. As a result, they will pave the way to ask the next question: **how** was the crime committed? The outcome of this is a credible sequence of events which explains how the evidence that was gathered came to exist.

At no point during these proceedings will the police have decided who committed the crime or what their motive might have been. Of course, they may have their suspicions based on their past experience, but this has no bearing (or at least **should** have no bearing) on the evidence gathering process.

It's only after the basic evidence has been gathered that the police will ask themselves **who** the perpetrator might be and **why** they might have done it. At the point at which the case goes to court, no decision has yet been made as to whether the accused is actually guilty. The only thing that has been decided is that the evidence is sufficient for the real process of analysis to commence. Just before judgement is made, the prosecutor will sum up the case by **explaining** how it was that the conclusion was reached.

This regimented sequence of events was so central to our culture that there were many iconic TV cop shows produced which set it in stone, of which perhaps the most famous was *Columbo* (a personal favourite of the authors). Columbo would always spend the majority of each episode simply asking questions. By this means he would establish the **what**, **where** and **when**. Little by little, he would discover inconsistencies in the stories of the protagonists and, without making any accusations, would drill down on the details surrounding those discrepancies. By the end, he would have enough information to be able to piece together a timeline of events which constituted the **how**. This would lead him to become sure of both the identity of the murderer (the **who**) and their motive (the **why**). At that point, the only thing left would be his breaking the news to them with the catch phrase "D'ya know : there's just one thing I don't understand". In doing this he was able to **explain** his reasoning for coming to his conclusions.

Of course, it hasn't always been like this. For example, on March 23rd 1692, in Salem, Massachusetts, Rebecca Towne Nurse (née Towne) was accused of witchcraft by Edward and John Putnam. The two families had been in various protracted land disputes for some years prior to the accusation. Nurse was arrested and put on trial in the spring of 1692. At no point was she ever accused of any specific crime, either real or invented, so her defence consisted of the testimony of her friends and family as to her respectability of character. As the trial proceeded, however, the young Ann Putnam and, on occasions, other children of the two Putnams who were also present in court would break into fits and claim Rebecca was tormenting them. Nurse was eventually found guilty and hanged for her "crimes" on July 19th 1692.

Along the way, Rebecca's sister, Mary Eastey, was also accused of witchcraft. In her case, this came about because, when Mary clasped her hands together, Mercy Lewis (an alleged "victim") imitated the gesture and claimed to be unable to release her hands until Mary released her own. On September 9th, Mary suffered the same fate at the gallows as her sister.

Ann Putnam later apologised to the Towne family for having made the false accusations, and this prompted the Massachusetts State Government to compensate the family. This closure to the story was, however, nearly twenty years in the coming.

What we see here is a clear example of the disastrous consequences that can ensue when there is a deviation to the *Trivium*'s order of questions, especially for those who might easily be mistaken for a being a witch. In this case, the first question that the court asked was **why** the crime had been committed. Their assumption that witchcraft was the motive possibly arose because this was the hot topic that was on everyone's mind at the time and because the idea was suggested by the Putnams' accusations. Soon after this, they moved on to the question of **who** had committed the "crime". The assumption that Rebecca and Mary were to blame was presumably also made as a result of the plaintiffs' accusations. It was only after the answer to these questions had been established that the court considered the **what, where, when** and **how**.

If we look at society over the ages, we might measure the "health" of the era by examining how close its legal system was to either the "Witch" or the "Columbo" model. So how about today? We like to think we live in an age of reason and that we have moved on from the age of witch hunts, but is this really the case? Let's have a look at an example to see.

On September 11th 2001 in New York, three buildings were destroyed. The first to be destroyed (but the second that was alleged to have been hit by an airplane) was the South Tower, at 9:59am EDT. A little later, at 10:28am EDT, the North Tower was destroyed. Much later on, at 5:21pm EDT, Tower Seven was destroyed. Ignoring the other events (in Washington DC and Shanksville), these three events constitute the **what, where** and **when**. At this point, without careful forensic investigation, it would have been impossible to work out the **how**, let alone the **who** and **why**.

Yet before the first two towers had even been destroyed, Ehud Barak, a former Israeli prime minister, appeared in London on the BBC news and suggested that Osama Bin Laden may have been responsible, and that his actions were motivated by terrorism. In doing that, he was clearly attempting to establish the **who** and the **why**. At that stage, since the first two towers had still to be destroyed, and the third would not be destroyed for another seven or so hours, he could not have established the **when** (not fully, at least), since to do so would have required a time machine.

And he wasn't the only one to sing this tune: there were numerous government officials and news anchors on multiple channels in the US all saying both that Bin Laden was responsible and that a war would be the likely result. Rita Cosby of Fox News, for example, announced this at 9:32 EDT. We should remind ourselves once again that this was shortly **before** the "collapse" of the first two towers, many hours before the "collapse" of the third and many months before the start of any attempt at an investigation.

What is noteworthy here is not so much that the mechanism of the *Trivium* was turned on its head that day, but that the whole nation went along with it. In the space of just a few hours, the whole of the US had been thrust back into the seventeenth century, taking most of the Western world with it. In a manner of speaking, hundreds of years of scientific and legal progress were repealed on 9/11 and the law of the jungle was erected in its place.

It may well be that our propensity to be taken in by propaganda which focuses on the **why** stems from some inherent flaw in our thinking. This shortcoming, which goes by the name of "promiscuous teleology", is the tendency we have to falsely attribute a purpose to an event for which we are seeking an explanation.

Deborah Kelemen and Evelyn Rosset, psychologists at Boston University[xl], are amongst a number of researchers to have written papers on this subject. Kelemen was aware that children aged seven to eight showed a preference for false explanations based on intelligent design, such as: "Rocks are jagged so animals can scratch themselves", but that this inclination seemed to diminish as their tuition in science progressed.

In order to determine the factors involved, Kelemen took two hundred and thirty university students and flashed various statements onto a screen in front of them for just a few seconds at a time, asking them to judge whether the statements were true or false. The list of statements included some false teleological assertions such as: "Earthworms tunnel underground to aerate the soil", and some true statements to act as a control. What they found was that the shorter the time the subjects were given to make their judgments, the greater their tendency to accept the false teleological statements as true. They found that this tendency was independent of the extent of the subject's scientific education and independent of their religious beliefs.

Given these findings, it should be easier to see how propaganda might be constructed to play on this tendency. If it is presented to us in such a way as to give us little time to think about some new event or situation, then our inclination will be to focus on purpose and thus deviate from the correct order of investigation as stipulated by the *Trivium*. It would be interesting to see someone take Kelemen's study a step further by testing the effects of emotional trauma on our penchant for this form of childlike reasoning.

To employ an analogy, we might view the struggle between science and religion as a giant pendulum that has been swinging back and forth throughout history. In 1633, when Galileo was first imprisoned for his heretical (yet evidence based) theory that the Earth orbited the Sun, we can imagine the pendulum swung firmly towards religion. By the 1990s it had swung just about as far as it has ever done towards science. Since then, it seems that it has started its swing back towards religion again, and who knows where it will end up.

A lot of this may be to do with the way the state maintains its authority over us. In times when there is a powerful external bogeyman for us to fear, such as the threat allegedly presented by communism in the 1980s, the state has little need for authoritarian tactics, because our fear is sufficient to keep us subservient. Under these circumstances, science and liberty may be free to prosper. Conversely, in times of diminished external threat, the state may be obliged to resort to authoritarianism in order to maintain its control. Here, we are more likely to be submerged in propaganda and threats, to lose sight of the scientific method and to fall prey to religion. When the pendulum swings this way, the "truths" that underpin our world are led by the religious mantra of repeated propaganda, rather than the beacons of logic and reason.

At the same time, on an educational level, we see the gradual dumbing down of the population accompanied by a gradual decrease in the academic level of the program of education supplied by our schools. The fact that this has been happening over the course of the last thirty years or so is not in doubt, but the question that remains to be answered is the direction of causality which operates here (assuming that there is one). On the one hand, we might conjecture that the dumbing down has been done by decree of the state in an attempt to make us more susceptible to their religious propaganda. But, on the other hand, one might suggest that the religious "spirit of the age" has made us dumber, and that our education system has merely diminished in academic level in its efforts to match this.

Reading these last few paragraphs, one might be forgiven for thinking that science and religion were somehow mutually exclusive, but nothing could be further from the truth, for, as we will see, there lurks religion even within science itself.

A great example of this is the "science" of plate tectonics. In 1912, Alfred Wegener, having observed that the shape of the West coast of Africa bore a striking resemblance to that of the East coast of the Americas, came up with his theory of Continental Drift. To see this clearly, one could use a pair of scissors to cut out the continents of America (north and south) and Africa from a map and note that the two shapes tessellate (fit together without any appreciable gap). He suggested that the continents that we see today were once joined together as parts of one large supercontinent which split into sections and gradually drifted apart over the course of millions of years. Nobody took him seriously until the 1950s, but today his theory is almost universally accepted.

In order for this to be possible, Wegener argued, huge "plates" which bear the continents must be migrating around the Earth. At any point where two plates were moving apart, to which he gave the term "constructive plate boundary", he said that new crust was being formed. There is plenty of evidence to suggest that this is true since, if one draws a map of the Earth colour coded by age of rock, one finds that the newest rocks are to be found in the mid-Atlantic, at the point from which both land masses are moving away.

To match this process, Wegener suggested that there were also "destructive plate boundaries" where the edge of one plate buckled and passed underneath the adjacent one whereupon it was consumed. Because of this "passing underneath" motion, he termed these boundaries "subduction zones". The rate of subduction, when aggregated across the whole planet, must be equal, according to Wegener, to the aggregate rate of movement of the constructive boundaries. If this were not the case, it would imply that the Earth was changing in size as time progressed.

The big problem with this is that, although a few potential subduction zone candidates have been located, nowhere near enough have been identified to balance out the effect of the construction. Nevertheless, the idea of their existence has been ratified by "scientific" canon to the extent where to argue against them is considered to be scientific heresy.

More recently, scientists such as Neal Adams and James Maxlow have noted that the tessellation effect which can be seen on the continents on either side of the Atlantic can also be observed on those on either side of the Pacific. If today's continents were joined across the Pacific as well as the Atlantic, then we would see a sphere that is substantially smaller in diameter than the Earth which exists today. The transition from this hypothetical smaller Earth to the one we see today can be seen in some beautiful animations that are easy to find on the internet ("Neal Adams Earth is growing"). These ideas have been made more accessible to a wide audience in recent years thanks to the work of Liam Scheff, Andrew Johnson and Richard Hall.

Of course, it is not our place to say which (if either) of these two theories is "true". The important point is the attitude of the current followers of Plate Tectonics with respect to their adherence to the theory of subduction zones, despite the lack of any substantial evidence to support the idea that they exist. Starting with their unfounded belief that the Earth has not changed in size appreciably over its lifetime, but faced with the compelling evidence of the constructive boundaries, they are forced to cling to their *ad hoc* hypothesis of "subduction zones".

Whatever you think about Scheff's theory, what is clear is that it represents a very interesting, new theory and a fascinating topic for research, but that anyone attempting to carry out such research will first have to overcome the religious dogma before they are awarded a grant.

In this chapter we have seen how the temptation towards religious thinking is always with us, even when we are most convinced that we are behaving in a scientific manner. If we follow the path that is set out for us by the *Trivium*, however, we will find that there is light to be found in the midst of the darkest of storms.

# - 23 -
# Which One Should I Believe?

> *"Nihil audio sententiam non esse. Videmus omnia esse prospectum, non veritas."*
> *(Everything we hear is an opinion, not a fact. Everything we see is a perspective, not the truth.)*
>
> Marcus Aurelius, Roman emperor

---

Human beings are inherently social animals, so it's no accident that society throughout the ages has been focused on the communication of information and ideas. The modern age presents us with an ever increasing capacity for this, both in terms of the volume of information and the speed at which it can be transmitted. Many of us can find this all a little overwhelming at times, and in these situations there is a tendency to latch on to the narratives with which we are presented as if they were a lifeboat on a rough sea. In this chapter we look at the problems that can result from this approach and some simple steps we can take to mitigate them.

Once we step outside of the domain of the mainstream media, it's possible to find as many narratives as there are sources of authority. For those who are used to feeding solely from the TV, such a plethora of sources can seem a little off-putting. We can imagine that dialogue similar to the following example is, perhaps, quite common:

> **Barry:** "Hey, look at this report live on CNN. They are saying that there has been a shooting."
>
> **Edward:** "That's weird. If you look here on GlobalResearch, they are saying it's a hoax."

**Barry:** "Huh? But how do I know which one to believe?"

So how are we to answer Barry's question? Before we consider this, we must first ask ourselves whether the question is to be fielded by our *explorer* or our *believer* mind.

From the *believer's* point of view, the answer is simple. You should believe whichever one your religion demands that you believe. If you are a devotee of *TVism*, then you should believe the one from the TV. If, on the other hand, you are a devotee of some particular "alternative media" source, then go for that one. For the *believer*, life is simple.

If we look at the question again from the *explorer's* point of view, on the other hand, we immediately run into some problems with the question which we need to iron out before we proceed:

"But how do I know which one to believe?"

The first problem is that word "one". This word implies that we are to select exactly one of the two opinions on the table, and then regard that one as the "truth". But what if both are wrong? What if each contains some morsel of truth but, even if put together, these do not represent the whole truth? What happens if both are true? After all, if one is true according to the Correspondence Model and the other true according to Constructivism, then it is possible for them to both be "true" even if they directly contradict each other. This is a topic which requires further discussion, and we'll pick it up again a little later.

The second problem, of course, is that word "believe". As we saw in chapter 2, for the *explorer*, the truth is a somewhat transient concept, because we are always on the lookout for new evidence and new hypotheses. If the word "belief" can be applied at all to the thought processes of an *explorer*, then it is the involuntarist form of belief that we dealt with in chapter 16, rather than the voluntarist form that contrasts it.

If we take the question as a whole, we see that it is no more than another example of a logical fallacy. This time, it's the Complex Question Fallacy in which we see a question which contains a controversial or unjustified presupposition, often a presumption of guilt. The nature of the question ensures that no matter how we answer it, the presupposition remains unchallenged. Perhaps the most often quoted example of this fallacy is the following question:

"When did you stop beating your wife?"

It's just not possible to answer the question without getting trapped by the falsehood.

The problem is that life just isn't as simple for the *explorer* as it is for the *believer*. Instead of comparing the two sources of authority, the *explorer* must perform an analysis of the full details of each proposition presented. In his book, "Official Stories"[xli], Liam Scheff introduces us to the "scratch technique" of analysis, which he describes like this:

- **Scratch 1** – Take only the information provided by the selected source, and analyse it for consistency.
- **Scratch 2** – Add into the mix additional information from other sources to try to build up a complete picture.

In many cases, the first step is all we need to check the veracity of a story from a certain source.

As an example, we might take the alleged Ebola Virus Disease (EVD) outbreak that was said to have occurred in October 2014 in West Africa. Some people say that Ebola was a real threat, and that a worldwide pandemic was a potential outcome. Other people claim that the whole thing was a hoax and that there were no real cases of Ebola. Others have even argued that Ebola is a man-made virus, manufactured in the West under the direction of the CIA and released into West Africa either by mistake or by design. Various sinister reasons for the supposed release of the virus have been proposed, such as the depopulation of the region, profit for big pharma, biological weapons testing, and so on. As before, it's not the purpose of this book to say which, if any, of these views is "right".

Instead of trying to make a judgement, let's use "scratch 1" to look at some evidence that was presented by the mainstream media. In Figure 19 you can see a photograph that is similar to many that were shown on TV channels and newspapers around the world during the height of the crisis. It was presented as a depiction of an Ebola patient being transported to a hospital in the US for treatment. Take a few moments to study the image in detail. Of the six figures depicted in the photograph, the first, third, fourth and fifth (starting from the left) are dressed all in white, the second in yellow and the sixth in a blue shirt with dark trousers.

As you can see, the photo shows six people and a wheeled stretcher. Four of the people are dressed in white hazardous materials suits (or "hazmat suits"). These suits are impermeable whole-body garments worn as protection against hazardous materials. The suit can be combined with self-contained breathing apparatus (SCBA) to ensure a supply of breathable air, as can be seen in the example of the third person (from the left) in the image.

We can assume that those in the photo are medical personnel who are wearing the suits in order to prevent them from contracting Ebola from the patient. This is reasonable because Ebola, so we have been told, is a highly infectious disease which is transmitted either by direct contact with an infected person or by the inhalation of their bodily fluids. Furthermore, the World Health Organisation (WHO) has deemed that Ebola is transmissible through contact with surfaces and materials, such as clothing and bedding, which have been contaminated with these fluids. The WHO has claimed in their "fact sheet 103"[xlii] that health-care workers have frequently been infected while treating patients with suspected or confirmed EVD. If this is true, then we must suspect that this has occurred as a result of close contact with patients in circumstances where infection control precautions have not been strictly adhered to.

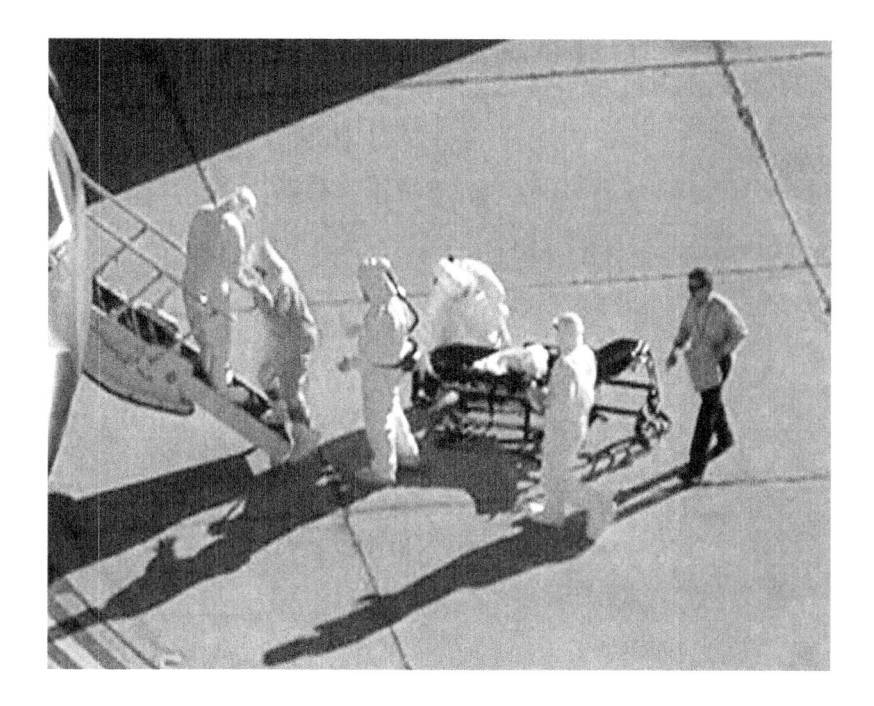

**Figure 19**

But the problems that are alleged to be presented by Ebola do not stop there. The onset of the symptoms of Ebola is said to be very rapid and the effects so debilitating that a sufferer can be rendered incapable just a few hours after being exposed to the virus. This makes treatment very difficult and death the most likely outcome. It is reasonable to suppose that anyone who is aware of these facts and values their life would want to wear protective clothing, rather than subject themselves to these risks.

So that covers the four people in the white hazmat suits. But there are still two further people depicted in this image for us to consider. First there is the person in the yellow suit. It is reasonable to assume that this is supposed to be the patient, as he or she is being helped up the steps of the aeroplane on the left of the picture.

If we take together our understanding of the debilitating effects of Ebola, the presence of the stretcher and the fact that the patient seems able to climb the steps; we see the emergence of our first contradiction. If the patient is able to walk up steps, then we must ask ourselves what the purpose was of the stretcher, when surely a wheelchair would have sufficed to transport the patient. Although this may appear to be a minor anomaly to some, and many will come up with reasons why logic wasn't applied here, it is important that we don't simply ignore details like this.

Lastly, we can see the person following along behind with the clipboard, the only person in the shot who is not wearing a hazmat suit. We will call him "Clipboard Guy". He presents us with a more obvious inconsistency because, if Ebola is as virulent as the WHO tells us it is, why is it that Clipboard Guy seems to believe that he's not in any danger? His relaxed body posture seems to suggest that he is either unaware of the danger that faces him, or, alternatively, is cognizant of the fact there is no danger.

These two points alone are sufficient to make us question the authenticity of the story that was woven from this image. As noted earlier, a photo similar to this was presented in the US mainstream media as an example of the treatment of an Ebola patient. But, given the analysis we have just performed, we have good reason to suspect that the true narrative is likely to be somewhat different.

The situation was compounded further when the anomaly, Clipboard Guy, was brought to CNN's attention by a fastidious viewer. CNN saw fit to air an "explanation" for his presence and the broadcast is easy enough to find on the internet ("CNN tries to explain Ebola Clipboard Carrying Guy").

The "explanation" they offered was that Clipboard Guy's presence was due to the fact that medical staff wearing the suits find it difficult to see, their view being restricted by the large hoods. For this reason, so CNN told us, they needed someone, in this case Clipboard Guy, to spot the way for them and give them directions. In addition, they suggested that he was in no danger as, according to them, Ebola is not an airborne disease. This assertion directly contradicts the contents of the WHO's fact sheet.

One's initial reaction to CNN's explanation might be that it seems to follow the form of an *ad hoc hypothesis* like that which we examined in chapter 9. In response to their explanation, one might point out that Clipboard Guy appears to be too far away to provide any meaningful help and, as seen in the CNN clip, half way through the stair-climbing activity he seems to lose interest and wanders off. One could be excused for thinking that these observations turn CNN's explanation from unlikely to untenable. If we were to argue these points with them, we might expect that they would go through another iteration of *ad hoc hypothesis*, thus extending it into a *religious reasoning chain*.

So what are we to make of this? With only one hypothesis to consider so far and an abundance of evidence that contradicts it, we are forced to look for others to see if we can find something that gives us a better fit. The first two possibilities that spring to mind are that this particular scene is a drill or that it is some kind of staged event or hoax. Without a doubt, there are likely to be many other hypotheses that fit the facts better than the narrative supplied to us by CNN.

For completeness, we could think a little harder and make a guess at which of these two alternatives is the more likely. If this were a staged event or hoax, we might surmise that it would be unlikely for the hoaxers to place Clipboard Guy at the scene, because to do so would surely make it obvious to any critical thinker that the event was not real. On the other hand, if we were witnessing footage of a drill, then it is probable that Clipboard Guy is there to monitor things to make sure the participants follow all the safety procedures. For this reason, perhaps the second hypothesis offers us a better fit for the observations.

Needless to say, we cannot deduce from this one example that the whole Ebola story was a sham, but we can say two things:

- It is very likely that the image we have scrutinized and the accompanying footage shows an Ebola (or similar) drill in progress, rather than an instance of **actual** Ebola.
- CNN's airing of their *ad hoc* hypothesis suggests that they might be complicit in the attempt to pass this drill off as the real thing.

There is, however, one more important question we need to address. If we are indeed seeing a drill or a hoax (or anything other than an instance of real Ebola) in this photograph, then what is the purpose in the perpetrators' trying to pass it off as the real thing? One possible answer to this conundrum might be that the event is an example of a *Video News Release*.

Pick up an average newspaper and leaf through the pages. The chances are that you will encounter at least one news item claiming that scientists have discovered a cure for cancer from some new source. Sometimes it's not a cure for cancer they have discovered, but, instead, something that **causes** cancer. If you were to gather all these stories together, you would find that we are told that some things both cause cancer **and** cure it! There are some websites which, very amusingly, seek to correlate these, "dailymailoncology" being just one example. The one thing that all these cures and causes have in common is that you are very unlikely to ever hear about them ever again. Cancer hasn't been universally wiped off the face of the planet by, for instance, the simple inclusion of a sturgeon's swim bladder in our breakfast cereal, or by the eradication of chalk from our drinking water. So why then are these stories published?

The true purpose of these "news" stories, in all probability, is to act as an advertising campaign for drug companies. When adverts masquerading as news are presented in this way, the term Video News Release is used to describe the phenomenon. One problem with normal TV advertising is that most people have learned to switch off (sometimes literally, usually metaphorically) when the adverts come on. Another problem is that people are gradually moving away from the TV and towards online media where the adverts are easier to avoid.

When people watch the news, however, either on the TV or online, they are more likely to accept what they see as the "truth". Presenting advertisements as news stories allows the advertisers to overcome the faculty we all have to "switch off".

At this point, one might argue that if no particular cancer drug is mentioned in the story, then how is a revenue stream for a drug to be generated? The answer is that the advert is a lot more subtle than that. What is going on here is an example of a concept called "Problem, Reaction, Solution". First, a problem is created: in this case it is the idea of cancer or, more generally, any kind of ailment or perceived ailment. Next, we see the reaction, the concern or fear of disease and ailments on the part of the viewer. Lastly we are presented with the solution, the purchase of some drug from one of the companies running the advert. It doesn't really matter what the ailment (or imagined ailment) is, or which company might benefit from the sale, since the purpose of this kind of advertisement is to heighten our awareness of disease in general and create a reaction of fear. The lack of specificity of the advert (in terms of which drug or treatment is being promoted) is more than compensated for by the ability of the advert to get past our "switch off" reflex. With a traditional advertisement, a company might expect to see a certain reward for their investment. With a Video News Release, the reward is likely to be greater since, though they might receive a smaller proportion, it will be a smaller proportion of a much larger pie.

Once this strategy is understood, it's easier to see how the purpose of the Ebola narrative delivered with this picture (and others like it) might be to create, in the eyes of the viewer, an artificially elevated fear of disease. This fear encourages the production, purchase and consumption of more vaccines and other prescription drugs. If it's the end users of the vaccines who are successfully manipulated by this strategy, the result will be an increase in revenue for the drug companies. Even more significant, however, is the case where it's a government which is manipulated. In this case, they may well try to introduce compulsory vaccination programs, and that could result in the drug companies' revenues going through the roof. We'll leave Ebola to rest there, but, before we can finish this chapter, we must return once again to the question of "which **one** to believe", and, in particular to that word "one". We saw earlier how, just by using this word in a sentence, we are coerced into excluding some possibilities from consideration. To put this more formally, what we see here is yet another logical fallacy: this time it's the Fallacy of the Excluded Middle (sometimes called a False Dilemma). In this case, the use of the word "one" has caused us to exclude the possibility that **both** of the opinions might be false. We are faced with an apparent dilemma as to which we should choose, but the dilemma itself is an illusion.

Consider the following example:

> **Edward:** "2,353 professional architects and engineers have signed a petition to say that the three towers destroyed in New York on 9/11 were brought down by controlled demolition."
>
> **Barry:** "There are around 250,000 architects and engineers in America, so the ones that haven't signed the petition must think that the official story is true. That means that the 2,353 signatories must be nuts and so we can conclude that Osama Bin Laden did 9/11."

In Barry's mind, there are only two distinct groups of architects and engineers. As a result, he is forced to place them all into one or other of these two subsets. The process of forcing different ideas like this into one category or box is often known as "conflation". The reality is, of course, that there are many possible groups into which we could divide the architects and engineers. Here are just a few of the possibilities:

- those who think it was controlled demolition
- those who believe the official story

- those who think it was controlled demolition but are too frightened to speak out
- those who have never considered the question
- those who have considered the question, but were unable to reach a conclusion
- those who do not believe the official story and do not believe it was controlled demolition

It is worth noting that Barry's *believer* mind has been careful to orchestrate the conflation in such a way that it reinforces his religious beliefs. By allocating the "controlled demolition" group into the first category and conflating all the others into the second, he has artificially weighted the data in line with his prejudices, regardless of which explanation is "true".

So why is it that we fall prey to this fallacy so often? Could it be that our desire to "know the answer" outweighs our desire to think rationally? *TVism* supplies us with our opinion on every topic where it seeks to control the narrative, and, in many cases, it does this by presenting us with two choices and telling us that one of them is "true". In other cases, the two choices on offer are presented in the form of a debate. When these two choices are both false, the likely intention is to draw our attention away from the real truth by making us focus on the debate. This tactic is known as a "false bone of contention". Whichever tactic is used, it is likely that our repeated exposure to issues presented in the form of two choices is responsible for our tendency to fall into the Fallacy of the Excluded Middle.

The selection of the truth from a set of two possibilities sits well with the Constructivist model of truth, but does not tend to fit with the Correspondence one. The latter is, by definition, the more malleable model, since, at any moment in time, a new hypothesis or some new evidence may come along which may necessitate a change of view. The former, however, is fixed by the narrative that comes from the TV and rarely alters with time, unless the TV dictates a change of canon. Somehow, we have been conditioned to regard our changing of our mind as a form of weakness. We have been fed the notion that, when confronted with someone with whom we don't agree, to ask them a question about their point of view is an indication of defeat.

On a final note, we shouldn't ignore the fact that Barry's comment includes an additional logical fallacy: *Argumentum ad Populum* (appeal to the people). In this fallacy, the speaker wrongly concludes that a proposition is true just because the majority (or a large number) of people believe it. A great example of this is when Galileo came up with the idea that the Earth orbits the Sun. At the time, the popular view was the opposite, and Galileo was persecuted for his heresy. Ultimately however, his theory came to be regarded as true.

In this chapter we have looked at the problems we face when we are presented with two options, especially if we expect to be able to choose one of them, or have been coerced into doing so. We have seen that one way to avoid the trap is to pick one of the options and subject it to a detailed analysis. In many cases, doing this will reveal the elements of the narrative which are false and give us important clues as to the motives of those who seek to manipulate us. In the next chapter we will investigate further by attempting to guess the identity of the manipulators.

# - 24 -

# Who Controls the TV?

*"The CIA owns everyone of any significance in the major media."*

William Colby, ex CIA director

---

Over the course of this book we have made the suggestion that the TV operates as a source for a belief system that, in many ways, closely resembles that of a fundamentalist religion. This begs the question as to who is pulling the strings: a question we hope to answer in this chapter.

Back in the 1950s, the CIA instigated a secret plan called Operation Mockingbird. Initially under the directorship of Cord Meyer and Allen W. Dulles, the outfit was soon handed over to CIA agent Frank Wisner. The goal of the plan was to present the views of the CIA to the American public.

Not only were leading American journalists in various media outlets recruited into a network, but also some magazines (for example "Encounter") were set up as wholly-run CIA ventures to be used as fronts. As time went on, the remit of the operation was broadened to exert influence on foreign media outlets as well as domestic ones, with a view to casting influence over a wider population. In 1966, it became apparent that the scope had been augmented still further when Ramparts Magazine published an article revealing that the National Student Association was funded by the CIA.

In 1979, it became apparent that all these activities were intertwined when the label "Operation Mockingbird" was first brought into the public eye by Deborah Davis in her book, "Katharine the Great"[xliii]. A little investigation into the operation reveals that it was by no means a shoestring affair, having initially been supported by Marshall Plan funds to pay for its activities. CIA agent Gilbert Greenway recalled a meeting with Wisner:

> "We couldn't spend all [the money]. I remember once meeting with Wisner and the comptroller. 'My God', I said, 'how can we spend that?' There were no limits, and nobody had to account for it. It was amazing."[xliv]

As a result of all this funding, Wisner's influence spread far and wide. He is said to have "owned" respected members of, among others, the New York Times, Newsweek and CBS. In addition, he controlled around five hundred "stringers": part-time, freelance contributors who moved from one organisation to the next. According to Davis, each of these assets was run as a separate operation,

> "requiring a code name, a field supervisor and a field office, at an annual cost of tens or hundreds of thousands of dollars."

For an example of this, we need look no further than the media's treatment of the Warren Commission's report on President John F. Kennedy's assassination. This was accepted almost universally, without criticism by the US media. Investigative reporter Fred Cook recalled:

> "I have never seen an official report greeted with such universal praise as that accorded the Warren Commission's findings when they were made public on September 24th 1964. All the major television networks devoted special programs and analyses to the report. The next day the newspapers ran long columns detailing its findings, accompanied by special news analyses and editorials. The verdict was unanimous. The report answered all questions, left no room for doubt. Lee Harvey Oswald, alone and

unaided, had assassinated the president of the United States."[xlv]

Influencing the opinion of the public in this way is one thing, but perhaps of greater importance is the ability to influence the opinion of the government itself, right up to and including the president. In order to appreciate this fully, we must turn our attention once more to the concept we touched on briefly in the previous chapter, the Video News Release. Let's imagine that the CIA has some propaganda it wishes to force on Congress. There are at least two different ways that it could go about doing this. The first would be to write a report and have it published internally to various members of the government. The problem with this, of course, is that they would be unlikely to read the report and, even if they did, the message would probably fall on deaf ears. The second way would be to have the same message broadcast on CNN (or some other mainstream channel) and have it disguised as a news item. Just as we saw before, if the message appears to come from what we assume to be an independent source, and is narrated by someone whom we assume to be an "expert", we are more likely to trust it. Under these circumstances, our tendency to doubt the message (as a consequence of our perception of the bias of the speaker) is reduced. Using this technique, the CIA quickly found that it could influence government policy without the government's being aware of it.

The fact that all this was (and probably still is) going on is not a matter of conjecture, as it was all but admitted to Congress in 1975 at the Pike Committee hearings. Congressman Otis Pike asked DCI William Colby:

> "Do you have any people paid by the CIA who are working for television networks?"

To this, Colby responded:

> "This, I think, gets into the kind of details that I'd like to get into in executive session."

Once the chamber was cleared (which means that we only have anecdotal evidence for this), Colby admitted that, in 1975:

> "The CIA was using 'media cover' for eleven agents."

If the CIA's network of news shills could be used to deliver propaganda, it could also be used to stifle news of events whose publication might be harmful to the CIA. Perhaps the most striking example of this is Operation Gladio, a covert operation conducted in the '60s, '70s and '80s in Europe by the CIA, NATO and various other alphabet organisations. The purpose of this campaign, fully described in Ganser Daniele's "NATO's Secret Armies"[xlvi], was to conduct terrorist bombings on civilian targets in Western Europe and blame them on various "terror cells" both left wing (under the alleged control of the Soviet Union) and right. Perhaps the most notable incident was the bombing of the Bologna Central train station in Italy on August 2nd 1980, which killed 85 people and wounded more than 200. The revelation that the bombing was the result of state-sponsored fake "terrorism" must surely be viewed as an important one, so, if this bombshell of a story (if you will excuse the pun) had hit the press in any major way, it most surely would have been the scoop of the decade. In fact, only a handful of references were ever made in US publications: three in the New York Times and one brief one in the Tampa Bay Times. No US TV station, as far as we are aware, has ever made reference to this example of state-sponsored terror, even though, in 1990, Italian Prime Minister Giulio Andreotti publicly admitted Italy's participation in the proceedings.

Arguably the most damaging PR disaster that the CIA had to cover up was that created by Gary Webb's 1996 exposé in the San Jose Mercury News of the CIA's involvement in cocaine trafficking during the 1984 Iran-Contra scandal[xlvii].

In 1984, the Contras, a group of Nicaraguan anti-government fighters under the command of the CIA's Oliver North, found themselves in need of some substantial funding. Not wanting to see their mercenary army go bust, the CIA stepped up to the challenge to find ways to support them. Perhaps the most well publicised result of their efforts was their supply of arms to Iran, a country which was under US embargo at the time following the overthrow of the Shah of Iran, Mohammad Reza Shah Pahlavi. This was the Shah who had himself been installed in 1953 as a result of the overthrow of the democratically elected government of Mohammad Mosaddegh in a CIA orchestrated coup ("Operation Ajax").

The arms were actually supplied to the Iranians by the Israelis and the Israelis were subsequently resupplied by the CIA who received their payment directly from the Israelis. The funds thus accrued were channelled to the Contras in their fight against the Sandinista government in Nicaragua.

Less widely-known is the second strand of the Contra's funding: the supply of weapons directly to the Contras in exchange for cocaine which was later traced to the manufacture of "crack" which ended up in the hands of residents of California and other US States. This all came to light with the shooting down, in October 1986, of CIA asset Eugene Hafenfus's plane during one of its resupply runs to the Contras. Documents were discovered in the plane which linked him directly to the US government, and one of the dead crew-members, Wallace Sawyer, had been previously identified as a CIA pilot bringing cocaine from Colombia to the US.

Before Webb arrived on the scene, news of these drug trafficking activities had already been published by scholars such as Alfred McCoy and Peter Dale Scott, and had even been revealed in Congress as a result of the 1989 Kerry Committee Report on Iran-Contra. But it was Gary Webb's "Dark Alliance" series of articles in the San Jose Mercury News that really popularised the issue, and so prompted the CIA to begin their counter-strategy. Even though the findings were upheld in a 1999 study by the CIA Inspector General, CIA spokesmen would enigmatically remind reporters that Webb's series "represented no real news, in that similar charges were made in the 1980s and were investigated by the Congress and were found to be without substance."

On December 10th 2004, Webb died from two .38 gunshot wounds to the head. Astonishingly, the coroner declared his death as a "suicide", yet in 2005 Ted Gunderson, a senior FBI special agent, came to the more believable conclusion that Webb had been murdered when he said:

> "He (Webb) resisted the first shot [to the head that exited via the jaw], so he was shot again with the second shot going into the head [brain]."

As reported by Charlene Fassa, Gunderson went on to say that, like many others, he regarded the idea that Webb could have been able to shoot himself twice as "impossible".

We have looked at various aspects of the CIA's control of the TV and of other media, but the CIA's reach is much broader than this restricted view we have so far considered. According to Tom Hayden in the LA Review of Books, the CIA employs "entertainment industry liaison officers" to "plant positive images of itself" in numerous Hollywood productions, recent examples of which include such blockbuster movies as "Argo" and "Zero Dark Thirty". Hayden goes on to say that:

> "So natural has the CIA–entertainment connection become, that few question its legal or moral ramifications. This is a government agency like no other; the truth of its operations is not subject to public examination. When the CIA's hidden persuaders influence a Hollywood movie, it is using a popular medium to spin as favorable an image of itself as possible, or at least, prevent an unfavorable one from taking hold."

The control the CIA exerts over the entertainment industry is complex and far reaching, and a detailed analysis would probably fill a few volumes. Some aspects of it are covered in Tricia Jenkins's "The CIA in Hollywood"[xlviii], in Carl Bernstein's "The CIA and the Media"[xlix] and in Mark Devlin's

"Musical Truth"[1], but this topic is one which is very much still under investigation by many researchers.

More worrying than this, perhaps, is the evidence that suggests the CIA's reach spreads into less traditional spheres of the media such as websites, alternative media outlets, chatrooms and, more recently, social media. There is sufficient evidence to indicate that, for many years, the authorities have been involved is setting up an abundance of websites, the sole purpose of which is to spread disinformation. Two of the more prominent ones, "Metabunk" and "ContrailScience", were confirmed as examples of this by government whistleblower Kristen Meghan on January 18th 2014. The problem that the authorities face is that these websites are, more often than not, quickly exposed by researchers and people like Meghan. Their response has been to broaden their tactics.

Cass Sunstein, the former administrator of the White House Office of Information and Regulatory Affairs and one of Barack Obama's closest confidants, co-wrote a controversial paper[li] in 2008. He proposed that the US government employ teams of covert agents and (supposedly) independent advocates to "cognitively infiltrate" online groups and websites that focused on anti-government "conspiracy theories". He wrote that such activity would increase citizens' faith in government officials and undermine the credibility of so-called "conspiracy theorists".

In 2014, Sunstein gave an interview in which he talked freely on the topic of Cognitive Infiltration and gave us an interesting insight into it. He revealed that there are at least two different methods that have been used to orchestrate this kind of subversion. The first is to send government agents ("shills") into chat rooms or onto websites to pose as researchers. Initially, these people would provide genuine research so as to gain the trust of their followers, but, after a while, they would start to introduce disinformation and even some entirely false topics. The second method is to target genuine researchers who have already made a name for themselves on social or alternative media and "persuade" them to deliver disinformation. Sunstein did not specify the exact nature of this persuasion, so we have no choice but to leave that to our own imagination.

Of course, the infiltration of opposition groups is nothing new. In 1971, the Citizens' Commission to Investigate the FBI burgled an FBI office in the borough of Media (*sic*), Pennsylvania and took several dossiers. These dossiers exposed an FBI program known as COINTELPRO (Counter Intelligence Program) which had been set up by Director J. Edgar Hoover to infiltrate, discredit and disrupt domestic political organizations. President John F. Kennedy had given his personal authorisation for some of their activities, yet, in a twist of Orwellian fate, was also to become the unwitting target of some of them.

Documented targets of COINTELPRO included the US communist and socialist organisations, black nationalists, the Ku Klux Klan, the National States' Rights Party, but, perhaps most disturbingly, those organising protests against the Vietnam War. Into these groups were placed FBI agents whose aim it was to undermine trust and create internal schisms. Once suspicions had been raised as to the presence of the agents, these were turned to the FBI's advantage by the creation of rumours to smear genuine activists. False media stories were created and bogus publications were printed in the name of targeted groups. False information about meetings and events was also promulgated, and the FBI even set up whole pseudo-movement groups run by government agents in order to divide the opposition into a number of camps intent on attacking each other.

Needless to say, the examples we have covered here are just a scratch on the surface of this operation. For the reader who wishes to delve a little deeper, Nelson Blackstock's "COINTELPRO: the FBI's War on Political Freedom"[lii] might be a good place to start.

One excellent example of Cognitive Infiltration is the recent "Flat Earth" phenomenon. This topic, which seemed to appear on the scene out of nowhere, was quickly taken up by many on social media such as Twitter and Facebook, becoming a popular topic of debate virtually overnight. Although most have avoided it, some highly respected researchers have substituted their normal output with stories relating to the subject. We can only wonder as to which of these people are actually shills, which are researchers who have been subjected to "persuasion" and which are simply misguided.

Even if we were to ignore the evidence of the CIA's control, we are still left with a credibility gap between our perception of the TV and its reality. In the UK there seem to be a fair number of news channels, but this number is eclipsed by the apparent number of channels on offer in the US. When we see the same message coming from what we perceive to be many independent sources, both TV and newspapers, we naturally get the impression that the message has been independently investigated and, as a result, represents the truth.

But is this really the case? In fact, this view is just another example of the situation we see so often in which the simplified (*believer*) examination points in one direction, whereas the detailed (*explorer*) one points in another. Take a detailed look at the ownership of all these "independent" US news outlets (see Figure 20) and we find that ninety percent of them are owned by just six large corporations: Comcast, News Corp, Disney, Viacom, Time Warner and CBS. By contrast, in 1983, this same arena saw owners from no less than fifty companies. As time has passed, the never ending impetus of globalisation has taken its toll in the form of mergers and acquisitions, and the companies with the more wealthy backers have consumed the rest of the field.

Sudden changes in the world have tended to attract attention, criticism and even protest; but iterative change as a result of a sequence of slow, relentless and minor events (such as these) tends to take us unawares. There was never any announcement that the world (or the US, at least) had moved from a state with many independent news sources to one where these have been largely replaced by a small cartel. But, then again, there was no single event that reified this change.

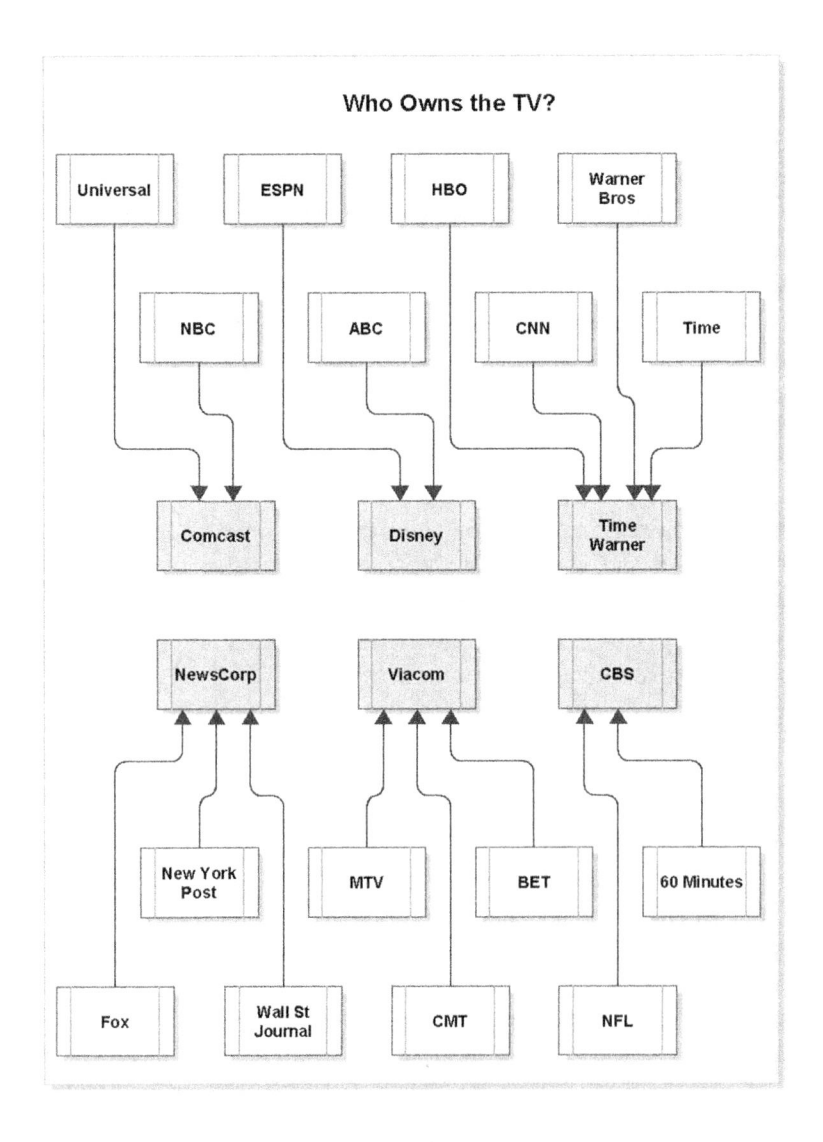

**Figure 20**

With six corporations controlling ninety percent of the media, we might suppose that there would be six different versions of the news fed to us each day. Yet just a little bit of investigation will lead us to evidence that this is far from the truth. The fact is that, in many cases, it would seem that the big six are all singing the same song. The fact that the "news" is centrally scripted has garnished from researchers a wide range of reactions from dismay to hilarity. There are a number of light hearted treatments of this which are easy enough to find on the internet ("Proof that the news is scripted"). Laughing aside though, we must take the investigation one step further and ask ourselves who is writing the script. Given what we have learned in this chapter, it's not hard to come up with a pretty good guess.

Like it or not, the main way most people seem to construct their view of the world around them is by watching and digesting the TV news. For the past sixty or so years, the TV has presented to us a narrative of a world consisting of ideologies such as capitalism, communism, Islamism and fascism; which have allegedly been struggling against each other for supremacy. Perhaps a more accurate view, however, would be that of a world of large corporations and powerful individuals struggling against each other for revenue streams. For instance, if an arms company wants to make more money, what better way is there than to invent the idea (and lodge it into the forefront of our minds) that we are being attacked by some unseen enemy against whom we must defend ourselves? This is nothing more than an example of the concept of "Problem, Reaction, Solution" that we looked at in chapter 23. In this case, the "problem" is the (fictional) external threat, the "reaction" is the public's fear and the "solution" is increased government spending on arms resulting in increased profit for the arms companies and banks.

Whatever your feelings about the big corporations that own the TV and the extent to which they exercise control over its content, most people would argue that the CIA's involvement in the proceedings is taking things a little too far. To build a potent instrument of control like the TV, then to hand it over to an unregulated and unsupervised organisation such as the CIA is undoubtedly a bad idea. Having explored, in this chapter, the nature of the TV's controllers, we will now move on to look at some of the doctrine that is handed to us under their directorship.

# - 25 -

# The Canon of the TV

*"We'll know our disinformation program is complete when everything the American public believes is false."*

William Casey, ex CIA director

---

In chapter 7 we saw how the TV is able to create a worldview that is essentially a religious construct built upon a set of unfounded false narratives. The world thus presented is one which we have been conditioned to **want** to exist, yet is one for which there is a significant weight of evidence to indicate that it does not. Conversely, in chapters 15 and 23, we looked at some analysis methods that can be used to reveal a worldview based on a Correspondence Theory of truth. In this chapter we will look at some real examples of events (in no particular order) whose nature varies dramatically depending on which of these two approaches we happen to adopt. The list we present is by no means an exhaustive one: there are many other examples of events which exhibit a similar degree of divergence when subjected to a process similar to that which we demonstrate here. There is no particular reason, other than that of brevity, why the following set has been selected for inclusion.

For each event presented, there is a brief description, including an outline of the purpose or motive. This is done twice, once from the TV perspective and once from the perspective of Correspondence. Following these, there is a section entitled "Elephant [in the room]" which describes a number of key facts or observations which, when taken together, can be viewed as the "pivot point" between the two narratives.

The purpose of this chapter is not to preach a certain point of view, but to present both perspectives, highlighting the divergence between them, with the aim of encouraging questions. Rather than taking the information presented at face value, our intention is to inspire the reader to use this as a platform for further independent research.

The reader's approach to each of the examples below will depend largely on which part of the mind he or she chooses to engage. For the *explorer* mind, the Elephant might be the starting point for a full analysis similar to that described in chapter 15. For the *believer*, on the other hand, the Elephant is likely to present itself as an opportunity for the application of the *believer* skills discussed in earlier chapters: principally Erasure, *Coincidence* (Miracle) and Religious Reasoning Chain.

# 9/11

## TV Narrative

On September 11th 2001, a terrorist conspiracy was brought to fruition by nineteen men (under the command of one in a cave) in which four airplanes were flown into one field (in Shanksville, Pennsylvania) and three buildings (two in New York and one in Washington DC). In addition, a third building in New York fell down as a result of office fires. The motive for the attack was that the conspirators "hated America because of their freedoms".

## Correspondence Narrative

With a little help from MOSSAD, some rogue elements within the US government conspired to bring about a terrorist event in which three buildings (in New York) were destroyed by some means resembling controlled demolition, while part of a fourth building (The Pentagon) was destroyed by a either a bomb or a missile, or possibly both of these. In addition, a field (in Shanksville) was hit by one or two missiles. The main purpose of the attack was to justify endless war in the Middle

East, thus generating a substantial revenue stream for the arms companies and banks that profited as a result of the false-flag attack.

## Elephant

Buildings cannot collapse on their own, at free fall acceleration, without a constant application of energy during the progress of the "collapse". It should be noted that this assertion concerns only the few seconds of time that comprise the "collapse" itself, as the events which precede these few seconds have no bearing on the assertion. A lack of any such suitable source of energy would imply a violation of the laws of conservation of energy. Even if such energy is supplied, for example by controlled demolition, it has to be applied evenly and precisely across the whole width and depth of the building in order to avoid its tipping to one side or the other as it falls. Such a finesse of timing is not possible as the result of a "natural" process such as a fire, even if such a fire could provide the necessary energy.

When airplanes crash, they leave in their wake substantial amounts of wreckage such as engines, wings, fuselages, seats, tail planes and so on. With the exception of a few small fragments, no such wreckage was observed by eye witnesses, media or amateur video footage at two of the alleged crash sites (Pentagon and Shanksville). Although some plane parts were observed at two of the other sites (Twin Towers, New York), detailed analysis of these parts has cast doubt on whether they actually came from the airplanes that were said to have been involved.

It was reported that a number of passengers made telephone calls to their loved ones from more than one of the planes that were said to have been involved. It has been officially stated that some of these calls were made from cell phones, while others were made from the planes' passenger satellite phones. The FBI has recently admitted that, in 2001, it was not possible to make a cellular telephone call from an aircraft flying at any significant altitude. Since the alleged cell phone calls (which formed the bulk of the "evidence" for the claim that Muslim hijackers carried out the attacks) were reported to have been made from altitudes well above that from which a call would have been possible, we are forced to conclude that the official narrative is a fiction. In addition to this, serious doubt has been cast on the assertion that the passenger satellite phones were functional (or even present) on the planes at the time. If these doubts are valid, they would render this second set of calls a fiction as well.

## References

There have been so many books written on this subject that it is difficult to know where to start. The books which are available tend to focus on one particular aspect of the events, so the starting place depends, to a large degree, on the interest of the reader. For an exploration of the physical process of the collapse of WTC7, the reader should refer to David Ray Griffin's book, "The Mysterious Collapse of World Trade Center 7"[liii]. For an exposé of the dubious telephone calls from the supposed passengers, the best reference source is undoubtedly Elias Davidsson's book, "Hijacking America's Mind on 9/11" (*op cit*). For a broader look at the political tapestry behind the events, David Ray Griffin's "The New Pearl Harbor Revisited"[liv] is recommended. For a detailed investigation of the real perpetrators, the reader might want to take a look at Christopher Bollyn's "Solving 9/11"[lv].

# 7/7

## TV Narrative

On July 7th 2005, a terrorist conspiracy in London, England was brought to fruition by four Muslim men. Three underground trains and one bus were blown up with bombs consisting of "hydrogen-peroxide and pepper" packed into their rucksacks. The motive for the attack was that the conspirators "hated Britain because of their freedoms".

## Correspondence Narrative

Rogue elements within the UK security services, perhaps with the help of MOSSAD, conspired to bring about a "terror event" in which three underground trains and one bus were blown up with pre-planted military grade explosives. The purpose of the attacks was to maintain the public's fear of an unseen external "enemy" in order to justify the government's spending on armaments and continued involvement in the "war on terror".

## Elephant

On the morning of the attacks, Peter Power of Visor Consultants was conducting a terror exercise in London which involved around one thousand participants. Power told us that the exercise was being run for an unnamed client whom he insinuated had US and Israeli connections. On the ITV news on July 7$^{th}$ 2005 at 8:20pm Power said:

> "We chose a scenario, with their assistance, which was based on a terrorist attack because they're very close to a property occupied by Jewish businessmen, they're in the City and there are more American banks in the City than there are in the whole of New York. [It was] a logical thing to do."

The exercise consisted of a number of mock events of which he said that three had almost precisely matched the "real" events in terms of the locations of the underground stations involved, the direction of the trains which were attacked, the details of the scenario of the events and their exact timing. The odds of such an eventuality happening by chance have been estimated to be in excess of a trillion to one, which would make this coincidence, if that's what it was, a miracle of biblical proportions.

On the morning of the attack, it was announced on the ITV news that three of the attackers had been shot in London's Canary Wharf by the police, a few miles from the alleged train bombings. This story, which was dropped after being aired just once, was also reported in various newspapers such as the New Zealand Herald and the South London News. There were also numerous eye witness accounts of the event, all of which add to its veracity. It is hard to comprehend how the "suicide bombers" could have died on the trains they were said to have bombed if they were later to be shot at Canary Wharf. Alternatively, if they were different "terrorists" to the ones who "died" on the trains, then it is hard to understand how this fact was removed from the news, given its potentially high relevance to public safety and interest.

At first, it was announced that the bombs used had been comprised of military grade explosives. A few days after the event, this story was changed, the new narrative asserting that the bombs had been made out of hydrogen-peroxide and pepper. There is no evidence to suggest it is possible to make a bomb from these constituents. Until such evidence becomes available, we are obliged to regard this assertion as a fantasy.

### References
Perhaps the only authoritative work on this is Nick Kollerstrom's book, "Terror on the Tube" (*op cit*).

## Sandy Hook

### TV Narrative
On the morning of December 14th 2012, 20 year old Adam Lanza, a crazy lone gunman, shot and killed twenty-six people at Sandy Hook Elementary school in Newtown, Connecticut along with his mother and, finally, himself. Apart from those who were killed, only two people were said to have been injured in the shootings. No convincing motive for the alleged killing spree has ever been ascertained.

### Correspondence Narrative
Rogue elements of the US government conspired to organise a staged active-shooter drill conducted by crisis actors in which no children (or anyone else) were hurt. The drill was passed

off as reality by the mainstream media. The motive for the stage-show was to promulgate an anti-gun narrative with the ultimate goal of repealing the Second Amendment to the US Constitution.

## Elephant

H. Wayne Carver, the chief medical examiner of the State of Connecticut, confirmed in a press conference on December 15th that the principal weapon used to shoot the victims was a Bushmaster AR-15 XM15-E2S, a high powered rifle weighing 2.82kg when empty. According to Carver, all the victims (including Lanza himself, but not Lanza's mother) were shot inside the school building.

Shortly after this, speculation arose that the Bushmaster was actually found locked in the boot (trunk) of Lanza's mother's car, which was parked outside the school. This was evidenced, so it was claimed, by video footage of police officers removing the weapon from the car and clearing the ammunition from it. In response to this development, ABC, CBS, NBC and many others all changed their story, now reporting that it was not the rifle that had been the murder weapon, but that two pistols, a Glock 20SF and a SIG Sauer P226, had been used instead.

It wasn't long after this that it came to light that the weapon that was removed from the car was actually an Izhmash Saiga-12 shotgun, and not the Bushmaster, as the earlier claims had stated. Looking at the footage of the weapon being cleared, the action used by the police officer is commensurate with that required to empty a shotgun, and does not match the removal of a magazine as would be required to empty the Bushmaster. Confusingly, some reports state that there were actually two weapons recovered from the car, the shotgun and the Bushmaster, but the evidence for this is weak.

Regardless of how many weapons were found in the car, the circulation of the rumour was sufficient to cause some of the mainstream media to modify their narrative of the events. Now two contradictory stories of the events had emerged: Carver's assertion that the weapon was the Bushmaster and the TV channels' assertion that the two pistols were used. At the time of writing, there has still been no clear, definitive statement as to the nature of the murder weapon or weapons. According to Carver, the shooting took place over the duration of around six minutes. In this time, so he maintains, each victim was shot between three and eleven times. If we average this out to seven shots per victim, we get a total of 182 shots, all of which met their mark. If we make the unlikely assumption of a one hundred percent hit rate and exclude from the count the two people who were injured, we end up with a fire rate of one shot every two seconds. Assuming that all these shots were made with the Bushmaster, as Carver suggests, and assuming we accept that ten thirty-round magazines were recovered from the school, as the official report claims, then we can conclude that Lanza would have had to have reloaded the magazine at least six times. If we now factor in some additional time for missed shots, which must surely seem reasonable, it's easy to surmise that the rate of fire would have had to have been as great as one shot every second. It seems unlikely that an individual such as Lanza, who, if the images we have of him are to be trusted, seems to be a somewhat scrawny individual, would have even been capable of carrying the weapons and ammunition he was said to have used.

After the event, no bodies were removed from the premises until after dark, no evidence was presented of any shots or blood and no definitive list of the deceased has ever been forthcoming. In addition, gag orders were placed on the families of the "deceased", and threats were made against those who sought to publish information that contradicted the official narrative.

## References

Readers wishing to investigate this event further might start by reading Jim Fetzer's "Nobody Died at Sandy Hook"[lvi] or Sabrina Phillips's "The Unofficial Story of Adam Lanza"[lvii]. Alternatively, there are many documentaries which have been made on the subject ("We need to talk about Sandy Hook", "The Life of Adam" and "Unraveling Sandy Hook").

# Vietnam War

### TV Narrative

On August 2$^{nd}$ 1964, the USS Maddox, while on patrol in the Gulf of Tonkin, reported that it had been attacked by three North Vietnamese Navy torpedo boats. The Maddox was said to have retaliated, and a sea battle was claimed to have ensued. Four Vietnamese were said to have been killed, but there were no US casualties.

The incident paved the way for Congress to pass the Gulf of Tonkin Resolution, which granted the authority to the US navy to assist any government of south-east Asia which was considered to be threatened by communism. This led to a huge deployment of US forces that quickly resulted in an escalation of the pre-existing hostilities (initiated by the French) and this led to the war against North Vietnam.

The war claimed the lives of around 2.5 million Vietnamese and forty-seven thousand US servicemen, and caused catastrophic devastation to Vietnam's environment and that of its neighbours, not to mention a legacy of birth defects and illnesses that persist to this day.

### Correspondence Narrative

The Gulf of Tonkin incident was a fabrication resulting from a conspiracy between, amongst others, Captain John J. Herrick, the commander of the 7th Fleet's Destroyer Division (who was aboard Maddox in charge of the mission), Commander Herbert Ogier, the captain of the Maddox and George Stephen Morrison, commander of the U.S. naval forces in the area (and father of James Douglas Morrison, of the 1960s rock band "The Doors"). Some say that it was just a coincidence that Jim Morrison, a widely known proponent of peace, was the son of a man whose actions led to one of the most pointless and bloody acts of mass slaughter since WW2, while others say that there was more to this than meets the eye.

The purpose of the war in Vietnam was neither that of retaliation against the Vietnamese, nor an effort to combat the "evil of communism". In all probability, the purpose was to create a revenue stream for the companies who provided the vast supply of arms that were used by the US military during the course of the war and the years that followed.

### Elephant

As a result of a Freedom of Information request on November 30th 2005, the NSA admitted that the Gulf of Tonkin incident had been a fiction.

Up until this point in the book, we have looked at many examples of false-flag attacks, where one side attacks itself, but blames the attack on an enemy in order to justify some military action which had been planned all along. But there are also some variations on this well-worn theme. In some instances, for example the WW2 attack on Pearl Harbor, there is a weight of evidence pointing to the fact that the initial attack is perpetrated by the enemy (in this case the Japanese), but there is also strong evidence of foreknowledge, and even encouragement, on the side which is the target of the attack (in this case the US). In the case of the Gulf of Tonkin incident we see another flavour of the same theme where the false-flag "attack" is actually a hoax.

Robert S. McNamara, US Secretary of Defense at the time, has since admitted that the alleged attack on the USS Maddox didn't happen, thus corroborating the information provided by the NSA.

### References

An account of the incident can be found in Edwin E. Moïse's "Tonkin Gulf and the Escalation of the Vietnam War"[lviii].

# Moon Landings

## TV Narrative

$20bn ($110bn in today's money) was spent by NASA on a program to put some men on the moon.

## Correspondence Narrative

$5bn was spent by NASA on a program to put some men into low Earth orbit. The budget surplus of $15bn was spent on the development of nuclear armaments and other weapons.

## Elephant

The Saturn 5 (Apollo) rocket that allegedly took NASA's astronauts to the moon was said to have contained 3587 thousand litres of propellant (adding together the fuel and the oxygen, to make things simple). A breakdown of this is shown in Figure 21. The mass of the parts of the rocket that were to finally break free of the Earth's gravitational field totalled 61 thousand kilos. These parts comprised the Command Module (CM) and Lunar Excursion Module (LEM). This means that, as a simple rule of thumb, it takes approximately 59 (3587 divide by 61) litres of fuel for every kilo of useful payload.

The Ascent Module (AM), which is the top section of the LEM or, put another way, the portion that was alleged to have taken off from the moon's surface, had a mass (without the fuel) of 2.15 thousand kilos.

So how much fuel would be required to make this take off from the moon and reach orbit? A naïve answer would be 126.9 thousand litres (2.15 times 59). However, the gravity on the moon is one sixth of the gravity on Earth, so we must allow for this by dividing our answer by 6. This leaves us with an estimate of 21.1 thousand litres. So how much fuel was in the AM? According to the facts supplied by NASA, the volume of propellant was 2.3 thousand litres, which is short by factor of around 9. Or, put another way, the AM would have needed about nine times the amount of fuel it carried in order to attain lunar orbit and dock with the CM. Once more, we should remind ourselves that all of this is just an approximation. To perform this calculation accurately would require us to perform some integration, and the maths involved in this is outside the scope of this book. As ever, the reader is encouraged to do their own investigation.

| Stage | L (000s) fuel | L (000s) O$_2$ | Kg (000s) mass |
|---|---|---|---|
| 1 | 770 | 1204 | 2290 |
| 2 | 984 | 303 | 496 |
| 3 | 253 | 73 | 123 |
| Other | | | 61 |
| Total | 2007 | 1580 | 2970 |

Figure 21

Looking at the clip of the take-off, which is easy enough to find on the internet ("Apollo 17 lunar module lift off"), it's quite easy to see that the AM doesn't appear to have any engines or any burn of fuel, the initial small explosion that can be seen at the instant of launch being the result of the charge used to separate the bolts holding it to the Descent Module (the part that is left behind). Some have suggested that the absence of any visible burn is due to the supposed fact that the fuel used was able to burn without any visible flame. This does not explain how, later on when the AM is a little higher, we do see some fuel burn. It also doesn't explain the absence of any visible engine, when the engines are so easy to see on all the other powered components.

While we are looking at the clip, it might be fruitful to ask ourselves some additional questions. Who is taking the footage we see? Who is panning the camera upwards as the AM goes up?

### References
Many books have been written on this subject, some good, some not so much. A good place to start might be Bill Kaysing's "We Never Went to the Moon"[lix]

# Chemtrails

### TV Narrative
"Persistent contrails" are trails of ice crystals which appear behind an aircraft while it is in flight. Contrails can appear under certain atmospheric conditions at altitudes exceeding eight kilometres. While normal contrails can exist for a maximum of just two minutes, the persistent variety can last for as long as four hours. The huge variation in the duration of the persistence of these trails has been suggested to be due to the varying content of water vapour in the air. This water content is said to have a significant impact on the speed at which the sublimation of the ice crystals occurs.

### Correspondence Narrative
The word "chemtrail" is used to describe the trails of metal oxide (aluminium, strontium and barium) nanoparticle aerosol which are thought to be deliberately sprayed by passenger jets and dedicated tanker aircraft. In this form, these oxides are hygroscopic, which is to say that they attract moisture from the surrounding air. This accumulation of water molecules causes them to spread into thick bands and, ultimately, the thin, silvery sheets which have been observed to cover the sky under certain conditions.

In contrast with this, contrails are (still) trails of ice crystals which sublime very quickly, regardless of the prevailing atmospheric conditions.

Although the presence of chemtrails is clearly evidenced, the motive for spraying them is not known with any degree of certainty. However, a number of hypotheses have been posited. Some people maintain that the atmospheric haze resulting from the metal oxides is an attempt to increase the Earth's albedo so as to (supposedly) combat the effects of global warming. Others claim that it is an attempt to decrease rainfall which would support the market for the drought and aluminium resistant GM crops which are being pushed by Monsanto. Still others surmise that the aluminium in the air is a deliberate attempt to increase the rate of Alzheimer's disease or to decrease the world's population by decreasing the average lifespan.

## Elephant

In a normal contrail, ice crystals form when water droplets, a by-product of the combustion of the aviation fuel, are cooled by the air into which they are injected. If conditions are right, precipitation of ice occurs when the mixture of water and air finds itself in a localised region that is below the Dew Point. After a short while, the ice crystals are dispersed due to Brownian motion and soon, within a few seconds or up to two minutes, encounter new air that's above the Dew Point, at which point the ice dissolves into the air. It is important to note that, if the air were already below the Dew Point before the injection of the additional water, then a (natural) cloud would already be present. Therefore any contrail created outside of a natural cloud must be surrounded by air above the Dew Point and thus should dissipate after no more than a few minutes.

In a chemtrail on the other hand, the metal oxide particles are not soluble in air, and so do not dissolve. They persist, sometimes for many hours, and spread until the layer eventually becomes too thin to be detectable to the human eye.

Chemtrails are just one example of a broad range of activity known as geoengineering: the deliberate anthropogenic modification of the weather or climate. Geoengineering by means of aerosols released into the upper atmosphere has been proposed by many climate scientists as a way to reflect more of the sun's light away from the Earth. It has been stated that stratospheric aerosols seem to offer the most effective course of action to achieve this and could be deployed soon, despite presenting an unknown risk to the environment and to human health.

In the UK, the recently formulated Scientific Advisory Committee on Nutrition guidelines suggest that everyone should be taking ten micrograms of vitamin D per day in order to counteract the effects of reduced sunlight. The guidelines maintain that this supplementation is necessary because of the low levels of sunlight offered by the UK's climate. However, they fail to explain why this advice was not offered when the process of human synthesis of vitamin D from sunlight was first discovered, or why the sun's light might have diminished prior to the issuance of the new advice.

Starting around 1996 (in the US) or 1998 (in Europe), white trails, which have always appeared in the wake of jet planes under the right conditions, were observed by many to change their behaviour. Whereas before this point in time, the trails had always disappeared within one or two minutes; after this point, they have sometimes been observed to persist for four or more hours. Although the non-persistent variety has always been well understood, no alternative hypothesis has been offered for the sudden appearance of the persistent variety.

### References

A few words of caution are necessary here. The reader is encouraged to read a wide variety of sources and be wary of disinformation pertaining to contrails. A description of the science behind chemtrails can be found in William Thomas's "Chemtrails Confirmed"[lx].

# Cold War

### TV Narrative

In 1957, following the USSR's launch of their Sputnik satellite, the term "missile gap" was first used to describe the extent to which the US was lagging behind the USSR in terms of weaponry. From that time until the late 1980s, the Soviet Union was seen as an evil empire, armed to the teeth, who would not hesitate to invade the West if they saw an opportunity to do so. From this beginning there followed the Cold War and its accompanying arms race that dominated geopolitics for the following three decades.

## Correspondence Narrative

At the time, around 22,000 US companies were kept in business by the arms trade. New weapons and new weapons' technology resulted in huge profits within the industry. In order to generate a revenue stream to support this, a suitable source of funds was required. Since fear was (and still is) the best way to convince people to do what you want them to, the myth of the missile gap was created in order to make a gullible US public willing to part with their tax dollars.

## Elephant

Many prominent members of the armed forces have pointed out that the whole idea of a missile gap was ridiculous. For instance, Dr. Herbert York, one of the early pioneers of missile research in the US, admitted in his book "Race to Oblivion"[lxi] that the launch of Sputnik was seized upon by the US arms industry to act as a catalyst for an arms race. In fact the US was, and always has been, three to five years ahead of the USSR in missile technology, as admitted by Admiral Gene La Rocque in an interview with the Australian journalist, John Pilger.

## References

The interview with La Rocque and many others can be seen in the documentary "The Truth Game" by John Pilger[lxii].

# USS Liberty

## TV Narrative

During the Israeli Six Day War, on June 8$^{th}$ 1967, thirty-four US naval servicemen were killed and one hundred and seventy-four injured when their vessel, the technical research ship USS Liberty, was attacked by Israeli forces. At the time, the ship was in international waters just north of the Sinai Peninsula. The first phase of the attack came from three Mirage fighter aircraft using 30mm cannon and air to surface missiles backed up by several Mystere fighters using canisters of napalm. The second phase came from three motor torpedo boats. The attack was later explained away as a mistake.

## Correspondence Narrative

The event was a classic example of a false-flag attack in which Israel attacked the US ship in an attempt to blame Egypt. By this subterfuge, they hoped to drag the US into the Six Day War. Since it became widely known pretty quickly that Israel was the real perpetrator, the story that the attack had been an "accident" was quickly constructed.

## Elephant

Before the attack, the planes came close enough to the ship for the crew members to be able to see the pilots with binoculars. The ship was clearly marked with the US flag, but the planes were seen to have had all their identifying markings removed. The removal of the markings suggests that the attack and the intention to deceive may have been premeditated.

Fifteen years after the attack, an (unnamed) senior Israeli pilot came forward and was interviewed extensively by (former) Congressman Paul McCloskey. The pilot said that he recognized the Liberty immediately as a US ship, and informed his headquarters of this fact. He said he was given the order to ignore the US flag and attack the ship anyway. When he refused to do this and, instead, returned to base, he was immediately arrested. The radio transmissions involved in this exchange were picked up, and so corroborated, by many military units around the Mediterranean.

The fact that the US made no attempt to defend the Liberty and did not take any retaliatory action against Israel indicates complicity on the side of the US.

### References
A detailed examination of the events and the surrounding political context can be found in Alan Hart's "Zionism, the Real Enemy of the Jews"[lxiii].

# Gladio

### TV Narrative
On August 2nd 1980, a bomb went off in the waiting room of the main railway station in Bologna, Italy. The blast killed eighty-five people and wounded more than two hundred more. Shortly afterwards, the attack was blamed on a neo-fascist terrorist organization called Nuclei Armati Rivoluzionari, although they denied any involvement.

This was just one example of a string of broad ranging terrorist incidents that took place in Italy and all across Europe throughout the 1970s, 80s and 90s. Some of these incidents were blamed on left wing terrorist cells who, so it was said, owed their allegiance to the Soviet Union, but, as can be seen in this particular example, this was not always the case.

Perhaps the most high profile incident was the kidnap and murder of the then Italian Prime Minister, Aldo Moro, by the Red Brigades in 1978. Moro was on his way to parliament to vote on inaugurating a new government backed by the Italian Communist Party (PCI). He was held for 55 days before his eventual murder, ostensibly for his plan to bring the PCI into the government.

## Correspondence Narrative

In the early 1950s, the CIA set up a number of groups of "stay-behind" armies in Western Europe, so that, in the event of a Soviet invasion, they would be able to gather intelligence and form resistance movements. By the early 1970s, support for the PCI was growing, so the network was repurposed to collude with, fund and direct terrorist organizations throughout Europe to instigate what has been termed a "strategy of tension". Such a strategy is one in which one or more false-flag attacks are orchestrated and blamed on an external enemy. The result is the creation of fear in the population, making them less likely to rebel against their government and more likely to accept the removal of their civil liberties. This encroachment on freedom enhances a government's ability to control its people.

The activities of these groups are extensive, and cover a long period of time. In Turkey in 1960, the stay-behind army staged a coup d'état and killed Prime Minister Adnan Menderes. In 1967, the Greek stay-behind army staged a coup and imposed a military dictatorship. In 1971, once again in Turkey, the stay-behind army engaged in domestic terror and killed hundreds. In 1977 in Spain, the stay-behind army carried out a massacre in Madrid. In 1980 in Turkey, the head of the stay-behind army staged a coup and took power. In 1985 in Belgium, the stay-behind army attacked and shot shoppers randomly in supermarkets, killing 28. In Switzerland in 1990, the former head of the Swiss stay-behind army wrote to the US Defense Department to say that he would reveal "the whole truth". He was found the next day, stabbed to death with his own bayonet.

## Elephant

In 1990, Italian and Belgian investigators started researching the links between the stay-behind armies and instances of terrorism in Western Europe during the post-war period. In the same year, the Italian Prime Minister confirmed that Italy's stay-behind army, given the name "Gladio" (the Italian word for "sword"), had been created in 1958 following the approval of the Italian government.

In 2000, the Italian government released a 300 page report on the Gladio operations in Italy which revealed its close connections with the CIA. In examining why those who committed the bombings in Italy were rarely caught, the report said that

> "those massacres, those bombs, those military actions had been organised or promoted or supported by men inside Italian state institutions and, as has been discovered, by men linked to the structures of United States intelligence."

## References

This fascinating and very complex subject has been the subject of many books and documentaries. Ganser Daniele's book, "NATO's Secret Armies"[lxiv], is one example of these.

# ISIS

## TV Narrative

ISIS is a group of Islamic extremists whose aim is to set up a brutal Islamic "Caliphate" over much of the Middle East. Motivated by their hatred of Western civilization, because of our "freedoms", they would not hesitate to commit acts of violence wherever they can.

## Correspondence Narrative

ISIS is a group of proxy-terrorists set up and controlled by the US and Israeli security services. Mercenaries are paid by the CIA and their fellow alphabet agencies to fight on both sides of the manufactured conflicts within Iraq, Syria and other countries in the Middle East. The label "ISIS" is applied to whichever group the CIA or the media wants to demonize at any particular point in time. The various groups within Syria are described as "moderate rebels" when they need supplies of arms and money from the West, but as "ISIS" when it becomes more fruitful to supply their opponents. The perpetual war thus created acts both as a source of revenue for the arms companies that supply the weapons and as an aid to Israel by creating artificial conflict between its enemies.

## Elephant

According to Hakem al-Zameli, the head of the Iraqi Parliament's National Security and Defence Committee, on February 23$^{rd}$ 2015, two British planes were shot down by the Iraqi government while delivering supplies to ISIS fighters. In addition, he revealed that the government in Baghdad is receiving daily reports from people and security forces in Al-Anbar province concerning numerous flights by the US-led coalition planes that airdrop weapons and supplies for ISIS.

Much coverage has been given by the mainstream media to the ISIS beheadings that have been alleged to have taken place in Syria and Iraq. However, starting with the alleged beheading of James Foley, none of the videos that have appeared has actually shown a beheading. At the instant when this would be expected to occur, we see a fade-to-black sequence followed by a shot of what looks like a prosthetic "head" placed near a "body". In addition, detailed frame-by-frame analysis of these videos has shown that they are, in all likelihood, filmed using green-screen technology and advanced production techniques, neither of which is known to be typical of Islamic militants. On August 25$^{th}$ 2014, it was revealed in the Telegraph that top British forensic experts had concluded that the James Foley video was likely to have been staged using "camera trickery and slick post-production techniques".

Many photos from the region that are said to depict ISIS show fleets of Toyota trucks containing masked men clad in black. The fact that the trucks are supplied to ISIS by the US State Department has been freely admitted on a number of occasions. In addition to this, ISIS's well equipped armouries have been found to be stocked with US and Israeli made weapons.

On October 19th 2014, Serena Shim, Press TV's correspondent in Turkey, was killed in a car crash in suspicious circumstances. The identity of the driver of the truck which hit her car is unknown, and he (or she) has not been apprehended. Shim had been working on a report which included the documentation of allegations of collusion between Turkish Intelligence (MIT) and militant extremists to smuggle fighters and weapons into Syria. She had been accused of spying by the MIT, and had received death threats from them. Typically, whenever a journalist has died while on the job, this has been met with tributes of sympathy from the world's press. In stark contrast with this, the death of Shim was universally ignored by Western media.

More recently, on January 27th 2016, prosecutors asked an Istanbul court to issue life sentences to two of Turkey's most prominent journalists: Cumhuriyet newspaper's editor-in-chief Can Dundar and Ankara Bureau chief Erdem Gul. Their "crime" was to report that President Recep Tayyip Erdogan's government had tried to ship arms to insurgents in Syria.

## References

Although there are no books written on this subject, to the best of our knowledge; there have been some excellent documentary style investigations which are easy enough to find on the internet ("corbettreport who is really behind ISIS").

# JFK

## TV Narrative

John F. Kennedy was assassinated at 12:30 CST on November 22nd 1963, in Dealey Plaza, Dallas, Texas. He was shot by Lee Harvey Oswald while he and his wife were travelling with Texas Governor, John Connally, and Connally's wife in a presidential motorcade. Oswald, a twenty-four year old ex-marine, was arrested in a movie theatre in a Dallas residential district one hour and fourteen minutes after Kennedy was shot. He was charged with murder the next day. The conclusion of a ten month investigation by the Warren Commission was that Oswald had acted alone and that Jack Ruby also acted alone when he killed Oswald shortly before he could stand trial. Oswald's motive is unclear. It was suggested that he may have done it because of his alleged ties to Soviet Russia, but this does not sit well with the fact that Kennedy was arguably the most left-leaning president the US had ever seen.

## Correspondence Narrative

A group of as many as eighteen gunmen were located at various vantage points around Dealey Plaza into which the motorcade was redirected in an unplanned and unauthorised detour. Just before the attack from multiple shooters, Kennedy's bodyguards, who would normally be standing on the running boards of the president's vehicle, were ordered to stand down and move away from their positions. Shots were fired at the car while it was moving, but they all missed and it was only when the car was brought to a halt that the fatal shots were fired. After this, the vehicle resumed its progress.

It is well documented that there was considerable tension between Kennedy and many other people within the government. In particular, many senior members of the CIA were disgruntled with certain aspects of Kennedy's approach to his presidency. There were many factors which contributed to this, including his stance on Vietnam and his rejection of the CIA's proposed false-flag attack on Cuba, Operation Northwood. But perhaps the most pertinent reasons were his stated intention to disband the CIA and to abolish the US dollar, replacing it with a money supply created by the government rather than the privately owned Federal Reserve. Lyndon B. Johnson, Kennedy's vice president, also had much to gain from the assassination in that he was sworn in as president immediately after Kennedy's death.

## Elephant

According to the official narrative, a total of three shots were fired by Oswald. One of them injured a bystander, James Tague, while a second caused Kennedy's fatal head wound. This indicates that the third shot must have caused all the remaining injuries that occurred during the event. More specifically, this one bullet must have entered Kennedy's back, exited through his throat, then entered Connally's back and exited his chest before passing through his right wrist and coming to rest in his left thigh. This implausible sequence of events is what has given rise to the name that this bullet has attracted in popular culture: "The Magic Bullet."

Lee Harvey Oswald was allegedly standing at a window on the sixth floor of the Texas Book Depository. Although it is just possible to see the target from this position, it would have been an extremely difficult and unlikely shot, especially with the inaccurate 6.5 mm Carcano Model 91/38 Carbine (with a defective sight) that was alleged to have been used.

One of the most iconic portrayals of the events of the day, the Zapruder film, has been the subject of much analysis. It has been demonstrated beyond all doubt that this film has been tampered with. There are frames missing from around the moment of impact of the bullet with Kennedy's head, and the frames that remain have been subjected to manipulation.

On February 6th 1985, a court in Miami concluded that the CIA had been behind the plot, as described in some detail in chapter 11.

## References

Just as with 9/11, there have been so many books written on this subject that it is hard to know where to start. Some of these books have been written with the deliberate intent to deceive, so the reader should be advised to tread carefully. One suggestion is Colonel John Hughes-Wilson's "JFK - An American Coup d'Etat"[lxv].

# Oklahoma Bombing

## TV Narrative

On April 19th 1995, the Alfred Murrah Federal Building in Oklahoma City was partially destroyed in a bomb attack. At 8:57am, Timothy McVeigh parked a Ryder van containing 2,200 kg of ammonium nitrate fertilizer, nitromethane, and diesel fuel mixture outside the building. The bomb went off at 9:02am, killing one hundred and sixty-eight people and injuring hundreds of others. It was alleged that McVeigh's motive was an attempt to get revenge on the government for their part in the Waco siege of April 1993.

## Correspondence Narrative

In the days leading up to the event, an unknown group of people allied to the FBI, Bureau of Alcohol Tobacco and Firearms (ATF) and the government planted one or more explosive devices within the basement of the building. At 9:02am these were detonated simultaneously, along with the small bomb in the back of the Ryder van, parked by the patsy McVeigh and his accomplice. The FBI's motive for the attack was to instigate a "strategy of tension" as described in the Gladio entry above.

## Elephant

More than twenty eye witnesses reported having seen an accomplice leave the van along with McVeigh.

Many news reports on the day carried the story that multiple bombs had been discovered in the building and that these were being dealt with by the bomb squad. A few days later, all these stories had disappeared from the news.

Many government employees who had offices in the building did not turn up to work that day because they had been forewarned of the attack.

A bomb causes damage by pushing very hard on the objects around it. If it is in physical contact with solid objects at the moment of detonation, such objects will be subjected to large forces and so are likely to be destroyed. What is much less effective is when a bomb just pushes against air. In this case, the air acts a bit like a sponge in that it absorbs the force of the explosion. The force that remains to be exerted on the surrounding objects is thus dramatically reduced. In this case, the force from the explosion would have had to travel through a large volume of air before reaching the building. In such a scenario, superficial damage, such as the smashing of a few windows, would be expected, but certainly not the devastation that was actually observed.

## References

Although there have been some books written on this subject, for instance David Hoffman's "The Oklahoma City Bombing and the Politics of Terror"[lxvi], perhaps the most in-depth information can be found in some of the online documentaries that have been made ("corbettreport The Secret Life of Timothy McVeigh").

# Ottawa Parliament Shooting

## TV Narrative

On the morning of October 22$^{nd}$ 2014, at Parliament Hill in Ottawa, Michael Zehaf-Bibeau allegedly shot Corporal Nathan Cirillo, a soldier on duty at the Canadian National War Memorial, before driving to the parliament building. He eluded the armed guards protecting the building and got as far as the Hall of Honour in the centre block, where the adjacent rooms were filled with government and opposition MPs holding discussions on new efforts to crack down on home-grown terrorism. Here, the gunman engaged in a shootout with security staff during the course of which he was shot thirty-one times by six officers. He died at the scene.

Prior to the event, the lone gunman had recorded a video to set down his motives for the attack, these being focused on Canada's foreign policy and Zehaf-Bibeau's religious beliefs.

## Correspondence Narrative

Although it is possible that Cirillo was shot by Zehaf-Bibeau, it is unreasonable to imagine that the unfolding events could have occurred without some form of collusion on the part of the security services. Parliament Hill is known to have a relatively large armed presence covering the whole area and, specifically, the entranceway and doors. The team is comprised of Canada's national police force (the Royal Canadian Mounted Police), the local municipal police (the Ottawa Police Services) and two special federal forces (the House of Commons Security Services and Senate Security).

The fact that a hardening of Canada's foreign policy towards the alleged "ISIS" followed so quickly after the shooting, even though there were no demonstrable links between the shooter and "ISIS", leaves one to suspect that Zehaf-Bibeau was a patsy. It is likely that the events were orchestrated to create the necessary fear in the public that would persuade them to support war in Iraq. The synchronised nature of the events with parliament's debate on terrorism suggests that the operation may also have been intended to influence the MPs by means of the same mechanism.

## Elephant

Even before the events of the day unfolded, reporters, TV crew and many members of the security services were already on the scene at the parliament building. In addition to this, we find that, as is all too common with staged events like this, government exercises were taking place both on the day of the event and on the days leading up to it. From the 20th to the 29th of October, the "execution phase" of a joint Canada and US military-intelligence exercise named Determined Dragon 14 ("Ex DD 14") was in progress. This was corroborated when, in an early CNN report following the shooting, we were told that police and military were running a multi-agency drill nearby at the same time. Freelance journalist Peter Henderson (formerly of Reuters and NPR) was at the scene:

"The soldier appeared to have been shot in the back. Other soldiers who were nearby doing drills at the time ran to help."

The presence of the drills and of the TV reporters strongly suggests that there was foreknowledge of the events on the part of a cohort of people in authority.

Neither the video footage nor the photographic evidence taken in the minutes after Cirillo's alleged shooting suggests that the soldier was shot. No sign of blood is visible either at the scene or on the victim. More specifically, the footage of alleged CPR being performed on the soldier can readily be confirmed to be simulated rather than an instance of genuine CPR.

Earlier in June that year, Justin Bourque had shot and killed three Royal Canadian Mounted Police officers in Moncton, New Brunswick. At the time, the Canadian Prime Minister, Stephen Harper, made a minimal statement and made little or no reference to terrorism. Yet Bourque's actions and statements bore all the hallmarks of an ultra-right wing anti-state worldview reminiscent of that of the Norwegian, Anders Breivik. After the Ottawa events, the reaction was very different. Harper and the rest of the world were quick to label the events as terrorism and place the blame firmly on "ISIS" well before any investigation had been carried out to ascertain whether or not this had been the case. The first sorties of Canadian F-18s took place just a few hours after the acts of this so-called "home-grown" and "self-radicalized" supporter of "Islamic jihad". The difference between the two reactions suggests that the events had been orchestrated to fit a script and to justify an agenda.

At the time of the shootings, Zehaf-Bibeau, a drug addict with mental health issues and previous convictions, was already known to the Canadian government and was legally prohibited from possessing or acquiring firearms. It remains a mystery as to how he obtained the weapon.

## References

There have been no books written on this subject and, in addition, no quality documentaries have been made. For this reason, the reader is invited to do his or her own research.

# Virginia Shooting

## TV Narrative

On August 26th 2015, while conducting a live interview in Roanoke, Virginia, two journalists from TV channel WDBJ7 were shot and killed. Alison Parker and Adam Ward both died as a result of gunshot wounds to the head and body. A third victim of the shooting, Vicki Gardner, survived after being shot in the back by the gunman. Vester Flanagan, former WDBJ7 employee and alleged shooter, died later the same day from self-inflicted gunshot wounds after a five hour manhunt which culminated in a car chase with police officers. He was certified dead at 1:26pm at Inova Fairfax Hospital.

A couple of hours after the shooting, Flanagan uploaded a fifty-six second video of the incident, shot from a first-person perspective apparently with the camera on his own phone. The video was uploaded to both his Twitter and Facebook accounts before they were suspended.

It is alleged that Flanagan was a disgruntled employee who had claimed staff at the station had mistreated him during his time there. He had accused one of the victims of making racist comments, and alleged that the other victim had complained to Human Resources. Conjecture has it that these events constituted Flanagan's motive for his actions.

## Correspondence Narrative

Evidence from the video footage and the eyewitness interviews correlates best with the hypothesis that this event was a hoax. A detailed analysis of the evidence and the narrative provided by the mainstream media brings to light many anomalies and inconsistencies which lead one to conclude that the official story cannot be true. It appears more likely that the hoax "shooting" was part of an ongoing campaign in the US to create an atmosphere of tension and fear of crazy armed gunmen. Once the public's fear has grown to a sufficient level, they will more readily accept new laws to take away their rights under the Second Amendment to the Constitution: the right of the people to keep and bear arms. The ultimate confiscation of all arms from the public would enable the introduction of a draconian police state, just as it has in many other countries before it.

## Elephant

In the video that was posted, Alison Parker was seen to be shot at several times as she ran away, yet there was no sign of bullet impact or blood on her as she ran. While she is moving away from the camera, her velocity is not observed to diminish in magnitude or change in direction. After a few seconds, she reaches a distance whereby a direct hit with a shot from a handgun would seem unlikely, before disappearing out of frame.

Before being "shot", Alison Parker can be seen in the footage to glance over at the gunman while he points the gun at her. She then turns back to Gardner, the interviewee, without reacting. This is all some moments before the shooting starts. Gardner, who also ignored the gunman's approach, later explained this by saying she had been blinded by the television lights. However, the video footage clearly shows that the only lights present, those of the TV camera, were being shone away from her throughout the majority of the period of time corresponding to the shooter's approach.

Some striking inconsistencies are apparent in the interviews Gardner gave in the days after the "attack". For instance, in an interview with Greta van Susteren, shown on the Fox "news" show "On The Record", she clearly states that the gunman approached from behind, yet we can see in Flanagan's video that she was facing the shooter with her back against the railings. She also says that, after the victims had been shot, they both fell down next to her, yet the video footage clearly shows Parker sprinting off down the walkway.

Gardner also stated that two armed police officers arrived five minutes after the shooting and asked her if she was able to get up. She said that she got up and walked to a truck where she waited until the ambulance arrived. She then walked to the ambulance and was taken to hospital. This narrative is entirely inconsistent with what we would expect in the case of somebody who had genuinely been shot in the back. In such instances, the emergency services would need to stabilize the patient before carefully placing them on a stretcher and taking them to hospital. Stabilization is particularly important in trauma cases involving suspected spinal injuries, due to the damage that can otherwise result. The patient is first fitted with a cervical collar (neck brace) before requiring the assistance of as many as five medical staff to lift them onto a long spine board or vacuum mattress. Failure to do this correctly can cause permanent paralysis or even death.

One day after the shooting, Alison Parker's father and boyfriend were interviewed a number of times. Neither showed any noticeable signs of shock, sadness or loss, and even appeared to laugh and smile during the interviews, with her father talking about gun control. This behaviour seems to be far removed from that which most would expect from individuals who have recently suffered the loss of a close family member or loved one.

## References

At the time of writing, this event is too recent for any books to have been released which describe it. The footage apparently taken by the alleged shooter has also been censored many times. At the time of writing, the only online copy to be found is one in which peripheral detail has been deliberately removed ("Liveleak shooter's perspective Virginia hoax"). However, numerous interviews with the surviving "victim" and with family members of those who were allegedly murdered are still available to view online.

# San Bernardino Shooting

## TV Narrative

On December 2$^{nd}$ 2015, Syed Rizwan Farook and his wife, Tashfeen Malik, killed fourteen people and injured twenty-two in a terrorist attack in San Bernardino, California. The attack, whose target was a training event of eighty delegates in a rented banquet room in the Department of Public Health, consisted of a mass shooting and an attempted bombing. Farook, who was a Health Department employee, was said to have become "radicalised" by ISIS, although no details were provided of this process. After the shooting, the couple fled in a rented SUV and, four hours later, the police pursued their vehicle and killed them in a shootout.

## Correspondence Narrative

The available evidence is consistent with the hypothesis that the alleged suspects were unwitting patsies who were used to promote the public's fear of the threat of the ISIS bogeyman. The wider agenda, in all probability, is the extension of the War on Terror meme and the creation of an environment in which sweeping 'national security' changes can be passed with no public objection. Shortly after the event, Donald Trump chose to feed the blind hysteria by proposing a ban on all Muslims entering the US.

## Elephant

Numerous eye witnesses identified the shooters as three tall white men carrying assault rifles and dressed in black military attire including body armour and combat trousers. An hour after the shooting, Fox News reported that the police were looking for three white males dressed in military gear. The uniforms described by the witnesses match those worn by the US based mercenary outfit, Craft International, formerly known as Blackwater.

Malik, who was nursing a newly born child at the time, was of short stature and weighed in at a mere 90 pounds. Not one single eye witness report matches her description.

Two days after the attack, the media swarmed into the suspects' apartment and were shown on TV going through the couple's personal possessions with no restrictions or control over their actions. Needless to say, this is not normal protocol for a criminal investigation where the primary concern is to guard a crime scene against any disturbance which could pervert the course of justice.

As is the case with the majority of incidents like this, Malik was already known to the security services. The FBI admitted to the public that they were aware that the "terror couple" had been "radicalised" for quite some time. Malik was born in Pakistan, and her background suggests a (Pakistani) ISI/CIA connection, rather than an ISIS one.

Approximately a year prior to the event, employees of San Bernardino County's Environmental Health Services division had participated in a multi-agency "active shooter" drill in the exact same room where the incident was alleged to have taken place. If this were just a coincidence, then it was compounded by the fact that, at the time of the incident, there was already a San Bernardino Police Department SWAT drill going on nearby. This was confirmed by Lieutenant Richard Lawhead when he said in an in interview with KTLA that his men were "already suited up and ready to go".

### References

As with the Virginia shooting, at the time of writing, this event is too recent for any books to have been written about it. In this instance, the reader is encouraged to perform their own investigation.

## War on Drugs

### TV Narrative

Evil drug lords throughout the world seek to corrupt the public (and make a fast buck) by supplying them with addictive and harmful recreational drugs. The problem is, perhaps, most severe in the US, where the benevolent and protective government seeks to reduce it or eliminate it altogether. Their strategy for doing this is to target the producers of the drugs, seek out the drug lords who traffic them and reduce the demand by educating the public. In the 1960s, it was believed that at least half of all the crime in the US was in some way drug related. President Lyndon B. Johnson decided to introduce an anti-drug campaign in 1968, focusing his efforts on illegal drug use. Estimates have indicated that the US spends $51 billion *per annum* on anti-drug initiatives. Despite all this, there is little evidence to suggest that their efforts have advanced their goals.

## Correspondence Narrative

The term "War on Drugs" was popularized by the media shortly after a press conference given on June 18th 1971 by President Richard Nixon, the day after he declared drug abuse to be "public enemy number one". Estimates of the value of the global drugs trade range from around $400bn to $700bn per year. By comparison, the global arms trade is estimated to be valued somewhere between $100bn and $200bn per year. Concrete evidence exists to show that a good proportion of the drugs trade is orchestrated and controlled by the CIA; the illicit funds accrued being used, in all probability, to finance their numerous clandestine operations around the world.

## Elephant

The relationship between the Iran-Contra scandal and the CIA's drug running activities has been discussed at length in chapter 24.

Most of the opium consumed outside of the US comes from Afghanistan. In 2000, somewhere between 3,600 and 4,600 tonnes of opium was produced there. In 2001, the Taliban took control of the opium production and all but eradicated it, with the result that production fell to around 185 tonnes. One of the stated goals of the US led occupation was to stop the production of the drug in order to remove its debilitating and harmful effects on its Western consumers. Based on this, it may come as a surprise to learn that, after the West had taken control of the country in 2002, production had nearly returned to its pre-Taliban level, with 3,400 tonnes being shipped.

## References

If the reader is interested in the Iran-Contra drug running, they should refer to Gary Webb's "Dark Alliance" (*op cit*). For a broader investigation of the topic, the best source of information is undoubtedly Michael Ruppert's "Crossing the Rubicon"[lxvii].

# War on Terror

## TV Narrative

The term "War on Terror" referring to the international military campaign that started after the September 11th 2001 attacks, was first used by President George W. Bush on September 20th 2001.

Islamic militants throughout the world seek to attack America and its Western allies because they "hate us for our freedoms". Because they are crazy and have no regard for their own lives, they will stop at nothing to find ways to kill us. It is America's duty, in its role as the world's policeman, to identify parts of the world that "support" the terrorists and to drop bombs on them.

## Correspondence Narrative

The phrase "War on Terror" is an instrument of propaganda used as a bogus cover for the US's global military campaign. The real purpose of this campaign is a wider set of strategic geopolitical objectives.

In order for the arms industry to exist, it needs a plethora of international buyers to purchase its weapons and a large source of funding to pay for the sales. The most effective way to manufacture both of these is through the creation of fear by means of a "strategy of tension". If foreign governments fear an unseen bogeyman, they will continue to purchase and use armaments to "defend" themselves against this mysterious enemy. If the public fears a bogeyman in their midst, they will willingly surrender their tax dollars in exchange for apparent safety.

Up until the late 1980s, the bogeyman was Russia, but, when they stopped playing ball, a new enemy was needed and needed quickly. The spectre of international Islamic terrorism was fittingly invented in order to fill the gap that had appeared as a result of the Russians' attempt to upset the applecart.

A more accurate name for the "War on Terror" might be the "War of Terror".

## Elephant

War which is directed at a civilian population, by its very nature, is an act of terror. Any attempt to conduct a "war on terror" must, by definition, perpetuate and augment the very thing it is designed to oppose. The whole idea that a "war on terror" can ever exist is thus an oxymoron.

There is no evidence to suggest that any of the wars which have been waged against alleged terrorists have ever been successful. In reality, the very opposite would appear to be the case.

Evidence exists that plans for military action against Afghanistan and Iraq were in hand well before 9/11. In September 2000, the Project for the New American Century (PNAC) released a policy document named "Rebuilding America's Defences" in which it stated that

> "the process of transforming the US into 'tomorrow's dominant force' was likely to be a long one in the absence of some catastrophic and catalysing event - like a new Pearl Harbor."

The attacks of 9/11 conveniently allowed the US to press on with the PNAC agenda. The creation of false excuses to justify going to war is certainly not a new phenomenon and is often deemed a necessary first step in constructing public support.

On September 20th 2001, PNAC stated in a letter to Bush that:

> "It may be that the Iraqi government provided assistance, in some form, to the recent attack on the US. But even if evidence does not link Iraq directly to the attack, any strategy aiming at the eradication of terrorism and its sponsors must include a determined effort to remove Saddam Hussein from power in Iraq."

When it became clear that any link between Iraq and the alleged perpetrators of 9/11 was tenuous, quickly erected in its place was the "weapons of mass destruction" (WMD) smokescreen.

### References
By far the best source of information on this subject is Michel Chossudovsky's "Globalization of War"[lxviii].

## Orlando Shooting

### TV Narrative
On June 12th 2016, at about 2:00am, inside "Pulse", a gay nightclub in Orlando, Florida, Omar Mateen opened fire using a Sig Sauer MCX assault-style rifle. Forty-nine people were killed and fifty-three injured in what was described as a terrorist attack. Pulse, one of the biggest nightclubs in Orlando, was holding a Latin-themed event for around three hundred patrons when the shooting began. After a three hour standoff, the shooter was shot and killed by officers of the Orlando Police Department.

The gunman, a 29 year old Muslim security guard originally from New York, was said to have phoned the emergency services during the attack and pledged allegiance to Abu Bakr al-Baghdadi, the head of the "Islamic State". In the call he stated that his motive was one of retaliation for the US killing of Abu Waheeb in Iraq which had taken place the previous month. In a subsequent investigation into Mateen's background, the CIA found no evidence to suggest that there were any links between him and "IS".

## Correspondence Narrative

In a similar vein to the San Bernardino shooting, it seems likely that Mateen was a patsy used in a staged shooting or drill constructed to inculcate a sense of fear of Muslim terrorists. What remains unclear is whether there were any real victims, or if the whole event was a hoax. What we do know, however, is that there is much evidence to suggest that crisis actors were employed during the recording of the TV coverage.

Just as in the case of the Virginia shooting, the atmosphere of tension created by the idea of a "crazy lone gunman" seems to have been orchestrated to coerce a trusting American public into accepting new laws and so giving up their rights under the Second Amendment: the right of the people to keep and bear arms. The fact that, soon after the shooting, President Obama pledged to ban "AR-15 style rifles" would seem to give some credence to this hypothesis.

## Elephant

Angel Colon, one of those said to have been injured in the shooting, was interviewed at his hospital bed just a few days after the incident. The media reports that he was shot five times, including in the hand. Colon himself maintains in several interviews that he was shot six times, and that the shot to the hand occurred as he tried to defend himself when the gunman aimed for his head. However, during many of these interviews, both his hands are clearly visible and show no sign of any injury: no wound, blood or bandages can be seen. Despite his alleged injuries, there is footage taken just days after the event in which he can be seen in the hospital sitting up in a chair, wearing his own clothing, leaning to hug a police officer; and all of this with a smile on his face. No evidence can be seen of any drip or monitoring equipment in the vicinity, and he seems to be in remarkable health for a man who has been shot five or six times with an assault rifle.

Presented by the mainstream media we see plenty of footage depicting what can be easily verified as actors, pretending to be victims, being helped or carried after the shooting. In a number of these, they can be clearly seen being carried **towards** the club rather than away from it. In addition, a number of them can be seen being put back on their feet when they think they are out of sight of the camera, only to walk off normally on their own, unaided.

Three months before the shooting, Orlando Health and the FBI teamed up for a training drill at Orlando Regional Medical Center, just two blocks from the Pulse nightclub. Eric Alberts, Emergency Preparedness Manager, organised the drill featuring a hypothetical active shooter and hundreds of casualties. In a story featured on "News 6", Alberts said:

> "Working with our FBI partners they're going to have to interview the patients, their families, anyone that was in that situation to try and find out the story. We really need to practice this piece because we've never done that before."

One of those participating in both the drill **and** the alleged shooting was a Dr. Matt Lube, who was said to have been amongst the surgeons who treated Angel Colon. During a press conference after the attack, trauma surgeon Chadwick Smith said he phoned him saying:

> "This is not a drill. This is not a joke. We have twenty plus gunshot wounds coming in. I need you here as fast as [possible]."

An interesting recent development is the increase in number of mainstream actors, as opposed to crisis actors, who appear in leading roles in hoax events. Even just a few years ago, this was fairly uncommon, one notable exception being that of David Wheeler ("Farscape" 1999; "The Dark Redemption", 1999) who played the part of Sandy Hook "victim" Benjamin, and who also cropped up, so it would seem, as a rather hapless, heavily armed "FBI agent" in the same production ("David Wheeler Fake Newtown Sniper").

In comparison to this, we see more than one mainstream actor playing parts in the Orlando production and, even though they might not be household names like Wheeler, they are still big enough to have their own IMDB pages. The first of these is Luis Burbano ("The Sacred", 2009; "Less Lost", 2012). The part he played is a curious one, since, by his own admission, he held the club's exit door shut from the outside, trapping people inside with the gunman. One witness, Janiel Gonzalez, voiced his scepticism over Burbano's role, saying of him in an interview:

> "This guy is trying to prevent us from leaving. Maybe they're working together."

Perhaps even more curious than this is the case of the starring actor, the one who played the part of Mateen and had appeared as an actor in the mock-documentary, "The Big Fix", released in 2012, some four years before Orlando. Before his rise to notoriety, he had an IMDB page listing his career, but this has since been removed, presumably by IMDB themselves.

Lastly, we have the case of supposed victim, Patience Carter, a "Fox 29" intern and aspiring singer from Philadelphia. Whilst she can't really be described as a mainstream actress, she clearly does have connections with the TV, and many have suggested that she was a crisis actress. Other people have argued that her presence was a mere coincidence. It's up to the reader to make up his or her own mind.

## References

As with a number of similar incidents listed in this chapter, it is still too soon for there to have been any books containing detailed analysis. The difference in this case, however, is that the alternative narrative is so easy to see that the footage and articles already available on the mainstream media are all we need.

For instance, evidence of the uninjured Angel Colon is just one click away ("Orlando shooting survivor is reunited with police officer"). The original footage showing the "victims" being carried the wrong way is also freely available ("Orlando Shooting Crisis Actors Taken Wrong Direction"), as is a mountain of additional analysis to show the correlation between the actors' surroundings and Google Maps. Evidence of the "Active Shooter Drill" is also available ("Orlando Health FBI active shooter training response drill Pulse shooting"), as is material which describes the Burbano story ("Orlando survivor admits trapping club-goers inside") and the Mateen story ("Orlando shooter Omar Mateen award-winning BP documentary", "Omar Mateen's IMDB Page Scrubbed").

# - 26 -
# Fairy Tales

*"At every moment of our lives, we all have one foot in a fairy tale and the other in the abyss."*

Paulo Coelho

---

A common theme throughout this book has been the idea that simple words can often hide a sea of complexity. The words "true" and "would", for example, can give the impression of aiding communication, but, sadly, as we have already seen, often hinder it instead. Over the course of the preceding chapters, we have taken the opportunity to analyse these difficult words and use the fruits of our work to illuminate certain areas of our culture. As we're now approaching the end of our story, it's about time we made good the promise that was made in chapter 7 and turn our attention to the noun phrase "fairy tale".

As with many words and phrases in English, and indeed in many other languages, this has an original meaning plus a number of transferred meanings, each of which has arisen as a result of some initial metaphoric use that has been repeated often enough to earn its place in the dictionary. The root definition:

> (1) "A children's story about fairies or mythical beings."

is perhaps not the sense alluded to when the phrase is normally used, at least not in a conversation between adults.

The first thing to understand is that the idea of a fairy tale is distinct from that of an untruth. An untruth is a false statement that **could** correspond to an event in the real world, yet does not do so in the context within which it is intended to be understood.

For instance, let's assume that Barry introduces the following proposition, which he claims is true:

> **Barry:** "Last week I went to France on vacation."

Assuming for a moment that we have some secondary source that enables us to be certain that Barry did **not** do this, we can conclude that his proposition is false. But there is nothing intrinsically wrong with the statement. Many people do go to France on vacation, and it may even be true to say that Barry did so too at some point in time. It just so happens that we know that he did not go there last week.

If a subject chooses to believe Barry's proposition and we are to try to allocate responsibility for this uptake of disinformation, then, although some of the blame may rest with the subject for not investigating more deeply, the majority of the blame must surely rest with Barry, who presumably has introduced the proposition in a deliberate attempt to deceive.

Now, let's allow Barry to modify his proposition a little, as follows:

> **Barry:** "When I went on vacation to France last week, I walked the twenty miles over the English Channel to reach my destination."

This time, things are very different, for we no longer need to make reference to some secondary source in order to reach the conclusion that the proposition is false. We can deduce its falsity just from the information provided in the proposition itself and, in this example, a basic understanding of the laws of physics. Most, if not all, readers will immediately see that Barry's proposition is impossible, but, for those unfamiliar with the relevant laws, and in the interests of completeness, the reason is as follows.

When we stand upright on solid ground, the force of gravity acts downwards on our body and can be modelled as acting on our centre of gravity, a point approximately at the second sacral vertebra, just below the solar plexus for most of us. An equal and opposite force, called The Normal Contact Force, pushes up on the soles of our shoes or feet. If we simplify things by considering the case where we stand at one of the poles, thus affording ourselves the luxury of ignoring the effects of circular motion, these two forces balance each other out, and the net effect is that we remain motionless in a stable position. At the same time, Newton's Third Law dictates that a third force, The Normal Contact Reaction Force, equal in magnitude to the other two, acts downwards on the ground beneath our feet. Since the ground is a solid, it has the structural integrity required to withstand this force without any noticeable deformation, and that's why we remain upright.

On the other hand, water is a fluid and so lacks the structural integrity enjoyed by solids. When we try to exert onto its surface a force equal to the Normal Contact Reaction Force of the previous example, it deforms and moves away from us. Since it is unable to sustain the force, it is similarly unable to exert the Normal Contact Force on the soles of our feet, since to do so would imply a violation of Newton's Third Law. Without the expected Normal Contact Force holding us up, our weight now exceeds the upward force acting upon us and we accelerate downwards as a result. This is why we cannot walk on water.

A basic understanding of High School physics is all it takes to demonstrate the impossibility of the second proposition, and it's this fact which enables us to categorise it as a fairy tale, rather than as a simple untruth. We can regard the following definition as the primary transferred meaning of the phrase, and it is this definition we allude to on the few occasions where we have used it in this book.

> (2) "A proposition which is demonstrably impossible without reference to any external circumstance."

Just as we did with the first proposition, we must now consider who is to be held responsible for the uptake of disinformation in this modified scenario, and here we are confronted with a very different picture to the one we saw before. In this case the majority of the blame must surely lie with the recipient. Since they have in their possession (if we can assume a basic knowledge of physics) all the information required to deduce the falsity of the proposition, their choice to ignore it must be, at least in part, a voluntary one. This deliberate act is what puts them into a position of Wilful Blindness, as discussed at length in chapter 16.

However, this is not the end of the story for the concept of the fairy tale. There is a second level of transferred meaning, and this is what, unfortunately, tends to muddy the waters. The reason for what many perceive to be the emotive nature of the phrase is this more recent pejorative sense, in which it is used to indicate the speaker's disapproval. To make things even more confusing, when we see the phrase used in this way, we often see it referring to a simple untruth, along the lines of our first proposition. As an example of this, we might consider the following:

> **Barry:** "On June 10th 1996, I received a degree from Stanford University."
>
> **Edward:** "To be quite honest, that's just a fairy tale."

Since there is nothing intrinsically impossible with Barry's proposition, we cannot demonstrate its falsity without reference to some secondary source of information, and this means that we can rule out definition (2). It is clear that Edward is using the phrase to express his contempt rather than simply his disbelief.

When the subject is presented with a fairy tale, as delineated by definition (2), it should now be clear that the rational option is to reject it, due to the fact that it is, by definition, false. But what would happen if the subject chooses to believe the fairy tale, nonetheless? What would happen, for instance, if he or she were to believe that Barry can walk on water, that a man could turn water into wine, or that three towers could violate Newton's Third Law? Well, it turns out that there are a number of options.

The first, and perhaps the simplest, is for the subject to withdraw from the matter and to cease any further thought about it. As an example, we could take Thomas Aquinas's "first-cause argument" for the existence of god. Once the subject has made a voluntarist belief in god, perhaps as a result of Aquinas's argument, he or she stops thinking about the question of god's existence. This, in turn, means that he or she neglects to ask the question as to who or what created god. Asking this question is all that is necessary to destroy Aquinas's argument, but the believer is rendered unable to see this as a result of their cognitive withdrawal, the consequence of their voluntarist belief.

To see the danger that this choice presents to the human race as a whole, it is necessary to conduct a short thought experiment. Imagine, if you will, that all human knowledge is drawn out on a piece of paper in the form of a map. You can imagine it as islands of knowledge linked together by bridges to represent the interconnections between related ideas. For want of a better term, we will refer to the map as the "Epistemological Plane" (EP). Imagine that, starting at birth, it is our goal to explore the entirety of the EP, in as much as such a feat can ever be possible. If we stray from our exploration, however, and choose to accept a fairy tale, we must erect a small circular fence around the appropriate area on the EP. We might coin the term "cognitive fence" to describe such a construct. The fence is there to stop us from facing up to the paradox that exists between the fairy tale and reality, and represents our decision to withdraw from this paradox. A small, hard-to-spot fairy tale might warrant a fence which encloses a small area of the EP, whereas a big, glaring one would entail fencing off a larger area.

The danger comes when the fenced areas enlarge and start to join up. As the forbidden area grows in relation to the totality of the EP, the cognitive ability of the subject diminishes. If we imagine this process proceeding to its logical conclusion, we would end up back at the start of the journey, as an individual with the cognitive ability of a newly born child. At some point in between the two extremes, we could model the subject as being in some stage of childhood, a state induced by their own cognitive withdrawal in response to their voluntarist belief in fairy tales.

It is interesting to note that there are some mainstream religions which demand that the subject engages in this process. For instance, in the Christian Bible, the author of the section known as "The Gospel of Matthew", whoever he or she may have been, says, through the mouthpiece of the fictional character denoted as "Jesus", the following:

"... and said, 'Truly, I say to you, unless you turn and become like children, you will never enter the kingdom of heaven.'" (Matthew 18:3)

So, is there any evidence to suggest that the rate of erosion of the EP is increasing in the way we describe? Taking a look at the catalogue of fairy tales of the last fifty or so years, some of which are described in chapter 25, we notice a couple of trends. The first and most obvious of these is the fact that the rate at which new fairy tales are introduced into and assimilated by society seems to be increasing as time goes by. The effect of this, for the majority, seems to be the erection of an ever-increasing number of cognitive fences.

The second trend is perhaps a little more subtle. In the early years, these events were elaborate affairs with multiple levels of deception woven together to form a complex weave. September 11th 2001 is a great example of this in that there are many strands to the story, and this can make it a difficult nut to crack, for some. Because these strands draw our attention away from the facets of the deception which make it obvious, the area enclosed by the cognitive fence is small. If we compare this to some of the more modern fairy tales, the San Bernardino Shooting or the Orlando Pulse Shooting, for instance, we see a very different story. Here it is a simple matter to spot the fairy tale just by watching one or two mainstream news reports. The unresolved contradictory stories, the implausible narratives, the uncanny coincidences, not to mention the unconvincing performances of the crisis actors, all join together to make the task a relatively simple one. In these cases, a swallowing of the fairy tale involves a cognitive fence of far greater proportion.

Many researchers have questioned the reason for the increase in the number of these events and the ever-decreasing level of plausibility of the TV narrative, and it certainly is a perplexing question. Perhaps the motive for this is the very effect we have outlined, a deliberate attempt to decrease the cognitive capacity of the population? If this is true, and things continue the way they are, we will soon see a society in which we have voluntarily entered into slavery, victims of our own self-created cognitive dysfunction.

One way to substantiate this hypothesis might be to look for other common examples of cognitive fencing. These are not hard to find when we consider the changes that have been made to society in the last fifty years or so. Political correctness, for instance, the scourge that swept through society in the 1980s and 90s, has rendered us unable to vocalise the mildest of criticisms for fear that we might hurt someone's feeling somewhere. Needless to say, this kind of societal force can lead to self-censorship, a sure way to lead a population away from truth. The link between our thoughts and our speech is perhaps an obvious one, and it's easy to see how our inclination for self-censorship might result in the erection of a cognitive fence to surround the forbidden area.

So much for the path of cognitive withdrawal, but now we must turn our attention to some of the other avenues open to those who choose to accept fairy tales. By now it should be obvious that any approach other than withdrawal must lead to some degree of cognitive dissonance, a concept we first introduced in chapter 8. This means that there will always be an emotional content, usually anger, to the behaviour of the subject when the area of dissonance is approached.

One option we see played out time and time again is the attempt to reconcile the fairy tale with reality by means of an *ad hoc* hypothesis or Religious Reasoning Chain. As we saw in chapter 9, the twists and turns imposed by this approach can become so convoluted, when the dissonance is fierce, that the behaviour can border on the comical.

Arguably the most perilous choice, at least for the individual, is to try to deal with the dissonance directly. In this case, the subject is forced to believe a thesis and its antithesis at the same time. Since this is impossible in the rational mind, we must now think of the subject, at least in some sense, as being divided into two separate individuals, one believing the thesis and one believing the antithesis. In some cases, such a division might have little consequence, but this all depends on the nature of the thesis. If the dichotomy is powerful enough and is introduced early enough in childhood, the damage can be catastrophic. For instance, if a child is brought up in an environment where he or she suffers abuse at the hands of one or both parents, yet receives frequent verbal reinforcement of the "your parents love you" maxim, then this can lead to the subject experiencing bouts of schizophrenia in their 20s and beyond.

That just about wraps it up for the transferred meaning of the phrase "fairy tale", but no discussion of the term would be complete without visiting its original meaning: the children's story. Many people regard these as simple forms of entertainment for children, and there is no doubt that this is true in many cases. But some have a rather macabre air to them, so much so that the memory of being frightened by them as a child can stay with us into adulthood. Many will probably agree that it's hard to accept entertainment as being the sole purpose for tales such as these.

Little Red Riding Hood (LRRH), a story which can be traced back to its roots in $10^{th}$ century France, will be familiar to many. The story goes like this:

> "LRRH is told by her mother to take some food to her incapacitated Granny in her cottage deep in the

forest. On the way, LRRH meets a wolf, who strikes up a conversation during which LRRH tells him where she is going. The wolf rushes on ahead of her, walks into Granny's house, eats her, puts on her bonnet, jumps into her bed, then waits for LRRH to show up. When LRRH arrives, she sees through the deception in the nick of time and manages to escape the house just as the wolf pounces. Later, she meets a woodcutter who accompanies her back to the cottage where he kills the wolf, slits open its stomach and rescues Granny. To finish the story, LRRH helps the woodcutter to fill the wolf's stomach with stones."

A story such as this may be used as an instrument of control for an unruly child, and many of us will be able to recall a parental threat such as: "Do as I say, or the wolf will get you". However, in "What Do You Say After You Say Hello" (*op cit*), Eric Berne tells us that there may be some additional function for tales like this.

A cursory examination might lead us to believe that we are presented with a simple story about an aggressor (the wolf), a saviour (the woodcutter) and some innocent victims (LRRH, Granny and the mother). But Berne's more thorough analysis brings with it some difficult questions. Why would an innocent mother send her daughter, alone, into a forest where there were wolves? Did she intend her daughter to come to harm? Why would she leave Granny alone in her cottage in the forest? Why did LRRH tell the wolf where she was going then fail to leave the cottage as soon as she saw the wolf in Granny's bed? Did she intend to be attacked by the wolf? Was it LRRH's intention to be rescued by the woodcutter all along? Perhaps her real goal was to engineer an opportunity to fill the wolf's stomach with stones?

Berne's penchant for questioning the motives of the protagonists leads him to some interesting real-life parallels with the tale. He tells the story of a patient, Carrie, who approaches Dr. Q (Berne is obliged to ensure the privacy of those he writes about) for psychiatric treatment. Arriving at the doctor's office, perhaps coincidentally wearing a red coat, she explains that she is suffering from depression, and finds herself unable to locate a satisfactory boyfriend. She goes on to describe how, at the age of ten, her mother would send her over to her grandparents' house where she would be abused by her grandfather. When asked what made her split up with her string of imperfect boyfriends, her answer was that "They were all just junior wolves."

It goes without saying that this is just one isolated case, and there is no suggestion that it is common for people to spend their lives acting out this particular script, but Berne does describe many similar examples in which the patient follows a script either taken from a fairy tale or from some other source. The pattern of behaviour he describes certainly invites us to do some thinking about the human mind.

In Berne's branch of psychology, Transactional Analysis (TA), the basic unit of currency of human interaction is termed a "stroke". For instance, when you pass an acquaintance in the office corridor and each say "hi" in passing, you have each given and received one stroke. TA tells us that we adapt our behaviour over the course of our lives so as to maximise the receipt of stokes. Starting from the age of around four or five, we experiment with different behavioural motifs, drawing on the stories we are told and the behaviour we observe to provide a pool of examples. Many of us choose a script quite early in life and spend the rest of our lives acting out our part within it.

If this is true, then it may well be that the idea we have of ourselves as fully cognizant beings, able to react rationally to stimuli from the world around us, bears only a passing resemblance to the truth. A more accurate view might be to see ourselves as actors in a play of our own creation, where the script is either one we create for ourselves or one which is drawn from our environment. This is an idea which is developed in the fascinating, yet enigmatic movie, "My Dinner with Andre" (Louis Malle, 1981). Describing this unique piece of social commentary would probably take a book in its own right, so we will just restrict ourselves to one rather poignant quote:

> "The doctor didn't see my mother. People at the public theatre didn't see me. We are just walking around in some kind of fog. I think we're all in a trance. We're walking around like zombies. I don't think we're even aware of ourselves or of our own reaction to things. We're just going around all day like unconscious machines, and there's all this rage and worry and uneasiness building up."

If there is any truth in this theory, then it could explain a lot. For instance, the seventy-five percent of the subjects in the Solomon Asch experiment (chapter 17) who conformed with the false decision of the majority in at least one of the critical trials could be viewed as being stroke or script-driven, with only the remaining twenty-five percent being reality-driven. In short, it could be the reason why the majority of us are unable to see the truth about the world, even when it is right in front of our noses.

Over the course of this chapter, we have looked at the concept of fairy tales from a number of different perspectives. Whether the story forms part of a traditional religion, the modern religion of TVism or is just a form of children's entertainment, the result can be the modification of our process of cognition and of our behaviour. If we accept that this is the case, we must then decide whether this alteration is just an accidental consequence of the stories we've been told, or whether the modification was the true purpose all along. If we come to the conclusion that this manipulation is deliberate, then this will naturally lead us to question who, or what, is pulling the strings. Musings of this nature are perhaps best left as an exercise for the reader.

An important goal for the human race as a whole must surely be to recognise fairy tales for what they are as soon as they are presented to us. It doesn't matter where they come from, a holy book, the TV news, the mouth of an authority figure;

and it doesn't matter what trickery is used to disguise them. They will lose their ability to control us as soon as we are able to see them in their true light. This may be difficult at first, but it gets easier with a little practice, and is a vital step for us all if we are to regain control over our own minds.

We are fast approaching the end of our journey and the point at which we must gather this all up into some kind of conclusion. But before we do so, it's worth pausing to recap on some of the topics we have covered.

Right from the start, we saw how differing Constructivist narratives can draw us into shallow, inescapable arguments, but how the beacon of Correspondence truth can lead us to a more detailed and verifiable understanding of our surroundings. We have seen how collections of fairy tales can be woven together by the elite who control the power structures that masquerade as the religions of today: Christianity, Islam, TVism and many others. "The TV Delusion", a book about religion in all its guises, has shown how these tapestries of deceit can act as a trap for the unwary, and how, once caught, we will develop elaborate forms of behaviour and cognitive dysfunction to justify our own captivity. Perhaps we are all susceptible, in some way to Stockholm syndrome?

On a more positive note, whatever the reasons for our propensity to conform to the norm, to believe in the impossible, to trust the untrustworthy and to be the perpetrators of our own deception, we always retain the capacity to change our reality, if we choose to do so.

# Conclusion

*"Truth is by nature self-evident. As soon as you remove the cobwebs of ignorance that surround it, it shines clear."*

Mahatma Gandhi

---

If there's one thing that mankind is good at, it's the creation of fairy tales for people to believe in. Some of these, such as the Tooth Fairy and Father Christmas, are designed purely for children and we soon grow out of them as we approach adulthood; but others, those designed for consumption by adults, can remain with us for our whole lives.

Closely associated with these myths, we often find various forms of ritual behaviour. Indeed, the construction of ritual to surround belief is so commonplace that it could almost be viewed as normal, and there is even evidence to suggest that this behaviour might exist in animals other than humans. It would seem that this is somehow connected with our tendency to assume, erroneously, that correlation, or apparent correlation, is synonymous with causation.

This was rather amusingly demonstrated in "Trick or Treat", a series of TV shows by the British illusionist and hypnotist, Derren Brown. The episode in question, first shown in the UK in June 2008, focuses on superstition and ritual. A clip of the show is easy to find on the internet ("Derren explores superstition and BF Skinner").

Brown invites a small group of people consisting of a few TV celebrities and some members of the public to take part in a televised experiment which starts with them being locked inside a large room. Above the only exit is displayed a "score", and the participants are told they will be allowed to leave the room and collect the prize money if it reaches one hundred within a limit of thirty minutes. In the room with the contestants are a number of objects, but there is nothing to suggest that these have any connection with the "score". As the show proceeds and the participants interact randomly with the objects, the "score" increases. Initially their actions are indiscriminate, but, over time, the participants become convinced that certain actions are causing the "score" to increase, and, as a result, they develop patterns of ritual behaviour in an attempt to enhance this.

In reality, none of the participants' actions has any bearing on the "score". In a separate room, away from the proceedings, there sits a tank which contains two goldfish. As either fish passes a central line fixed to the tank, a volunteer presses a button which adds one point to the "score".

Brown explains that his experiment is based on a similar one conducted by B. F. Skinner in which pigeons take the place of the human participants and the scoring mechanism is replaced by a random delivery of food pellets. Although the pigeons were not given a collection of objects to interact with, they were observed to engage in seemingly ritualistic behaviour, such as walking around in circles and pecking at specific points, in their attempts to be rewarded with the food.

Back in the real world, examples of ritualistic behaviour are easy to find. In the case of the Tooth Fairy, for instance, the ritual is as simple as placing a tooth under one's pillow, supposedly in exchange for a small financial reward. In the case of mainstream religion, on the other hand, we see adherents congregating in ornate buildings and engaging in repetitive behaviour consisting of spoken words and gestures, supposedly in exchange for an enhanced status in the "afterlife".

Moving on to the case of *TVism*, the rituals become more complex and reveal themselves in a number of phases. In the first phase, we allow our wealth to be stolen by our governments who then pass it on to arms companies in exchange for munitions. These munitions are then used to bomb people to whom we have assigned the religious label, "terrorists". The second phase of the ritual consists of our attempts to absolve ourselves from the guilt associated with our having partaken in the first phase, these often materialising as wilful blindness. It's this that allows us to either turn a blind eye to the first phase or to forget about it altogether. Some might argue that this sequence of events does not constitute a ritual, yet it does fit the broad definition of the word, in that it is an irrational behaviour which is not subject to critical analysis on the part of the participant.

The exact point of origin of many of these fairy tales is lost in the mists of time. All we can really say is that, in some cases, the point lies thousands of years in the past. Some are so powerful that they can survive their own death, only to be recycled and re-invented in the context of new power structures. For instance, Osiris, the Egyptian god of the underworld, is said to have had twelve disciples during his earthly life, was murdered by the evil god Set and was resurrected (some days later) before going on to live in the sky with the other gods. When this religion died out, the same sequence of events was taken by those who constructed Christianity and recycled into the myth of Christ.

Throughout the course of this book, we have discussed a number of these myths and encountered a number of recurrent themes along the way. "We're OK. They're not OK," for instance, has appeared during our study of both mainstream religion and the modern day religion of *TVism*. This "life position" has been seen to underpin some of the more basic and unpleasant human psychological characteristics, such as those we saw coming to the forefront in the Stanford Prison experiment and those that drive the racism we still see all too commonly today.

So what are we to make of all this?

Ernest Becker, in what many have described as the culmination of his life's work, "The Denial of Death"[lxix], tells us that one of the principle drivers for human psychoses is the fear of our own death. Becker, basing much of his material on the work of Danish philosopher, Søren Kierkegaard, notes that this fear is not something with which we are born. Indeed, in their early years, infants have no concept of death, let alone a fear of it. In fact it's actually somewhat the opposite. As a child, our every need, both physical and emotional, is taken care of for us. We just need to utter a word and that which we desire is normally made available. This even works before we are able to utter any words at all: we just need to make any sound, and someone will figure it all out for us. As a result of this, so Becker posits, we form the opinion that, at least in some sense, we are immortal.

It is only around the age of five that we normally get our first glimpse of the concept of death. Maybe this begins when we see a pet die, or perhaps it's the death of an elderly relative that kick-starts our process of awareness. Whatever the trigger, at some point we become aware of our fear of death and we also begin to observe that same fear in those around us, especially the adults. At the same time, we see in people's behaviour a strong tendency to avoid any mention of this fear and to avoid the topic of death in general.

This transition from a state of presumption of immortality to one of the recognition of the inevitability of death, coupled with the near absence of any counselling along the way, comes as a big shock for the young child. Not only that, but there is no escape from the immediacy of the paradox. Inside our mind there is a system of logic and symbols which seems infinite and enduring, yet outside our mind there is a physical body which is subject to age and decay. The perpetual presence of this dichotomy can act as a compelling motive for repression, or a powerful potion for psychosis.

Becker tells us that we all live for the myth that somehow we can cheat death and return to the state of immortality which we imagined ourselves to have had as an infant. Of course, a moment's consideration would be enough to tell us that this is impossible, yet we ignore this fact and cling to our belief regardless. The burden of this knowledge of mortality, coupled with our attempts to convince ourselves of the veracity of the myth of immortality, demands that we develop the ability to hold in our minds simultaneously a proposition and its own opposite, and regard them both to be true. Of course, it has been known for thousands of years that such a thing is impossible, but this paradox is so deep-rooted that we are barely aware of its existence. It is this which is the driver for our belief in the veracity of our fairy tales, and it may well be that we view the cognitive dissonance resulting from the paradox as being preferable to the pain of facing up to the reality of death itself.

For Christians, the purpose of their belief system is not really to provide reassurance as to what happens after they die, but, moreover, to reinforce the myth that they can escape death altogether. It's not so much an afterlife that Christianity offers, but a life eternal and, for many other religions, the story is the same. The notion of a god and the price of avoiding "sin" are just the stepping stones of *ad hoc* hypothesis in the Religious Reasoning Chain from which we derive our myth of immortality.

In days gone by, when traditional religion was still in its prime, the myths which comprise the doctrine were sufficient to act as a soma for the population. However, in our modern age, religion, at least religion in the traditional sense of the word, has lost its previously dominant position in society. For us, the duty of granting immortality no longer rests with the church, but has, so it would seem, been transferred to the state. We live under the assumption that the state loves us and will protect us from all evil, harm and death. In our madness, we suppose that, if the state does its job well enough, its protection will be eternal.

It is reasonable to suspect that it is this false assumption that makes us reticent to question authority. After all, who in their right mind would ever question the authority of an entity who is granting them immortality? If we were to challenge the state's authority, we might imagine that this will lead to the withdrawal of its protection, leaving us to fend for ourselves in what is, so we are told, an ever increasingly frightening world. In addition, it is reasonable to assume that a very strong challenge, such as one which might result in revolution, will result in the state's taking active steps to kill us. Given all of this, it's highly likely that it's our fear of death that drives us to submit to the authority of the state and accept whatever lies are foisted upon us. Perhaps it is only those of us who have a smaller measure of this fear who will ever be able to face the truth.

With these thoughts in mind, we should move on to answer a few questions that remain outstanding.

## What Happens To You After You Die?

As we have already seen, the lack of a clear answer to this question may well be at the heart of all the modern world's problems. Our fear of what lies ahead entices us to accept the fairy tales that are offered to us, even though, deep down, we know that they are not true. So how can we dispel this fear and free ourselves from the chains which bind us?

In essence, the problem we face is just another manifestation of the same one we have seen so many times over the course of the previous chapters. It all has to do with the source of authority. When we subject ourselves to the authority of others, the likely result is deception and slavery, but when we take on the responsibility of authority ourselves, truth and freedom are the more likely outcomes. Similar problems can often be addressed with similar solutions, and our current question is no exception to the rule. To give ourselves a better chance of uncovering the mystery of what happens to us after we die, we should follow the same process that has brought us so much success already. In short, we need to gather evidence, subject what we find to a careful analysis, formulate some hypotheses then evaluate each in turn. Of course, our process will be subject to the same potential pitfalls as it has been previously. For instance, if we were to confine ourselves to just a subset of the available evidence, then we would be likely to go astray.

To illustrate this, we need look no further than what we might term the "scientific" view of life and death. Cosmologists tell us that the universe is some fourteen billion years old. For the vast majority of this time, right up until a few decades ago, you were, not to put too fine a point on it, dead. If you prefer to think of that state as being one of non-existence, that's fine: it amounts to the same thing. In another few decades you will return to this state of death.

So what are we missing here? Is there some way in which we can we gather more evidence? If only we could find someone who had died, then come back to life to tell us what they experienced!

As it turns out, there is no shortage of people who claim to have done just that. In 1981, a Gallup poll found that around five percent of the US adult population, a total of about eight million people, claimed to have had a near-death experience. For those unfamiliar with the term, a near death experience is an incident in which a patient is pronounced clinically dead, only to later be resuscitated by medical staff. In many cases, the "death" has been verified by using an electroencephalogram (EEG) to show an absence of all brain activity. But, far from being simply an American "new age" phenomenon, it would seem that experiences like this are virtually universal, as is evidenced in records going back for over two and a half thousand years.

No serious attempt to answer the Big Question can be made without reference to the testimony of these witnesses. Many authors have done just that and have written at length of their findings, but perhaps the best all-round appraisal is to be found in Michael Talbot's "The Holographic Universe"[lxx].

## Does Religion Make You Less Intelligent?

This is an assertion that one often hears coming from the lips of atheists. Not surprisingly, it is denied, almost without exception, by those who follow some kind of religion. So who is right? In order to answer the question, we must first find out what is meant by the word "intelligence".

Being a good researcher requires us to possess two different qualities in equal measure. In some ways, these two qualities can be considered to be opposites, while in other ways, we might regard them as companions. Perhaps that's why individuals who possess the perfect balance of each are so thin on the ground.

The first of these qualities is called "analysis". Using this skill, we take an idea and break it down into its constituent parts. Once this is done, we turn our attention to those constituent parts, breaking them down further until we reach the individual "atoms of truth" that lie within. One way to imagine this process is as if we were proceeding down a tree trunk towards the tree's roots. The "atoms" are to be found at the tips of the roots. This process of progression towards detail describes the mechanism of analysis when functioning at full efficiency. The problem we all face is that, at every turn, our *believer* mind, armed with its box of religious labels and fairy tales, is waiting to seize its opportunity to stop us in our tracks. When we encounter an offering from the box that satisfies one of our desires to believe, the process of analysis comes to a halt, at least for that particular root under consideration, and all the tendrils that emanate from it.

The second quality is "synthesis". This is the process that enables us to piece together a number of disparate facts or ideas so as to form some kind of continuity. We must look for the fixed patterns that underlie the observations we have made, whilst taking care not to ignore any differences along the way. Here, just as before, the *believer* mind is ready to thwart us with an offering from its box of tricks. If there comes a point when we are about to reach a realisation that might threaten an element of our core belief system, it pipes up with a cry of "*coincidence*" (miracle), or formulates an *ad hoc* hypothesis as appropriate. Once this happens, our ability to piece things together evaporates.

It's the combination of the qualities of analysis and synthesis that is normally known by the term "intelligence". As we have seen time and time again, it is the *believer* mind that acts to constrain each of these faculties: sometimes, albeit, with the best of intentions. It's therefore reasonable to conclude that this natural phenomenon, which exists in all of us to some extent, is one of the key limiting factors that we face in terms of our intelligence.

As we have seen throughout this book, it is in the domain of religious fundamentalism, in all its shapes and forms, where we see the *believer* mind as a dominant force. Here it has such a power that it is able to create a form of psychosis or even a mild schizophrenia which renders us unable to distinguish fairy tale from reality. As we have covered at length in chapters 6 and 7, the striking similarities between traditional religious fundamentalism and the modern day equivalent, *TVism*, are inescapable. It is reasonable to assume that the fundamentalism associated with the *believer* mind has not gone away, but has merely changed its habitat.

The best way to see how this works in practice is to look in detail at an example. Referring to Figure 22, the reader can see how this relates to a study of the events of 9/11. Each box in the diagram represents a stimulus, a 9/11 truism, along with two different approaches we might adopt in response. The list of facts is by no means exhaustive, and the order in which they are presented has no significance. There is no reason why these particular facts have been chosen from the much larger set that can be found with just a little research.

The first bullet point in each box describes the truism. For each of these, the *believer* mind offers us a religious repost, and *ad hoc* hypothesis, which is shown in the second bullet point. This represents the attempt on the part of the *believer* mind to interpose a barrier to our process of analysis. The process of analysis that the *believer* seeks to avoid is shown below this in the form of a series of questions. These are the sort of questions we should be asking in order to provide an *explorer* response to the truism.

## 9/11 : Example Analysis & Synthesis

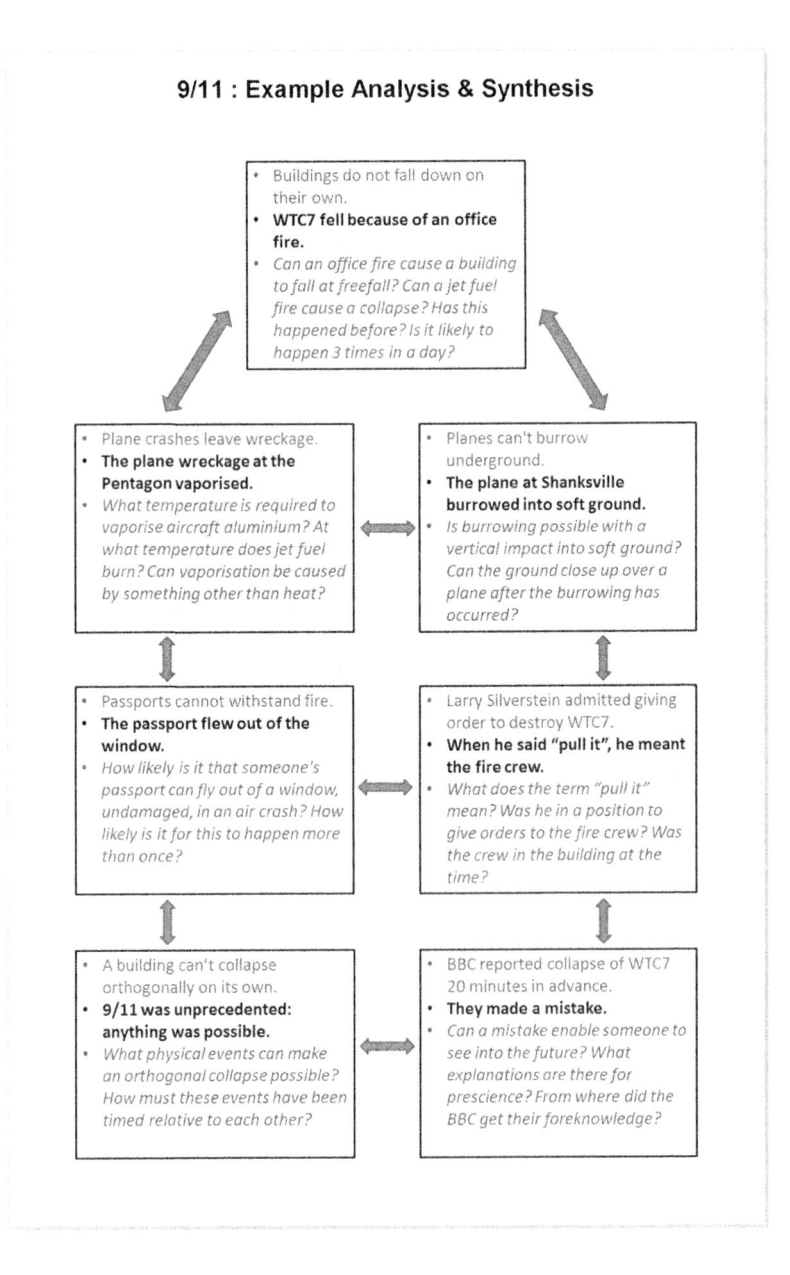

- Buildings do not fall down on their own.
- **WTC7 fell because of an office fire.**
- *Can an office fire cause a building to fall at freefall? Can a jet fuel fire cause a collapse? Has this happened before? Is it likely to happen 3 times in a day?*

- Plane crashes leave wreckage.
- **The plane wreckage at the Pentagon vaporised.**
- *What temperature is required to vaporise aircraft aluminium? At what temperature does jet fuel burn? Can vaporisation be caused by something other than heat?*

- Planes can't burrow underground.
- **The plane at Shanksville burrowed into soft ground.**
- *Is burrowing possible with a vertical impact into soft ground? Can the ground close up over a plane after the burrowing has occurred?*

- Passports cannot withstand fire.
- **The passport flew out of the window.**
- *How likely is it that someone's passport can fly out of a window, undamaged, in an air crash? How likely is it for this to happen more than once?*

- Larry Silverstein admitted giving order to destroy WTC7.
- **When he said "pull it", he meant the fire crew.**
- *What does the term "pull it" mean? Was he in a position to give orders to the fire crew? Was the crew in the building at the time?*

- A building can't collapse orthogonally on its own.
- **9/11 was unprecedented: anything was possible.**
- *What physical events can make an orthogonal collapse possible? How must these events have been timed relative to each other?*

- BBC reported collapse of WTC7 20 minutes in advance.
- **They made a mistake.**
- *Can a mistake enable someone to see into the future? What explanations are there for prescience? From where did the BBC get their foreknowledge?*

Figure 22

The arrows between the boxes represent our synthesis of the facts that will lead us towards the big picture. In stopping us from properly considering the truisms, the *believer* mind prevents us from completing the synthesis.

The TV plays to our *believer* mind by presenting us with a set of superficial, dumbed down and phoney analyses. At the same time, it offers up its own false synthesis, and this discourages us from forming our own. Exposed to the TV from an early age, we quickly start to hunger after the neatly packaged narratives it feeds us, because these play on our childhood need for security and comfort. Once some erroneous ideas become lodged in our minds, these act as a magnet for further false narratives that correlate with them, and it seems we tend to place a greater degree of importance on the cohesion of narrative than we do on the truth. The upshot of all this is a snowballing of the need for the TV's fairy tales, a need that soon becomes an addiction. The unwavering trust we have come to place on the TV as a result typically exceeds that which we place on any parent, peer or authority figure.

## Is Religion Responsible for Violence?

Over the years, there has been much talk about how religion is to blame for much, if not all, of the violence we see today in the Middle East, and indeed throughout the world and throughout time. For instance, Shia Muslims differ from Sunnis in that they maintain that Ali, the son-in-law of the Prophet Muhammad, and his descendants have the holy right to lead the Islamic community. According to some, the belief (or not) in this story has caused many deaths. But how many deaths are we really talking about? And how do we know that it was this belief in particular that caused the deaths?

At the same time, we must compare this to the millions of lives that have been lost in all the US led wars in the Middle East over the past few decades, all of which have been justified by the religious mantra of *TVism* and its false narrative of nineteen men armed with box cutters, controlled by one in a cave with a beard, acting in the name of Islam.

It is very clear that religion can sometimes lead to violence, but, as we have seen throughout the book, it's often all too easy to point the finger at the wrong religion. In attempting to answer our question, we must make sure that we consider religion in all its forms, not just the mainstream varieties that the TV identifies for us. When a powerful religion, such as *TVism*, stirs up violence and plants the blame on another religion, such as Islam, we must be very sure that we don't fall prey to the propaganda and, in doing so, misappropriate blame to the wrong party.

## Why Are We Here?

There are many who postulate that religion is an essential part of our reality, since within its doctrine lies the answer, supposedly, to that most tantalising of questions: why are we here? If we surmise that religion is nothing more than a power structure created by an elite group of men, are we then forced to conclude that life has no meaning?

Needless to say, we don't have the answer to the question, but we shouldn't let that fact dissuade us from having a guess. Throughout this book we have looked at the ways in which we think about the world around us, and placed our focus on the analysis of evidence as the guide to keep us on the right course. In this section however, we deviate from this well-trodden path to offer our opinion, and the reader is reminded to regard it as no more than that.

When each of us is born, we enter the world having been allocated one very special gift, a gift more precious than any other: the authority over our own mind. If the bearer seizes it, he or she is asserting their right to determine for themselves how the world works, what's right or wrong and what's good or bad. But, as with all gifts, the receiver is free to do with it whatever they like.

Unfortunately, the problem is that when we are born, we are not in a position to be able to recognise the gift or its importance. Sadly, this means that most of us, in the West at least, are tricked into giving it up at a very early age, thanks to the misinformation that is fed to us through our "education" system. We are systematically lied to about many fundamental truths pertaining to our nation and our place within it. We are lied to about what we have been in the past, lied to about what we are in the present and lied to about what we are striving to be in the future. The cycle of lies is perpetuated from each generation to the next when unwitting adults, victims of the same abuse in their childhood, pass the stories on to the children in their care.

As children, we have very few skills with which to defend ourselves against the onslaught. When we see adults around us who have the appearance of being more world-wise than us, it is all but inevitable that we place our unquestioning trust in them. This, of course, is our biggest mistake since, over the course of the centuries, the disinformation has grown to become a vast body of "knowledge" which reflects not the real world, but the fictional construct that stands in its place.

As we get older and develop the ability to think critically, the web of deceit takes on a new twist. Presumably concerned that the lies might one day wear a little thin, the elite who rule over us, whoever they might be, turn up the heat. The new trick up their sleeve is to use our own fear as a weapon against us to encourage us to continue to sing to their tune.

Returning again to the idea of purpose, it may well be that there is no meaning to life at all, and that our imagining otherwise is the result of the defect of promiscuous teleology, as discussed in chapter 22. Those who believe this to be the case are free to construct their own purpose and do with life whatever they see fit, hopefully without causing any unnecessary harm to anyone or anything else.

On the other hand, if we imagine that there *is* a purpose to life, then we think it's safe to say that making ourselves the slave of another person's fairy tales does not put us in a good place from which to discover it. And it makes no difference where they come from: a priest, a holy book, a newscaster or a TV set; it's all the same. Any journey to seek life's real meaning must surely start with our reclaiming the gift, the seizing of control of our own minds. In all probability, this will be the first step of many on the path to self-realisation. The alternative route, the path of fear, would leave us at the mercy of those who seek to advantage themselves from our self-created slavery.

In any situation with a negative outcome, it is the tendency for many to try to identify a single external source on which to pin the blame. A more rational approach, however, might be to accept that we must take on some responsibility for our own lives. In this case, it should be clear that some of the blame must rest with the tricksters who have deceived us, but, equally, it's hard to deny our own culpability when we sell our birth right for a fistful of lies.

## What Happened to the Positive Advice?

Back in the Introduction we promised to provide some positive advice on how to take back the control of our thoughts, and, in doing so, avoiding slavery. The time has come to make good on that promise.

The first and most important step is to get rid of the TV set. There is no surer way to free oneself from the shackles of a religion than to eliminate its source. For many people, this idea may seem unappealing. Surely it can't all be bad? In reality, we have to accept that the medium as a whole represents a pretty wide range of toxicity. The most damaging, perhaps, are the twenty-four hour "news" channels: the ones which repeat their corporate propaganda at hourly intervals. At the other end of the spectrum, it's hard to see how a program about the narrow-striped mongoose can do you much harm. If you can't get rid of your TV, then try to be more selective in your viewing choice.

To fill the gap this leaves, you could select some YouTube channels or independent on-line media sites which might provide an alternative view of the news, or follow some independent researchers on social media. There is no shortage of worthy material: you just need to go and seek it out. Whatever the source, be it TV or alternative media, the important thing to remember is that the content will always be coloured, at least to some extent, by an agenda. If your expectation is to be handed the facts on a plate, then you are likely to be disappointed. If, on the other hand, you start to regard everything you read and see as merely an expression of opinion, you'll soon find that the content you previously saw transforms to become just one part of a bigger picture encompassing the message, its presenters, their promoters, and their agenda. A source has the capacity to deceive only in as much as you believe it to be feeding you the truth in the first place. Once you have become accustomed to subjecting material to critical analysis, you will soon be able to see it for what it is.

But how can we ensure that we are always in a position to decide whether our *believer* or *explorer* mind gets to do our thinking for us? Just as with all decisions, the first and most important step is to recognise that there is indeed a choice to be made. Once we are aware of the existence of the *believer* and *explorer* minds, it's easy to observe the interplay that goes on between the two, an interplay that continues throughout our waking life. Whenever we are presented with the opportunity to think, the *believer* will be there to tell us what's what, while the *explorer* will always want to ask questions. It's really just the act of questioning that's the key to making the choice.

One simple technique for engaging the *explorer* might be to force yourself to ask a question as your immediate response the next time somebody tells you something new. Try and do this whether you agree with what they say or not. Remember that asking someone a question is not a sign of weakness, not a signal that you agree with them, not an admission of defeat and is not an expression of servility or stupidity. The asking of questions is the one vital tool we have for finding out more about the world around us, and there is certainly more to gain in using it than there is to lose. If we agree with the speaker, it may enable us to break new ground together in our understanding of the world. If we disagree, on the other hand, we still have the opportunity to gain a fuller understanding of the speaker's point of view. This information may also come in handy at a later date in acting as a balance for our own thoughts or for those of others. If it turns out that the speaker is talking nonsense, then a well-placed question is often a good way of letting them destroy their own argument in a way that is non-confrontational and, sometimes, quite amusing.

On occasions, it may be that we don't know what to ask. Accurately locating the central thesis of an argument can be difficult and, more often than not, the right question either occurs to us too late or not at all. However, this should not put us off since, under most circumstances, asking **any** question will be better than asking no question at all. Even though part of the purpose of questioning is to explore the response, perhaps a more important goal is to ensure the engagement of the *explorer* mind.

## Close

One of the greatest failings we face as human beings is probably our failure to accept that our own knowledge is incomplete and that, no matter how hard we strive to complete it, it will never be so. Often in our lives, we arrive at what we might term a pseudo-plateau: a point at which we assume we have won the battle, only to find that the real campaign is yet to start. This realisation can be a bitter pill to swallow, yet can also be a very humbling experience. When we realise that "truth" is just a mirage and that we are not shackled to the same beliefs for all of our lives, the result can be a feeling of illumination, liberation and, for some, almost like an awakening. At this point, new facts and insight cease to be a threat and, instead, become an opportunity. Today's nonsense may well turn out to be tomorrow's reality.

# Conclusion

As we have ascertained on so many occasions during the course of our journey, the truth is a tenuous and malleable commodity; one which changes continuously as the course of human history progresses. In many ways, we are like ants crawling on a giant sheet of paper in one instant of time. We assume that the portion of the paper we see represents the full picture, but this, in most cases, is just an illusion. In order to see the real full picture, we must step above the plane of the paper and beyond the mind of the ant.

The more evidence we seek out, assuming we have the strength to do so, the closer to some particular truth we may get. Yet we are always faced with the temptation of taking the easy path by buying in to the narrative that's presented to us. At the end of the day, we must make our own choice as to the route we take and be prepared to accept responsibility for the consequences.

Plato described the situation well with his "Allegory of the Cave", written around 380 BC. In this story[lxxi] he describes a gathering of people who have lived their whole lives chained to a wall of a cave, facing the blank, back wall. The captives spend their days watching the shadows of objects passing outside of the cave as they flicker over the surface of the blank wall inside, and they mistake their perceptions for reality. Plato goes on to imagine what would happen if a prisoner were to be freed and allowed to see the reality of the world outside the cave. If he were to return to the cave to inform his former companions of the falsity of their perceptions, he would, in all likelihood, be seen as deranged, and treated with contempt.

It takes courage for us to face the fact that the shadows we see are not true reality, and even more to free ourselves of our shackles and turn to face the real world outside. Perhaps this is best summed up in the words of William Blake[lxxii]:

> "If the doors of perception were cleansed every thing would appear to man as it is, Infinite. For man has closed himself up, till he sees all things thro' narrow chinks of his cavern."

# Glossary

*"The truth will set you free, but first it will make you miserable."*

James A. Garfield, ex US president

---

*Ad hoc* Hypothesis – An explanation for an observation that is made on the spur of the moment without consideration or evidence.

Authority Filtering – A mechanism of thought in which information and evidence from non-canonified sources is excised.

Authority Hierarchy – A construct in which more highly canonified sources of authority supersede lesser ones in terms of the extent to which information from them is trusted.

*Believer* – A person who uses his or her *believer* mind in the majority of situations, or one who is using the *believer* mind at a particular moment.

*Believer* Mind – That part of our mind which is inclined to make decisions and reach conclusions based on the opinions of some external source of authority rather than the available evidence.

Canonical – Conforming to a ratified aspect of religious doctrine or belief.

Canonical Filtering – A mechanism of thought in which information and evidence that does not conform to some ordained canon is ignored.

*Coincidence*/Miracle – An impossible event in the physical world that is ascribed to a supernatural cause (in days gone by) or to a random one (in more modern times).

Constructivist Theory of Truth – A theory which states that the truth of a proposition is defined by an authority.

Correspondence Theory of Truth – A theory which states that the truth of a proposition is defined by its correlation with a real event.

Empirical Falsification – A principle which states that an idea suitable for study is one for which there exists a mechanism by which it might be disproved.

Erasure – A mechanism of thought in which non-canonical observations are silently ignored.

*Explorer* – A person who uses his or her *explorer* mind in the majority of situations, or one who is using the *explorer* mind at a particular moment.

*Explorer* Mind – That part of our mind which is inclined to make decisions and reach conclusions based purely on the available evidence.

Fairy Tale – A proposition that can be invalidated by reference to information from within the proposition itself along with the application of empirically verifiable physical laws.

False-Flag attack – A covert operation in which a country or army attacks itself and blames the attack on an enemy. These events are often used as a psychological operation to prepare the public for war with the "enemy".

Learned Helplessness – A psychological trait in which the subject adopts a sense of futility as a result of some previous traumatic experience.

Logical Fallacy – An error of reasoning which results in the mandatory falsification of an argument that supports a proposition.

Popper-Compliant – A proposition which obeys the principle of Empirical Falsification.

Protect the Religion – A psychological game in which a *believer* must defend a position which contradicts logic, reason or evidence.

Religious Labelling – A process by which a *believer* can discard information or evidence by grouping it with something deemed to be undesirable.

Religious Reasoning Chain – A sequence of *ad hoc* hypotheses in which each is supposed to prop up the holes in the last.

Reversal – A bias removal technique in which the elements of a situation involving an out-group are temporarily replaced by the corresponding elements pertaining to the in-group.

Splitting – A practical application of the Fallacy of the Excluded Middle in which a topic is viewed as being polarised into two camps, at least one of which is subject to a religious label.

Superficial Processing – A mechanism of thought in which the subject avoids the detail in a topic in order to avoid the truth.

Systematic Processing – An analytical thought process in which the subject investigates a topic thoroughly in order to seek and find the truth.

*TVism* – A religious system of myths and fairy tales which emanate from the TV and are readily accepted as Constructivist Truth.

Wilful Blindness – A mechanism of thought in which the subject intentionally ignores facts which might cause discomfort.

# References

*"There are two ways to be fooled. One is to believe what isn't true; the other is to refuse to believe what is true."*

Søren Kierkegaard, Danish philosopher

---

[i] Obedience to Authority; Stanley Milgram; Harper & Row; 1974
[ii] Scientific Method; Barry Gower; Routledge; 1996
[iii] The Logic of Scientific Discovery; Karl Popper; Routledge; 1934
[iv] "Peter Power 7/7"
[v] What Do You Say After You Say Hello; Eric Berne M.D.; Penguin; 1997
[vi] The Collected Papers of Bertrand Russell, Volume 11; Bertrand Russell; Routledge; 1997
[vii] The Albigensian Crusade; Jonathan Sumption; Faber & Faber; 1999
[viii] Evidence for the Explosive Demolition of WTC7 on 9/11; David Chandler; AE911Truth; 2009
[ix] The Selfish Gene; Richard Dawkins; Oxford Paperbacks; 1976
[x] The Mysterious Collapse of World Trade Center 7; David Ray Griffin; Armchair Traveller; 2005
[xi] How to Win Every Argument; Madsen Pirie; Continuum; 2006
[xii] History of Experimental Psychology; Edwin G. Boring; Prentice Hall; 1950
[xiii] Studies in the Way of Words; Paul Grice; Harvard; 1991
[xiv] Social Psychology; Michael Hogg; Pearson; 2013
[xv] The Making of the Atomic Bomb; Richard Rhodes; Simon & Schuster; 2012

[xvi] Hijacking America's Mind on 9/11; Elias Davidsson; Algora 2013
[xvii] Understanding your Personality; Patricia Hedges; Sheldon; 1993
[xviii] Games People Play; Eric Berne M.D.; Corgi; 1974
[xix] On Death and Dying; Elisabeth Kübler-Ross; Scribner; 2014
[xx] Terror on the Tube; Nick Kollerstrom; Progressive Press; 2011
[xxi] Principles of Neural Science; Eric Kandel et al; McGraw-Hill; 2012
[xxii] Brain Systems Underlying Declarative and Procedural Memories; Endel Tulving; Sinauer Associates; 2001
[xxiii] Wilful Blindness; Margaret Heffernan; Walker & Co; 2012
[xxiv] Learned Helplessness; Martin E. P. Seligman; Oxford University Press; 1995
[xxv] Effects of Group Pressure upon the Distortion of Judgment; Solomon Asch; Carnegie Press; 1951
[xxvi] Conformity-Deviation, Norms, and Group Relations; Muzafer Sherif; Harper & Brothers; 1961
[xxvii] Introducing physical and emotional suggestibility and sexuality; John Kappas; Panorama; 1999
[xxviii] Eyewitness Testimony; Elizabeth F Loftus; Harvard; 1996
[xxix] Redefining medical students' disease to reduce morbidity; R. Moss-Morris & K Petrie K; 2001
[xxx] Groupthink; Irving Janis; Cengage Learning; 1982
[xxxi] Conditioned Reflexes; Ivan Pavlov; Dover Publications; 2003
[xxxii] About behaviourism; Burrhus Skinner; Mass Market Paperback; 1976
[xxxiii] The Lucifer Effect; Philip Zimbardo; Rider; 1971
[xxxiv] Nineteen eighty-four; George Orwell; Penguin; 2013
[xxxv] Propaganda; Edward Bernays; Horace Liveright; 1928
[xxxvi] Secret History; Nick Cullather; Stanford; 1999
[xxxvii] Beyond Good and Evil; Friedrich Nietzsche; Createspace; 2014
[xxxviii] Breaking the Spell; Nicholas Kollerstrom; Castle Hill; 2014
[xxxix] Hellstorm; Thomas Goodrich; CreateSpace; 2014
[xl] New Scientist; Ewen Callaway; March 2009
[xli] Official Stories; Liam Scheff; CreateSpace; 2014
[xlii] Fact Sheet 103; World Health Organisation; www; 2015

[xliii] Katharine the Great; Deborah Davis; Institute for Media Analysis; 1991
[xliv] The Cultural Cold War; Frances Stonor Saunders; The New Press; 2000
[xlv] Fifty Years of Investigative Reporting; Fred J. Cook; G.P. Putnam's Sons; 1984
[xlvi] NATO's Secret Armies; Ganser Daniele; Routledge; 2004
[xlvii] Dark Alliance; Gary Webb; Seven Stories; 2014
[xlviii] The CIA in Hollywood; Tricia Jenkins; University of Texas; 2012
[xlix] The CIA and the Media; Carl Bernstein; Rolling Stone; 1977
[l] Musical Truth; Mark Devlin; aSys; 2016
[li] Conspiracy Theories; Cass R. Sunstein; Harvard University; 2008
[lii] COINTELPRO: the FBI's War on Political Freedom; Nelson Blackstock; Pathfinder; 2000
[liii] The Mysterious Collapse of World Trade Center 7; David Ray Griffin; The Armchair Traveller; 2005
[liv] The New Pearl Harbor Revisited: David Ray Griffin; Olive Branch; 2012
[lv] Solving 9/11; Christopher Bollyn; Bollyn; 2012
[lvi] Nobody Died at Sandy Hook; Jim Fetzer; Moon Rocks; 2015
[lvii] The Unofficial Story of Adam Lanza; Sabrina Phillips; Createspace; 2014
[lviii] Tonkin Gulf and the Escalation of the Vietnam War; Edwin E. Moïse; University of North Carolina; 2000
[lix] We Never Went to the Moon; Bill Kaysing; Health Research; 1997
[lx] Chemtrails Confirmed; William Thomas; Bridger House; 2004
[lxi] Dr. Herbert York; Race to Oblivion; Simon & Schuster; 1970
[lxii] The Truth Game; John Pilger; (documentary); 1983
[lxiii] Zionism, the Real Enemy of the Jews; Alan Hart; Clarity; 2009
[lxiv] NATO's Secret Armies; Ganser Daniele; Routledge; 2004
[lxv] JFK - An American Coup d'Etat; Colonel John Hughes-Wilson; John Blake; 2015
[lxvi] The Oklahoma City Bombing and the Politics of Terror"; David Hoffman; Feral House; 1998

[lxvii] Crossing the Rubicon; Michael Ruppert; New Society; 2004
[lxviii] Globalization of War; Michel Chossudovsky; Global Research; 2015
[lxix] The Denial of Death; Ernest Becker; Souvenir Press; 2011
[lxx] The Holographic Universe; Michael Talbot; Harper Collins; 1996
[lxxi] Plato; The Republic CreateSpace; 2014
[lxxii] William Blake; The Marriage of Heaven and Hell; CreateSpace; 2014

Printed in Dunstable, United Kingdom